The Englishman's England

IAN OUSBY

The Englishman's England

Taste, travel and the rise of tourism

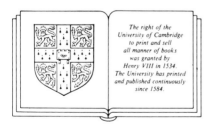

The right of the
University of Cambridge
to print and sell
all manner of books
was granted by
Henry VIII in 1534.
The University has printed
and published continuously
since 1584.

CAMBRIDGE UNIVERSITY PRESS

Cambridge   New York   Port Chester   Melbourne   Sydney

Published by the Press Syndicate of the University of Cambridge
The Pitt Building, Trumpington Street, Cambridge CB2 1RP
40 West 20th Street, New York, NY 10011, USA
10 Stamford Road, Oakleigh, Melbourne 3166, Australia

First published 1990

Printed in Great Britain at
the University Press, Cambridge

British Library cataloguing in publication data

Ousby, Ian, *1947–*
The Englishman's England: taste, travel and the rise
of tourism.
1. England. Tourism
I. Title
338.4'79142

Library of Congress cataloging in publication data

Ousby, Ian, 1947–
The Englishman's England: taste, travel, and the rise of tourism
Ian Ousby.
    p.   cm.
Bibliography.
ISBN 0–521–37374–3
1. England – Description and travel – History   2. British – Travel –
England – History.   3. Tourist trade – England – History.
4. Aesthetics, British – History.   5. Literary landmarks – England –
History.   6. Country houses – England – History.   7. England –
Antiquities – History.   8. Landscape – England – History.   I. Title.
DA600.087   1990
338.4'7914204 – dc20   89–9768   CIP

ISBN 0 521 37374 3

Contents

Illustrations

Acknowledgements

Most of the research for this book was done in the Cambridge University Library and I owe a great debt to many members of its staff, particularly those in the Rare Books Room, the Maps Room and the Photography Department. I am also grateful to the following for their help: P. A. Baldwin, Cholmondeley Estates, Houghton Hall; Kathleen Collier, The Wordsworth Trust, Dove Cottage; Mark Girouard; Anne Flavell, John Johnson Collection, Bodleian Library; Jane Fowles, Archivist to the Marquess of Bath, Longleat House; David Green, former Keeper of Archives, Blenheim Palace; Sarah Greenwood, Historic Houses Association; R. H. Harcourt Williams, Librarian and Archivist to the Marquess of Salisbury, Hatfield House; Eeyan Hartley, Keeper of Archives, Castle Howard; F. C. Jolly, Holkham Estate Office; David H. Jones, British Tourist Authority; I. M. Lang, Wilton Estate Office; Mairi R. Macdonald, The Shakespeare Birthplace Trust; M. A. Pearman, Librarian and Archivist, Devonshire Collections, Chatsworth; P. A. Rundle, County Record Office, Trowbridge, Wiltshire; Francesca Scoones and Pamela S. A. Stacey, The National Trust; Mrs D. A. Staveley, Secretary to the Duke of Rutland, Belvoir Castle; A. W. Stevenson, Leicestershire Libraries and Information Service; Edmund Swinglehurst, The Thomas Cook Group Ltd; Marquess of Tavistock, Woburn Abbey. Thanks also to Patricia Robertson for her encouragement, to my editor Andrew Brown for his patience, knowledge and enthusiasm, and to Trudi Tate and Victoria Cooper for all their help.

The illustrations are reproduced by kind permission of the Syndics of Cambridge University Library, except for the following: pages 34, 50,

52 and 53, courtesy of the Trustees and Guardians of Shakespeare's Birthplace; page 88, courtesy of the Thomas Cook Archives; page 135, courtesy of Dr Paul Hartle; page 164, courtesy of The Wordsworth Trust, Dove Cottage.

Introduction

I

Some friends of mine who live in Israel put a lot of effort into persuading their English uncle to pay them a visit before they finally managed to overcome the various objections which his sedentary, insular disposition readily suggested. He arrived late at night and was driven from the airport through darkened streets. As soon as he got to my friends' flat he fell into a jet-lagged sleep from which he did not wake until they were finishing breakfast on the balcony next morning. Virtually ignoring them, he went straight to the railings at the edge and stood in silence admiring the view spread beneath him: bright sunlight, white houses stretching higgledy-piggledy down the hillside, a glimpse of distant lemon groves. Finally, he turned to them and put his reaction to it all in words. 'Well', he said, 'you can certainly tell you're not in England.'

The whole world knows my friends' uncle. He has intimidated, amused and irritated waiters in Calais and tribal chieftains in the Congo. He has been making regular contributions to our literature of foreign travel for the last hundred and fifty years, and we can still hear his voice in the bars of cross-Channel ferries, in Alpine funiculaires, in guided parties being shown the Acropolis. If we cringe at the sound, devoutly hoping that nobody will identify us as his fellow-countrymen, that is because, in our hearts, we can't deny our kinship with him. Grappling with the mysteries of the New York subway system or staring in wonder at the Pyramids, to our secret shame we sometimes hear the ghostly echo of his voice in our own heads, whispering that we can certainly tell we're not in England.

In theory, there should be nothing humiliating in this discovery. Travel, like so many other transactions of life, forces us to measure the unfamiliar by reference to the familiar: to define the experience of being abroad, we need a concept of 'home'. Our special discomfort stems from the fact that of all nations we have perhaps the most strongly defined sense of national identity – so developed and so stylised, in fact, that we are frequently conscious of it as a burden or restraint. Willy-nilly, we take abroad with us a sense of England and our own Englishness like a precious family heirloom or, worse, like a sort of virginity to be preserved intact from all the dangers that threaten it.

The tongue-tied banality that can result is matched by the distinctive lyricism which the spectacle of 'home' itself can provoke. We hear it at its most eloquent from the mouths of returning travellers, at the moment they set foot again on native soil. Here, for example, is George Orwell at the end of *Homage to Catalonia*, gratefully exchanging the hardships of the Spanish Civil War for the comfort of a seat on the boat-train and a view of 'southern England, probably the sleekest landscape in the world':

The industrial towns were far away, a smudge of smoke and misery hidden by the curve of the earth's surface. Down here it was still the England I had known in my childhood: the railway-cuttings smothered in wild flowers, the deep meadows where the great shining horses browse and meditate, the slow-moving streams bordered by willows, the green bosoms of the elms, the larkspurs in the cottage gardens; and then the huge peaceful wilderness of outer London, the barges on the miry river, the familiar streets, the posters telling of cricket matches and Royal weddings, the men in bowler hats, the pigeons in Trafalgar Square, the red buses, the blue policemen – all sleeping the deep, deep sleep of England, from which I sometimes fear that we shall never wake till we are jerked out of it by the roar of bombs.*

It is worth pausing to unpack the subtleties of this passage, if only because its deceptive air of simplicity has misled one historian of travel literature into praising it for its 'acute sense of place'. In fact, it amounts to a cunning little essay on the stereotypes that make up the Englishman's sense of home, the image of England that can shape his experience of his own country as much as his reaction to foreign parts. To be sure, Orwell begins by presenting his list of sights as personal

---

* Notes, largely confined to giving the sources of quotations and making acknowledgement of other people's work, may be found at the end of the book. They are identified not by numbers but by the relevant phrase from the text. The notes for each chapter are preceded by a brief account of the studies I have found particularly useful.

observations backed by personal memory – evocative scenes glimpsed from the window of his railway carriage and described in an accelerating rhythm which mimics the train's approach to London. Yet, from the start, the plural nouns endow the items on his list with a generalised, representative force. By the end, Orwell has confessedly departed from a specific route and a specific occasion: we are not being asked to believe that the press was actually reporting a cricket match or a Royal wedding (let alone cricket matches and Royal weddings) on the day of his return from Spain and, besides, the boat-train does not run through Trafalgar Square. From the self-conscious poeticisms with which he evokes the scenery of Kent to the bright, primary colours in which he paints London, Orwell piles up a familiar rhetoric of cliché, half-surrendering to its potency and half-mocking its limitations. Here, he says, is the image of England we have constructed from the complex realities around us, ignoring the tensions of world politics, editing out the industrial cities of the north and sentimentalising the landscape of the south into a profoundly attractive, dangerously complacent picture.

The ambivalence with which Orwell here regards England and his own Englishness, and the rhetorical skill with which he dramatises that ambivalence, are characteristic of his work, however rare they may be in travel writing, a genre not usually notable for subtlety or self-awareness. Yet the selective, idealised image of England this passage presents so adroitly for our inspection belongs to a long history of image-making. We could usefully locate the view Orwell conjures up as he looks out of his train window in a tradition that stretches back at least as far back as those panoramic views which eighteenth-century poets, like James Thomson in *The Seasons*, delighted to survey, pluralising every river, hill and cottage into a representative type, and juggling the rules of distance and perspective to fashion a satisfying prospect. The source from which poets like Thomson created their image of the English landscape was Italian painting, and the result taught Englishmen to discern in their own rainy corner of northern Europe the pastoral charms and the harmonies of composition they already admired in the work of Claude and Poussin. The source for Orwell's cosy, still largely pastoral England, of course, is the imagery of tourism. Those larkspurs in the cottage gardens are familiar to him and to us, not from our own personal memories of such scenes, but from their status as conventionalised signs on postcards and travel advertisements. By the time his list reaches a rhetorical climax with the men in bowler hats, the pigeons in Trafalgar Square, the red buses and the blue policemen, its kinship with the London Transport posters of the 1920s and 1930s is more or less openly declared. British Airways still uses the same emblems in TV advertisements for foreign audiences.

There is an irony in this, of which Orwell himself is implicitly aware. In Spain he was by turns the committed partisan, the self-questioning intellectual and the investigative journalist, never simply the tourist. That fate waits to seduce him on his return to England where, as he sinks back into the comfort of his railway seat, he is far more tempted to view the scenery in terms of the conventionalised imagery of tourism than he ever felt while abroad. If we are all tourists now, we are perhaps never more so than when we are at home; like Orwell, we may protest against the limitations this role imposes, but we can never entirely escape its influence. Our communal sense of England has been codified into the familiar images of the travel poster and the accompanying rhetoric of the guidebook far more than we care to admit – making the countryside into cottage gardens with larkspurs, London into bowler hats, pigeons, buses and policemen, leaving the industrial cities of the north conveniently hidden from view by the curve of the earth's surface, and reducing our history and culture to a list of representative sights or specially selected attractions. If we doubt the role this tourist map has played in defining our national sense of identity, we need only remember what actually happened when the roar of bombs which Orwell prophesies at the end of *Homage to Catalonia* became a reality in World War II. Seeking to broaden their bombing campaign against military and strategic targets into an assault on English morale at a deeper level, the Germans launched the so-called 'Baedeker raids', directed at buildings and monuments which received a distinguishing star in Baedeker's guidebook.

II

This book is about how the tourist map of England has been created. (And, apart from an occasional infringement of the Welsh bank of the Wye, I do mean 'England' rather than 'Britain'; the creation by the English of a tourist map of Scotland, Wales and Ireland is a different issue.) I do not attempt anything like a formal history of domestic tourism, any more than I offer a survey of all the various sights to which it has devoted its energies. Instead, I approach the subject by concentrating on the growth of four types of attraction: literary shrines, or places connected with writers; country houses; ancient monuments and medieval ruins; and, in every sense the largest of my examples, the natural landscape. This is a modest and deliberately selective list, omitting as it does (for example) any consideration of purpose-built attractions likes spas and seaside resorts, if only because these are among the few aspects of the social history of tourism that have been widely studied. Yet it is sufficient for my purpose in showing how movements in taste have led to patterns of travel, and how these patterns of travel have in turn been expanded and systematised into a tourist industry.

By taste, which provides the initial cue, I mean the application of general tendencies of thought and cultural attitude to the act of judging one aspect of our environment as interesting, beautiful or otherwise worth attention and rejecting others as not. Travel quickly converts these judgements into practical, local and specific terms. In doing so, it creates a habit of vision and a corresponding habit of blindness: seeing our environment, getting to know a region of England or an aspect of its life, increasingly become a matter of appreciating particular sights from a particular angle. Tourism completes the process by turning the habits of travel into a formal codification which exerts mass influence and gains mass acceptance. Distinguishing stars in guidebooks, symbols on maps and road signs enforce its selections, raising them to the status of communal or official wisdom; the sights thus selected are professionally laid out for display, explained, preserved, restored and eventually endangered or spoiled by their very popularity.

I am interested, then, in tourism as a state of mind as much as in tourism as an industry. My discussion will need to take note of the social changes and technological changes that have made tourism possible, just as it will frequently record the signs of commercial activity that announce its growth. Yet my underlying concern is with the appetites that have prompted tourism, the assumptions that have shaped its form and the mentality that has resulted. In this regard, I am pursuing a topic already broached by several previous commentators, notably Roland Barthes, whose witty reading of the *Guide Bleu* to Spain in *Mythologies* makes as compact an introduction to the subject as one could hope to find, and Daniel J. Boorstin, Paul Fussell and Dean MacCannell, whose studies share a common fascination with the tourist as what MacCannell calls 'one of the best models available for modern-man-in-general'.

In the work of Professors Boorstin and Fussell the tourist cuts a particularly sorry figure. The passive victim of advertising and publicity, he travels without curiosity, without attachment and often virtually without information to 'pseudo-places' in pursuit of 'pseudo-events'. It is no part of my intention to defend the culture of tourism, but I hope to correct some of the mistakes into which this repugnance can quickly betray us. The discovery that we are all tourists now is depressing enough to prompt evasive action. Its customary form (we are all familiar with it) is to insist that we ourselves have miraculously escaped the disease: I am a traveller, you are a tourist, they are trippers. In fact, tourists are often distinguished not by the mindless complacency that Boorstin and Fussell so readily attribute to them but by precisely the *angst* about their role and the dislike of their fellows which this formulation expresses. They are not just people who carry expensive cameras, wear Hawaiian shirts, talk in loud voices and visit theme parks, but also people – like you and me – who are positively obsessive in avoiding such behaviour.

The 'I am a traveller, you are a tourist' formulation depends on the attempt to draw a more reassuring distinction between 'travel' and 'tourism' than I have made so far or will go on to make in the course of this book. Developing Boorstin's arguments, Fussell has identified three distinct figures, the explorer, the traveller and the tourist:

All three make journeys, but the explorer seeks the undiscovered, the traveler that which has been discovered by the mind working in history, the tourist that which has been discovered by entrepreneurship and prepared for him by the arts of mass publicity. The genuine traveler is, or used to be, in the middle between the two extremes. If the explorer moves toward the risk of the formless and the unknown, the tourist moves toward the security of pure cliché.

'The genuine traveler is, or used to be': the uncertainty about tenses here is revealing in an argument which is also being advanced under the guise of historical analysis. The explorer, the traveller and the tourist, Fussell explains, belong to different periods of modern history: the explorer to the Renaissance, the traveller to the 'bourgeois age' and the tourist to 'our proletarian movement'. By definition such epochs and their characteristic representatives do not lend themselves to precise dating, yet in Fussell's hands the boundaries prove suspiciously portable. Indeed, it appears that the 'genuine' traveller – in touch with the mind working in history and hard at work at 'real' experiences in 'real' places – still lives in the person of the author himself, died at some undefined point between the two world wars and fell victim to the railway in the nineteenth century.

Obviously, what is being proposed is not historical definition but a vision of a Golden Age. Observing and hating the contemporary triumph of tourism, commentators begin with the determination to view it as a peculiarly modern illness, a fall from grace that typifies the failings of our own culture. 'It was not always thus', they cry and turn back to contemplate the good old days when genuine travel was still possible, in their youth, before the plane was invented, before the American Express card, before the steamer, before Cook's package tours, before the railway. Like all such Golden Ages, the more closely it is sought, the more elusively it recedes from our grasp. It is a phantasm, compounded of modern self-dislike, intellectual snobbery and sentimentality about the past. And ironically enough, it ends up serving the very phenomenon it sought to denounce and escape, for the tourist industry well knows how to exploit our yearning to get off the beaten track and rediscover genuine travel, just as it well knows how to exploit our cosy, simplified view of the good old days in promoting unspoilt inns, medieval banquets, town criers, Tudorbethan teashops and all the more significant monuments now blandly classed as 'heritage'.

III

I don't think any study that seeks to describe the mentality of tourism, rather than just cataloguing the statistics of an industry, can completely avoid the vagueness and the confusions I have been criticising. Our implication in tourism is too deep – and too unhappy – for us to claim we can view it objectively, let alone compare it authoritatively with the experience of past generations. Yet, in seeking to explain how what I call the tourist map of England was created, I find a much longer and more complex history than any sentimental vision of a pre-tourist Golden Age destroyed by recent, modern corruption would admit.

Even a brief look at the medieval pilgrimage can administer a brutal correction to the sentimentality which afflicts our view of past travel. For the pilgrimage was definitely not what Paul Fussell would label exploration or even travel. It displayed, though in miniature, most of the structures we associate with tourism and at least some of the unpleasing atmosphere that goes inevitably with them. Pilgrims, by definition, trod a beaten path towards a communally agreed, indeed a well-publicised, goal. They went in groups under the supervision of guides like Harry Bailey, the innkeeper of the Tabard in Chaucer's *Canterbury Tales*. They stopped at intermediate points, in the form of inns, hostels or subsidiary shrines, which were as well-defined as the motorway restaurants and minor sights where modern tour operators arrange for their parties to break the journey. Along the route and at their final destination, they could buy religious relics, predecessors of the souvenir. And that final goal, the religious shrine, had at least some of the attributes of the professionally displayed tourist attraction. It was in the charge of a sacrist, or custodian, and it was sometimes accompanied by explanatory markers of a sort familiar to any modern tourist. The late fourteenth-century Magna Tabula which survives from Glastonbury, for example, was a large folding wooden frame pasted on two sides with parchment sheets telling the story of St Joseph of Arimathea and ending with a list of indulgences. The sale of indulgences – like the trade in minor, portable relics, a common target of attack by reformers – is a powerful reminder of the commercial aspect of the medieval pilgrimage. St Albans' dispute with Ely about which foundation displayed the true bones of the martyred Alban, or the similar quarrel between Glastonbury and Canterbury about St Dunstan's bones were not so much religious disagreements as business rivalry, for pilgrims' veneration was bringing Glastonbury an income of more than £120 a year by the end of the thirteenth century.

This might sound an uncharitable, even offensively cynical, description since it does not take the devotional purpose of the pilgrimage into account. Pilgrims embarked on their journeys to satisfy not a frivolous appetite for fun but a profound spiritual need. It is no part of my argument to deny this motive, yet it seems to me to increase rather than diminish the way that the pilgrimage anticipates tourism. However much the posters and brochures may promise us fun and pleasure, tourism does not depend solely on the appeal to these appetites and, even in its most debased forms, it usually makes some gesture towards higher motives. Like the spas before them, seaside resorts claim that they can minister to our health and mental well-being; the crassest theme parks sometimes allege that the theme to which they are devoted has some vaguely informative value. In the case of the tourist attractions I examine in this book the appeal to seriousness is more pronounced and less easy to dismiss. Tourists don't visit country houses or ruins or nature just for fun but out of the belief that the experience will in some way educate or uplift them – terms that express our own secularised, more vaguely defined equivalents of those precisely felt spiritual demands which impelled medieval pilgrims on their journey.

My first chapter will argue that the cult of literary shrines translates the cult of the pilgrimage into the secular language of tourism with remarkable fidelity. In that chapter, as in the others which make up this book, the bulk of my account will concern developments that took place, roughly, between the middle of the eighteenth century and the middle of the nineteenth century, for it is during this span that the progression from taste to travel to tourism I sketched earlier was effected. Canons of taste originating in Augustan and Romantic culture determined the selection of sights we still seek out today as major landmarks on the tourist map of England. By the end of this period most of the patterns, attitudes and dilemmas that characterise the experience of tourism today had been established.

Essential to converting the theories of taste into the practical organisation of tourism was an intellectual energy which assigned the act of travel itself special importance and a practical energy which made travel increasingly easy. When an eighteenth-century writer like Richard Twiss speaks of 'rambling about the world' he does not have in mind anything like the frivolous leisure pastime that phrase might now suggest: he is praising an activity which for him, and his age, 'proves the greatness of the mind of men, and the immortality to which it aspires'. Travel was a leading instrument of that post-Reformation spirit of inquiry which valued empirical knowledge over abstract speculation or book-learning derived merely from tradition. We learn by going out and seeing for ourselves, by becoming travellers. 'The use of travelling', said Samuel Johnson (and note that he said 'use', not 'pleasure'), 'is to regulate imagination by reality, and instead of thinking how things may be, to see them as they are.' By 'things', on the whole, Johnson meant 'people'. If travel was an instrument of inquiry, then the goal of inquiry was to understand mankind rather than inanimate objects. Knowledge consisted in a grasp of the great moral truths that govern human behaviour, and breadth of knowledge consisted in a grasp of the local variants that affect human behaviour in different places and different cultures.

This twin emphasis on the general and the local explains why the spirit of inquiry should have led travellers abroad for much of the eighteenth century. The scope of scholarly knowledge could be extended by voyages to exotic and distant lands, where both the consistency of morals and the variety of human manners could be affirmed. The gentleman's education could be completed by a more modest version of the same discovery in 'the *moving Academy*', the Grand Tour of Europe. Home ground, by contrast, was too tame and too familiar to furnish the scholar with conclusions of much originality or provide the gentleman with an education of much weight. At least, so it seemed until the latter part of the eighteenth century, when a growing body of opinion deplored how the 'universal rage for Foreign Travel has long occasioned an unaccountable neglect of the Beauties and Wonders of our own Country'. This reaction had several sources. At its simplest, it voiced the needs of those who were moved by the age's spirit of inquiry but lacked the purse or the leisure to embark on extended travel abroad. It took heart from that residual distrust of foreign parts which has made its contribution to English attitudes in virtually all periods: denunciation of French and Italian sophistication plays a part in the rhetoric used by several of the travellers I will be quoting in later chapters to praise the character of their native country. Above all, the growing interest in domestic travel was encouraged by technical advances in roads and communications which, by making it easier to travel round England, opened people's eyes to how much remained to be seen and explored.

The popular image of pre-railway travel in England is one of the prime examples of that falsification of the history of travel I have already attacked. Since the mid Victorian era we have been busy constructing a sentimental picture of overloaded stage coaches creaking their way through mire, burying themselves in snowdrifts and being held up by gallantly dressed highwaymen which tells us little about the realities of eighteenth-century and early nineteenth-century technology. The speed of horse-drawn vehicles was greatly increased by the introduction of Arab bloodstock into English horse breeds in the mid seventeenth century, the steel coach spring which began to replace leather braces in the mid eighteenth century and the refinement of the elliptical spring, invented in 1804. Road surfaces were improved by the engineering work of John Loudon Macadam, John Metcalfe and Thomas Telford. The proliferation of turnpike trusts, taking over from the older system which had left the care of roads to parishes often unable or unwilling to pay for them, began to establish a system of long-distance communication roads.

All these factors worked steadily to reduce journey times, shortening the London–Manchester run from four and a half days in the early eighteenth century to a day just over a century later, for example, and shortening the London–York run from five days in the seventeenth century to four days in 1706 and to thirty-one hours in 1790. This last time was achieved by the *Highflyer* coach, for even the names of the vehicles, particularly the mailcoaches, reflected the brash pride of an age impressed with its own achievement in making travel safer, faster, more modern: *The Protector*, *The Pilot*, *The Age*, *The Era*, *The Telegraph*, *The Enterprise*, *The Plymouth Fly*, *The Magnet*, *The*

Express. It is only a short step to Stephenson's *Rocket*, since in this regard as in so many others the railway age came as the next advance in a process which had already made a major impact on domestic travel.

This is not to claim that travellers filled their diaries and notebooks with praise for the ease and speed of modern travel. Travellers cherish inconveniences, and nowadays, after we have crossed the Atlantic in less than five hours, we still write home to tell our friends that we had to wait for over an hour in the departure lounge. Eighteenth- and early nineteenth-century travellers tell of delays and discomfort, of reckless coachmen and insolent tollgate keepers, of pot-holes, mud and impassable roads. Touring in the 1760s, the agriculturist Arthur Young complained enough about the failings of the English road system to have provided material for several volumes of the 'how quaint it all used to be' school of travel history. Such accounts miss the point by failing to detect in this grumbling the impatience of a generation already revelling in the excitement that comes from applying its spirit of inquiry to domestic travel and eager to extend inquiry as far as possible. The longing for a countryside penetrated by communication arteries which make it perfectly accessible to the traveller expresses a dream of knowledge as much as a demand for practical convenience. We can hear it satisfied when Young praises the improved road system of Oxfordshire in the first decade of the nineteenth century:

A noble change has taken place, but generally by turnpikes, which cross the county in every direction, so that when you are at one town, you have a turnpike road to every other town. This holds good with Oxford, Woodstock, Witney [&c.], and in every direction, and these lines necessarily intersect the county in every direction.

The same attitude underlies the annoyance we hear from the traveller who seeks out a particular spot only to find that he cannot lay his hands on proper information about it. The Honourable John Byng, whose tours in the 1780s and 1790s made him as great an expert on this sort of impediment as Young is on bad roads, vented his annoyance by recording specimens of the sort of conversation which 'almost daily pass'd between me, a country man or an inn keeper':

B. and countryman. – (B) what is that place? – (C) I am a straunger. – (B) Where does that road lead to? – (C) I am hard a hearing. – (B) Is your old priory, or any part of your old castle remaining? – (C) I never heard of such places; I'm sure there's none such here, or ever was!!

B. and innkeeper. (B) Do you know this county well? – (I) Aye, perfectly well. – (B) Anything worth seeing hereabouts? – (I) Nothing that ever I heard of. – (B) Do you know such a place? – (I) Know nothing of it. – (B) Which is the road to ——? – (I) I never was that way. – (B) Do many people go to see ——? – (I) Not that ever I was told. – (B) Have you any shews in town? – (I) I can't say. – (B) Whose house is that by the road side? – (I) I don't think I ever enquired. – (B) When will your fair be? – (I) I can't recollect exactly.

The solution, as Byng himself often suggested, lay in proper guides. It is significant to note how quickly and easily travellers like Byng, raging everywhere at the inadequacies of innkeepers, servants at country houses and the like, transfer the term 'guide' from people to books. The full term 'guidebook' was not apparently coined until the early nineteenth century – one of the first uses of it recorded by the *Oxford English Dictionary* occurs in Byron's *Don Juan* – but the concept of the guidebook and the colloquialism 'guide', as well as the cognate 'companion', are creations of the eighteenth century. The poem praising a country house gives way to the more factual catalogue of its art collection; the antiquarian study of the medieval ruin begins to make its appearance; the topographical poem yields to the picturesque description in prose. Their contents are subsumed into larger volumes, written not by local enthusiasts but by travellers covering a wide stretch of territory. Though these books are usually presented as personal narratives, including the various accidents and encounters of the journey, they are clearly written more and more with an eye to helping subsequent travellers along the same road, offering recommendations, warnings and information that ranges from practical details of prices to potted local history. Such books became one of the popular staples of late eighteenth-century publishing and Byng, for all his grumbling, could still begin his journey to the West Country in 1782 by admitting that 'Tour writing is the very rage of the times'. By the first decade of the nineteenth century one of the comforts of travelling in England, thought Robert Southey, was that 'wherever you go, printed information is to be found concerning every thing which deserves a stranger's notice'. From the mid nineteenth century onwards such information was codified into the synoptic, 'impersonal' handbooks of Murray, Black and Baedeker.

The country was thus becoming known in a double sense. It was being penetrated by roads intended for long-distance rather than just local traffic. It was being explained and interpreted by guides expressing the taste and outlook of the class of travellers themselves. Both aspects of this change are strikingly embodied in the change of conventions in mapping. The county maps John Speed produced in the early seventeenth century present the terrain as a series of separate and

One of Thomas Rowlandson's illustrations to *The Tour of Doctor Syntax in Search of the Picturesque* (1809) by William Combe. Despite the contemporary rage for travel books, Syntax is given short shrift by the bookseller to whom he offers the written account of his tour:

> 'A Tour, indeed! – I've had enough
> Of Tours, and such-like flimsy stuff.
> What a fool's errand you have made
> (I speak the language of the trade),
> To travel all the country o'er,
> And write what has been writ before!
> We can get Tours – don't make wry faces,
> From those who never saw the places.
> I know a man who has the skill
> To make your Books of Tours at will;
> And from his garret in Moorfields
> Can see what ev'ry country yields;
> So, if you please, you may retire
> And throw your Book into the fire:
> You need not grin, my friend, nor vapour;
> I would not buy it for waste paper!'

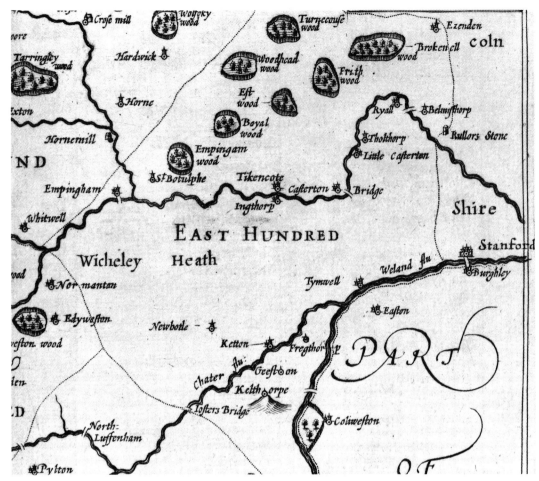

Part of the map of Rutland from John Speed's *Theatrum Imperii Magnae Britanniae* (1616). Rivers, woods and hills are prominent, and the approximate size of towns is suggested by the symbols that mark their locations, but the bridges at Stamford and Casterton are the only clues to the course of the Great North Road.

often apparently disconnected items, showing towns, cities and natural features like hills and rivers in detail but omitting roads. These appear prominently on John Cary's county maps at the end of the eighteenth century, but by then a more extreme form of communication map had been evolved in the strip-maps pioneered by John Ogilby's *Britannia* in 1675 and developed by Daniel Paterson in the 1780s. Designed for the traveller who wants to get from A to B, they divide the terrain into a succession of strips tracing the course of a long-distance route. The road itself is emphasised at the expense of natural features like hills and rivers, which, unless they constitute an impediment to the journey, are

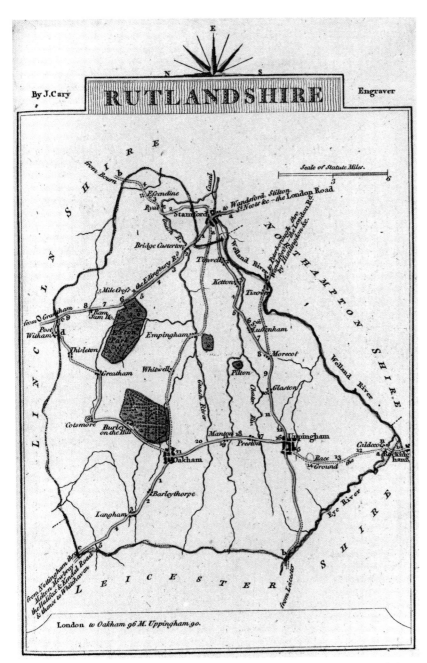

Map of Rutland from *Cary's Traveller's Companion, or a Delineation of the Turnpike Roads of England and Wales* (1791). The course of the Great North Road runs through Stamford from right to left. Cary labels it in terms of long-distance travel, as the London road and the 'Edingburg' road, and adds the mileage between major towns.

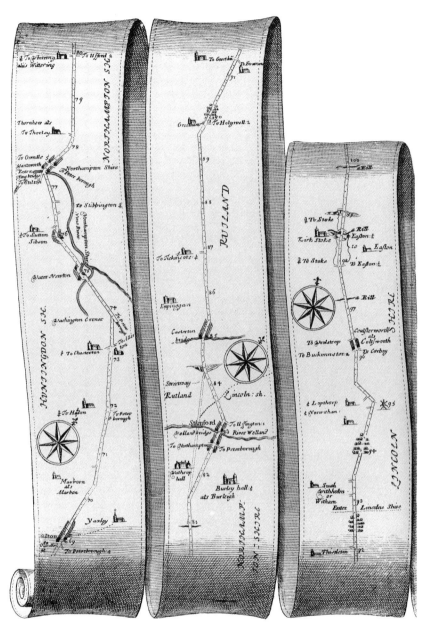

Strip-map from John Ogilby's *Britannia* (1675) showing the Stamford section of the Great North Road, with accumulated mileage from London. Rivers and county boundaries are relevant only where they intersect the route.

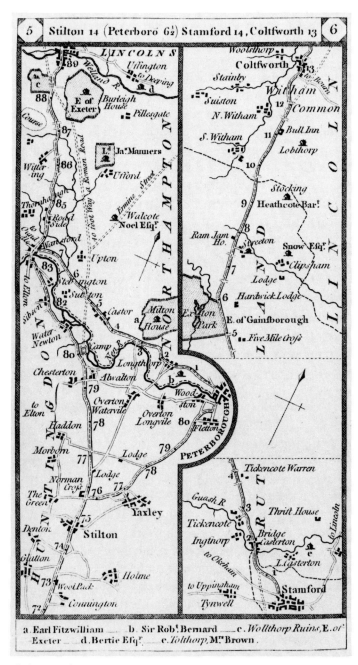

Strip-map from *Paterson's British Itinerary* (1785) showing the same section of the Great North Road. The rivers have dwindled in size and importance since Ogilby's *Britannia*, and the route is busy with information about country houses and their owners.

relegated to the same category as the country houses or churches marked along the margins of the route, as sights or features of interest falling within the traveller's view.

In a sense, these strip-maps embody the triumph of tourism: what is known, or worth knowing about a place, is what can be seen on the route to somewhere else. The active spirit of inquiry which sent people out to look at the country around them was achieving a knowledge less satisfying than its exponents had aimed at. That is why even so dedicated and energetic a traveller as Byng, eager to record every detail of his tours in his journal, could still admit to a curious sense of disappointment even at the moment of apparent success:

> If my journals should remain legible, or be perused at the end of 200 years, there will, even then, be little curious in them relative to travell, or the people; because our island is now so explored; our roads, in general, are so fine; and our speed has reach'd the summit.

This disillusionment is written into the shifting connotations of the very word 'tourist' itself. It was not, as some commentators have supposed, a creation of the railway age; leisure passengers who travelled by train were called 'excursionists' or, contemptuously, 'trippers'. Indeed, writing in the 1840s, Wordsworth could maintain that the term 'tourist' 'precludes the notion of a railway'. He meant that the railway excursionist went from A to B and back again on his return ticket, whereas the tourist made a tour or circuit. We still use 'tour' in that sense today, for actors, musicians and lecturers make tours, and soldiers perform tours of duty, but we do not call them 'tourists' when they do so, since the word now implies a leisure activity, incompatible with work or even seriousness of purpose.

This was not the case in the 1780s and 1790s when 'tourist' first comes into currency in the writing of people like Byng. 'Obstinate, solitary, traveller' though he is, he can still apply the word 'tourist' to himself without embarrassment, to indicate simply that he is making a tour, to describe the capacity in which he demands maps and information, and even, in his exuberant moods, to indicate the superior state of knowledge that travel can achieve: 'the only people who become acquainted with counties, are tourists'. The tourist was still someone pursuing a serious inquiry, so that when Arthur Young drew up his reports on the condition of English farming contemporaries labelled him an 'agricultural tourist'.

Yet at almost the same time that the word had achieved currency in this sense, it also developed negative connotations. Commenting in

1808 on the reports submitted to the Board of Agriculture, William Marshall challenged the claims of even so serious a figure as the agricultural tourist to become expert about the scenes he travelled through:

A mere tourist, it is true, may catch certain facts which pass under his eye in travelling: and, in this way, he may gather some general ideas of the nature of a country, and a few particulars of practice that may happen to be going on, *at the time of his tour*; and such facts may be entitled to public notice, *as far as they go*. But let him not claim, on such slight pretensions, a right to make a *general Report* of the nature and practice of the country or district thus passed over.

How quickly the qualifier 'mere' has attached itself to the noun, implying what Marshall goes on to argue openly: that the tourist's knowledge of what he travels through is, after all, a superficial matter of catching at passing sights and impressions. The tourist reduces the rich complexities of place to 'sight-seeing' – another revealing word, which enters the language in the 1830s, aptly conveying how the shifting human scenes which had first fascinated eighteenth-century inquirers had been reduced to a static list of objects and monuments. Perhaps those nuances of local knowledge which tourists had abandoned in their pursuit of routes recommended by strip-maps and guidebooks written by other tourists was better, after all? Yet the 'rattling Tourist', as Adam Walker had already dubbed him in 1792, did not merely ignore such local nuances: his influence blurred and destroyed the local character of the places he visited, exciting 'envy and false ideas of happiness among the peaceful inhabitants'.

And so, almost as soon as the vocabulary of tourism emerged, it was invaded by self-doubt and self-criticism of a sort we like to believe the exclusive property of us moderns. Writing in the days of coaches and turnpikes, when speed had reached its summit, Byng could already voice that familiar yearning for a lost Golden Age, which he located in the seventeenth century, when it still took two days to get from London to Huntingdon: 'I should have liked the travell of those times: the reception, and comfort at an inn; and the getting, at every distance of an 100 miles, amongst a new people with a new dialect; and where every thing was cheap too, because it could not be removed.' The faster and more widely we travel, the more we begin to doubt the value of travel itself, to suspect that the things we most admire are best appreciated and preserved through fixity rather than movement. That possibility occurred to Cobbett, and defeated him, when he got lost during his rural ride from Burghclere to Petersfield in 1826:

I rode up to the garden-wicket of a cottage, and asked the woman, who had two children, and who seemed to be about thirty years old, which was the way to LUDGARSHALL, which I knew could not be more than about *four miles* off. She did *not know*! A very neat, smart, and pretty woman; but, she did not know the way to this rotten-borough, which was, I was sure, only about four miles off! 'Well, my dear good woman,' said I, 'but you *have been* at LUDGARSHALL?' – 'No.' – 'Nor at ANDOVER?' (six miles another way) – 'No.' – 'Nor at MARLBOROUGH?' (nine miles another way) – 'No.' – 'Pray, were you born in this house?' – 'Yes.' – 'And, how far have you ever been from this house?' – 'Oh! I have been *up in the parish*, and over to *Chute.*' That is to say, the utmost extent of her voyages had been about *two and half miles*! Let no one laugh at her, and above all others, let not me, who am convinced, that the *facilities*, which now exist of *moving human bodies from place to place*, are amongst the *curses* of the country, the destroyers of industry, of morals, and, of course, of happiness.

And off he went, continuing his tour. And we, in spirit, go with him.

1

Literary shrines and literary pilgrims: the writer as tourist attraction

Christianity is the chief supplier of tourism.

Roland Barthes, *Mythologies*

I

There are many good reasons for visiting Lyme Regis. Its natural setting in a bay on the Dorset coastline gives it broad vistas of the sea and makes its streets quaintly crooked and hilly. As he walks them, the visitor comes across reminders of the Regency, when Lyme first enjoyed favour as a bathing resort. The town has something to tempt the scientifically curious, too, for the surrounding blue lias cliffs are rich in fossils; Mary Anning discovered the ichthyosaurus here in 1811. The historically minded will remember that in 1685 the Duke of Monmouth landed on the Cobb, Lyme's distinctive stone pier, to start his unsuccessful rebellion against James II. These charms were already acknowledged by the middle of the nineteenth century – the town had risen to the distinction of a royal suffix – but for the poet Tennyson they were outweighed by something else. Jane Austen had been here and made Lyme the scene of a memorable episode in *Persuasion*. 'Don't talk to me of the Duke of Monmouth', the Poet Laureate told his host, waving aside the sort of guidebook summary I have just offered. 'Show me the spot where Louisa Musgrove "fell down and was taken up lifeless".'

Of course, it was a disgracefully unprofessional, even philistine demand for a writer to make. Any academic specialising in the study of literature will tell you that proper consideration of Jane Austen's novel depends hardly at all on familiarity with Lyme Regis. Most, I think, would say our judgement should not be affected if we discovered that Jane Austen had never been there or even that Lyme did not exist. Yet Tennyson's attitude remains the popular one. To the common reader, and to those who get their reading from television serials, a large part of literature's appeal is its connection with place – real places that can be visited by car over a sunny Bank Holiday. To the leisure traveller, literary associations are as much a part of the landscape as country houses or historic buildings or beauty spots.

When we visit Lyme Regis now, we bring memories of John Fowles' *The French Lieutenant's Woman* as well as *Persuasion*. The countryside to its north, of course, is Hardy's Wessex and beyond that lie the Exmoor of R. D. Blackmore's *Lorna Doone* and the Devon coast of Charles Kingsley's *Westward Ho!* If we leave the south-west and make our way north towards the Scottish border, we can travel through the countryside of Housman's *Shropshire Lad* or Arnold Bennett's Five Towns or Shakespeare's Warwickshire or D. H. Lawrence's Midlands or the Brontës' Yorkshire moors, until we at last reach Wordsworth's Lake District. And as we go, we pass a host of specific sites. How many churches owe their trickle of donations to the presence of a writer's grave or monument? How many inns owe their passing trade to the custom they once enjoyed, or are supposed to have enjoyed, from a famous author? England now boasts about forty houses preserved and opened to the public because a writer was born, grew up, courted, lived, wrote or died there. Between them, they attract about two million visits a year. If we are all tourists nowadays, then at one time or another we are all literary pilgrims.

It is worth noting that word, 'pilgrims', and the usage which makes 'shrines' of writers' birthplaces, homes and graves. They are not peculiarly my own, but part of the common language of literary tourism, heard everywhere in the older accounts I shall be quoting in this chapter and still surviving even in the most up-to-date guidebooks. As my introduction suggested, the medieval pilgrimage established precedents for literary tourism we would do well to consider. Its distinctive blend of high-minded sanctity and debased commercialism is powerfully reminiscent of medieval Catholic culture in its later stages. So, too, are the underlying reasons for its popularity. When the Reformation purged saints from the calendar, stripped idols from the churches and denuded the landscape of shrines, the public need for these things had to find secular equivalents. The statesman and the soldier could fill this role, at least until the memory of their deeds faded into the recesses of history. The scientist and the explorer could serve their turn as well, until their discoveries became mere commonplaces of knowledge. But the writer could best endure, kept alive by his living book, his achievement at once majestic and familiar to later generations. He proved the ideal hero for a secular culture, the most satisfying object of national pride.

II

These forces have exalted Shakespeare to special heights of worship, and later in this chapter I shall look in some detail at the curious legacy he bequeathed to Stratford-upon-Avon. But, given the loose mixture of patriotic and religious feeling I have described, it is hardly surprising that Westminster Abbey should have led the way in literary shrines. As unofficial church of the nation, it already housed the bones of Edward the Confessor, the only English king to achieve sainthood, and was steadily being filled with monuments to later sovereigns and national heroes. The growth of Poets' Corner within its walls marked the creation of the first and still the most comprehensive attraction for the literary tourist.

The cornerstone was laid in 1400, when Chaucer was buried outside the Chapel of St Benedict in the south transept, his grave marked by a slab in the pavement and, later, by a lead plaque on a nearby pillar – hung there, it is said, by the printer Caxton. Though he had enjoyed royal favour in his time, Chaucer may have gained this distinction in death by more than his poetry. As Clerk of Works to the king he had supervised work on the Abbey's nave and he had died within the Abbey precincts, in a house whose site was later covered by Henry VII's Chapel. But it was Chaucer the poet whom Nicholas Brigham, himself a minor poet, commemorated in the 1550s with a splendid new tomb near the original grave. Its presence soon attracted another writer to the south transept. Since he died in nearby King Street the poet Edmund Spenser would probably have been buried somewhere in the Abbey in the normal course of events but, as his Latin epitaph pointed out, the actual spot for his grave was chosen so that he could lie near Chaucer. He was honoured there as the Prince of Poets, 'his Hearse being carried by Poets, and mournfull Verses and Pomes throwne into his Tombe'.

When the playwright Francis Beaumont was buried near by in the opening years of the seventeenth century the little group around Chaucer's tomb became a landmark, at least to fellow writers. It gave pride to a profession still struggling for its dignity to be recognised. William Basse wrote in his 'Elegy on Shakespeare':

Chaucer's tomb, the nucleus of Poets' Corner in Westminster Abbey. An
engraving from John Dart's *Westmonasterium* (1742).

Renowned Spenser, lye a thought more nye
To learned Chaucer, and rare Beaumont lye
A little neerer Spenser to make roome
ffor Shakespeare in your threefold fowerfold Tombe.

It was not, obviously, a serious proposal for exhumation from Stratford, but rather a complimentary conceit of a sort the age delighted in. Ben Jonson replied in the same spirit, insisting that Shakespeare's memory was ensured by his writings alone:

My *Shakespeare*, rise; I will not lodge thee by
  Chaucer or *Spenser*, or bid *Beaumont* lye
A little further, to make thee a roome:
  Thou art a Moniment, without a tombe,
And art aliue still, while thy Booke doth liue,
  And we haue wits to read, and praise to giue.

It was only fitting that Jonson himself should end up in the Abbey, particularly since he was a resident of Westminster and an old boy of Westminster School. He was buried not in the south transept but in the north aisle of the nave, where the magnificent simplicity of his epitaph triumphed over the misspelling of his name: 'O rare Ben Johnson'. With the death of Abraham Cowley, one of several now forgotten poets commemorated during the Restoration, Sir John Denham could congratulate literature on the place in public honour it had achieved:

These Poets near our Princes sleep,
And in one Grave their Mansion keep.

Yet when Addison paid a visit in 1711 the effect was still rather haphazard: 'In the poetical Quarter, I found there were Poets who had no Monuments, and Monuments which had no Poets.' The *Spectator* essay that offered this mild complaint is itself a striking expression of the spirit of the times, an eloquent tribute to the appeal which graves and monuments could hold. They induced a mood that the age particularly relished: 'the Gloominess of the Place, and the Use to which it is applied, with the Solemnity of the Building, and the Condition of the People who lye in it, are apt to fill the Mind with a kind of Melancholy, or rather Thoughtfulness, that is not disagreeable'. This pleasing, pensive melancholy led naturally to the vein of elegant truism which is the special hallmark of the age's reflective writing. Addison ended his stroll round the Abbey with a passage that few later guidebooks could resist quoting:

When I look upon the Tombs of the Great, every Emotion of Envy dies in me; when I read the Epitaphs of the Beautiful, every inordinate Desire goes out; when I meet with the Grief of Parents upon a Tomb-stone, my Heart melts with Compassion; when I see the Tomb of the Parents themselves, I consider the Vanity of grieving for those whom we must quickly follow: When I see Kings lying by those who deposed them, when I consider rival Wits plac'd Side by Side, or the Holy Men that divided the World with their Contests and Disputes, I reflect with Sorrow and Astonishment on the little Competitions, Factions, and Debates of Mankind. When I read the several Dates of the Tombs, of some that dy'd Yesterday, and some six hundred Years ago, I consider that great Day when we shall all of us be Contemporaries, and make our Appearance together.

To appreciate the importance such meditation would assume in eighteenth-century culture we need only point to the popularity of Gray's 'Elegy Written in a Country Churchyard'. To understand its local application to the Abbey and the Abbey's poetical quarter we have to descend to the writings of John Dart. Dart was a very minor antiquary whose *Westmonasterium* was remembered only to be castigated for its slovenliness; even at the time of its publication in 1742 the book had to be sold for less than the cost of its engravings. Its prose description of the Abbey is prefaced by a heroic poem which Dart had first issued separately some years before, an incautious gesture if he wished to establish a literary reputation but one the historian can now thank him for. It invites the reader to forsake distant Groves and murmuring Floods for tolling Bells and dusty Tombs, there to engage in solemn reflection on Man's feeble Power and Death's unbounded Sway. The various monarchs and dignitaries commemorated in the Abbey then march lifelessly through Dart's couplets. In this dull parade writers are given a place of distinction for reasons the muddled verse just manages to convey:

> The Poet's Name can strike a Pale around,
> And where he rests he consecrates the Ground,
> Can from rude Hands the sculptur'd Marble save,
> And spread a sacred Influence round the Grave.
> Thus *Virgil*'s Tomb attracts the Trav'ller's Eyes,
> While none can tell where great *Augustus* lies.

Significantly, Dart's prose guide begins in the south transept, where the collection of graves and monuments was growing more substantial and more coherent than it had been in Addison's day. In the Abbey's Gothic surroundings the age was trying to create a Temple of Worthies – one of those elegant, judiciously organised tributes in stone and verse with which they sometimes liked to ornament the picturesque land-scaping of their gardens. John Barber, printer and later Lord Mayor of London, put up a monument to Samuel Butler, who had died poor and obscure in 1680 after writing the satirical *Hudibras*. William Benson, Wren's successor as Surveyor-General, persuaded the authorities to allow a memorial to the regicide Milton, earlier denied burial in the Abbey by the Royalist Dean Sprat.

In an age so richly appreciative of monuments, so finely aware of the immortality one writer could confer on another with an epitaph, Alexander Pope became the arbiter of taste. He originally proposed to use the otherwise barren task of writing an inscription for Nicholas Rowe to complain that Dryden still lay 'Beneath a rude and nameless stone' near by. The real value of Rowe's memorial, the first version of Pope's epitaph suggested, would be as a signpost to the whereabouts of his great predecessor. When the Duke of Buckingham agreed to remedy the deficiency in 1720 Pope consulted with his friend Atter-bury, then Dean of Westminster, about the proper wording of a tribute until the verses originally proposed had been winnowed down to a simple statement of Dryden's name and dates. Its effect, said Dart, was 'a silent Reproach to abundance of others in this church, by showing how few Words are necessary to express real Merit, and how many are requisited to set off none'.

Pope was active, too, in the campaign for a monument to Shakespeare. The result, erected in 1740, had a surround and pedestal by William Kent, its corners decorated with portraits of Richard II, Henry V and Queen Elizabeth – where, remarked Horace Walpole, 'they have as little to do as they have with Shakespeare'. The full-length statue by Peter Scheemakers showed the poet leaning on the pedestal and looking 'natural, free, and easy', as *The Gentleman's Magazine* admiringly put it. For the scroll that unfurled from Shakespeare's hand, Pope mockingly proposed an epigram against the practice of making monuments commemorate their donors as prominently as their subjects:

> Thus Britain lov'd me; and preserved my Fame,
> Clear from a Barber's or a Benson's name.

Instead, the scroll was carved with a slight misquotation from *The Tempest*.

Pope and his contemporaries believed that a Temple of Worthies should find room for moderns as well as ancients: part of its purpose was to announce the continuity between writers of the present age and the examples they followed. In this spirit Pope contributed an epitaph on his friend John Gay, author of *The Beggar's Opera*, but made a finely theatrical gesture when it came to his own death in 1744. He chose to be buried in Twickenham near the villa, garden and grotto he had tended with as much care as he had brought to his poetry. The epitaph he wrote for himself remembered 'One who would not be buried in Westminster Abbey', thus neatly combining advertisement of his own and the Abbey's importance in the literary world.

Given the century's emphasis on the dignity appropriate to monuments, and the solemn feelings they could inspire in the spectator, we need to remind ourselves that these things are difficult of achievement. If we picture the Abbey and its poetical quarter as a hushed, reverential place haunted by the occasional pensive essayist, then we are forgetting that the monuments were intended for public gaze and that, even in the eighteenth century, such spectacles easily took on the trappings of a modern tourist attraction. It was not that Poets' Corner became slowly tainted by commercialism as it grew famous. Rather, it simply could not avoid being caught up in the commercialism of which the Abbey already had a long history. Space for monuments had always been for sale, and admission charges had been levied since the Reformation. 'If I had a mind to be angry', wrote Horace Walpole, 'I could complain with reason ... that the Chapter of Westminster sell their church over and over again; the ancient monuments tumble upon one's head through their neglect, as one of them did, and killed a man at Lady Elizabeth Percy's funeral; and they erect new waxen dolls of Queen Elizabeth, etc. to draw visits and money from the mob.'

Such accusations are made at length in one of the first published accounts to use the modern term, 'Poets' Corner'. Goldsmith's essay of 1760 in his *Citizen of the World* begins like a latter-day version of Addison's musings in *The Spectator*. 'What a gloom do monumental inscriptions and all the venerable remains of deceased merit inspire!' But Goldsmith is writing in the assumed character of a visiting foreigner, and this has always been a favourite device of the satirist. His Chinese dignitary is shocked at being asked for payment to get into the royal chapels:

I was surprised at such a demand; and asked the man whether the people of England kept a *shew*? Whether the paltry sum he demanded was not a national reproach? Whether it was not more to the honour of the country to let their magnificence or their antiquities be openly seen, than thus meanly to tax a curiosity which tended to their own honour? As for your questions, replied the gate-keeper, to be sure they may be very right, because I don't understand them, but as for that there threepence, I farm it from one, who rents it from another, who hires it from a third, who leases it from the guardians of the temple, and we all must live.

He is appalled when his guide, one of the 'ecclesiastical beggars' who haunt the place, rattles off lies and legends as historical fact, and disgusted when an extra tip is demanded at the end of the tour.

These practices continued into the nineteenth century, when various never quite satisfactory reforms were undertaken, but, of course, they did not deter visitors. The essay in Washington Irving's *Sketch Book* of 1820 shows how little sentiments and impressions have changed since Addison's day. Appreciation of the Gothic atmosphere has grown more richly sentimental, and now feeds openly on neglect of the building's fabric: 'every thing bears marks of the gradual dilapidations of time, which yet has something touching and pleasing in its very decay'. The resulting mood leads to the familiar vein of sober reflection, and Irving finds the tombs 'teaching no moral but the futility of that pride which hopes still to exact homage in its ashes, and to live in an inscription'. The monuments in Poets' Corner (a term by then fully established) prove a slight but not unexpected disappointment, since 'the lives of literary men afford no striking themes for the sculptor'. Nevertheless, he notes that 'visitors to the abbey remain longest about them'. His explanation for this seeming paradox neatly puts its finger on the attraction that literary shrines have for tourists:

A kinder and fonder feeling takes place of that cold curiosity or vague admiration with which they gaze on the splendid monuments of the great and the heroic. They linger about these as about the tombs of friends and companions; for indeed there is something of companionship between the author and reader.

Yet at the time of Irving's visit this pleasure was being partly abridged. When Lord Byron's body was shipped back from Missolonghi to London in 1824 and laid out, embalmed almost beyond recognition, for admirers to view, his friends confidently looked forward to a funeral in either the Abbey or St Paul's. 'I think the funeral apparatus cannot be too plain', one proposed grandly, 'or the crowd too great.' But the poet's scandalous doings at Newstead, his public romances in London society, his treatment of his wife, his friendship with the atheist Shelley, the train of mistresses, illegitimate children and pets with which he toured the Continent, the verse that struck even his publisher as licentious: the memory of all these things was too recent and too shocking. The Dean of Westminster declined the

Poets' Corner in the early nineteenth century, complete with a guide waiting for custom. An engraving from a drawing by John Preston Neale, published in Edward Wedlake Brayley's *The History and Antiquities of the Abbey Church of St Peter, Westminster* (1818–23).

honour and Byron's funeral cortège made its four-day journey up to Nottinghamshire, lining the streets with crowds wherever it passed, one of the greatest unofficial spectacles of the age.

Time, said Addison surveying the monuments, is a great reconciler of contending parties, but Time does not hurry to the task. Thorvaldsen's statue of Byron was refused a place by the Abbey in 1829 and eventually found a home in his old Cambridge college, Trinity, where it still sits brooding in the inappropriate surroundings of Wren's library. As late as 1924 the Dean of Westminster could reject yet another petition on Byron's behalf by citing his 'world-wide reputation for immorality among English-speaking people'. Hardy was provoked to write 'The Refusal', a satirical monologue in which the Dean denounces Byron in very unclerical language as a 'creed-scorner / (Not mentioning horner)' and contemplates future horrors:

> 'Twill next be expected
> That I get erected
> To Shelley a tablet
> In some niche or gablet.
> Then – what makes my skin burn,
> Yea, forehead and chin burn –
> That I ensconce Swinburne!

The present tablet to Byron was not unveiled until 1969.

The Abbey's long exclusion of him was only the first of a nineteenth-century catalogue. When George Eliot died in 1880 Dean Stanley remembered the novelist's atheism and her liaison with George Henry Lewes, and let it be known that he would require 'strong representations' before admitting her. The matter was dropped. Wilkie Collins, popular novelist but also a man with two mistresses and several illegitimate children, was turned away because of 'other considerations than ... literary excellence'. By 1909, when George Meredith was consigned to the outer darkness of Dorking cemetery, Thomas Hardy had begun to wonder if Poets' Corner might not need a 'heathen annexe'.

The change from earlier centuries is striking. The friendly and informal times when poets threw elegies into Spenser's open grave had gone. So, too, had the loose and tolerant standards which allowed the Restoration poet Sir John Denham to lie near Chaucer among rumours that he had poisoned his second wife. With the Victorian era Poets' Corner had been made official and forced into orthodoxy. Its monuments had become an index to those writers whom the Church of England could approve.

Dickens, Browning and Tennyson all survived clerical scrutiny; so in our own century did Thomas Hardy, which comes as a surprise, and Rudyard Kipling, which does not. To some contemporaries Kipling's funeral seemed the very apotheosis of literary fame – the Poet of the Empire being buried in the Church of the Empire – but Hardy's funeral was the more telling occasion. He had wanted to lie near his father and grandfather in Stinsford churchyard, but his executor Sydney Cockerell became aware of this unsurprising wish only after arrangements had been made for a grand occasion in Poets' Corner. By way of grisly compromise Hardy's heart was buried in Dorset and the rest of him in the Abbey.

Part of an atheist being buried in a church whose Dean he had mocked: it showed how empty was the dignity that Poets' Corner could bestow. And belief that the place was losing its meaning had by then a long history. Some of his contemporaries had noted that Dickens would have preferred to lie in Rochester cathedral and had

Mourners at Dickens' tomb in Poets' Corner. An engraving from *The Illustrated London News* for 25 June 1870.

been disturbed by the Abbey's swift appropriation of his body. The cold formality of Tennyson's funeral, when elderly peers and statesmen staggered under the burden of his coffin, had not struck friends as a fitting passage into death for the author of 'Crossing the Bar'. Years before, oblique criticism of Poets' Corner had already been voiced by writers about Stratford-upon-Avon. In Holy Trinity church Washington Irving had asked of Shakespeare:

What honour could his name have derived from being mingled in dusty companionship with the epitaphs and escutcheons, and venal eulogiums of a titled multitude. What would a crowded corner in Westminster Abbey have been, compared with this reverend pile, which seems to stand in beautiful loneliness as his sole mausoleum!

An early guidebook to Stratford had agreed, finding Shakespeare's fate preferable to Milton's or Spenser's: 'I do think it far happier to be buried in the quiet church of Stratford than, like them, in the bustle and roar of London. No poet, perhaps, rests so happily as Shakspere. This is better than being buried in Westminster Abbey or St Paul's, to lie at peace among your own.'

III

Perhaps Stratford was not such a peaceful contrast after all. The same forces that first created Poets' Corner and then drained it of meaning ensured that the 'proper little mercate town' (as William Camden described it in 1586) grew into a major tourist attraction, a literary shrine to rival if not eclipse anything the Abbey had to offer.

The Stratford tourist industry did not begin promisingly. Six years after Shakespeare's death the actors in his old company included the town in their tour of the Midlands. In all likelihood their main purpose was to pay tribute to the memory of their dead colleague, if only by taking a look round the scenes of his birth and death. Without some sentimental motive there was scant reason for making the journey, since the touring companies of actors who had once been frequent visitors were no longer welcome in the Puritan climate of 1622. The Borough Chamberlain recorded the outcome in his accounts: 'To the King's Players for not playing in the Hall 6/–'. The town would never number Shakespeare's plays among the most attractive or profitable aspects of his fame but this, surely, must be the only time it paid any visitor – actor or otherwise – to go away.

Yet Shakespeare had not been forgotten in Stratford and the King's

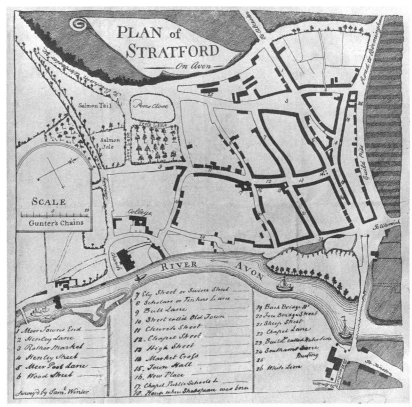

PLAN of STRATFORD — On Avon —

SCALE
Gunter's Chains

RIVER AVON

1 Moor Town's End
2 Henley Lane
3 Rother Market
4 Henley Street
5 Meer Pool Lane
6 Wood Street
Survey'd by Sam.l Winter

7 Ely Street or Swine Street
8 Scholars or Tinkers Lane
9 Bull Lane
10 Street call'd Old Town
11 Church Street
12 Chapel Street
13 High Street
14 Market Cross
15 Town Hall
16 New Place
17 Chapel Public Schools &c
18 House when Shakespeare was born

19 Back Bridge St.
20 Fou Bridge Street
21 Sheep Street
22 Chapel Lane
23 Build.t call'd Water side
24 Southam's Lane
25   Ducking
26 White Lion

Samuel Winter's plan of Stratford in 1759, when it was still Camden's 'proper little mercate town' or (as David Garrick would conclude) 'the most dirty, unseemly, illpav'd, wretched-looking Town in all Britain'.

Men need not have left completely disappointed. They could have visited Holy Trinity, where Shakespeare's gravestone was already set in the chancel pavement, offering its curse on future sextons who might disturb his grave to make room for additional occupants. They could probably have seen Gheerart Janssen's monument on the wall above as well, for it was certainly in place when the First Folio was published the following year. It typified the contemporary fashion in shrouds: a half-length bust of the poet gazed out from a square entablature decorated with, among other things, the coat of arms he had acquired. And if Shakespeare owed the honour of being buried in the church rather than the churchyard and the further honour of being so solidly com-memorated more to his local property holdings than his writings, then at least the inscription below went some way towards indicating his larger claim on posterity. With his death, said the epitaph, 'quick nature' died too; living art was merely page to serve his wit.

The earliest engraving of Shakespeare's monument in Holy Trinity, first
published in Sir William Dugdale's *Antiquities of Warwickshire* (1656) and
here reproduced from the edition of 1765. The rather different appearance of
the monument seen by later generations of tourists is presumably the combined
result of the engraving's inadequacies and the recutting of the monument itself
in 1746, though Baconians drew a sinister conclusion.

The popularity of Poets' Corner shows that the need for shrines could satisfy itself literally, in a fascination with funeral monuments. For some time to come the Stratford bust remained the chief focus of interest for visitors, and its varying fortunes expressed the history of Shakespeare's reputation in miniature. It was first engraved in Sir William Dugdale's *Antiquities of Warwickshire*, published during the lean years of the Commonwealth when, with the closing of the theatres, Shakespeare's reputation sank to its lowest point. After the Restoration and a consequent rekindling of interest in the drama it attracted enough curious visitors for the vicar of Holy Trinity to make a conscientious note in his diary: 'Remember to peruse Shakespears plays and bee versed in them, y^t I may not bee ignorant in y^t matter.'

The eighteenth century completed Shakespeare's return to the stage (though his plays were usually still performed in mutilated versions) and his recognition as England's greatest poet. By 1749 time, helped perhaps by souvenir hunters, had so eroded the soft stone of the Stratford monument that it stood in sorry contrast to the graceful statue by Peter Scheemakers recently unveiled in Westminster Abbey. Part of the cost for repairs was raised by a benefit performance of *Othello*, apparently the first time a play by Shakespeare was staged in his home town. The freshly renewed colours did not always meet with approval in an age whose taste in monuments ran to cool marble and dignified allegory rather than the waxworks realism of Shakespeare's day. 'Lady Caroline Petersham is not more vermilion', exclaimed Horace Walpole in his best allegro manner. At the end of the eighteenth century the Shakespearian scholar and editor Edmond Malone persuaded the vicar to have the bust whitewashed, but even in this chastened form it could still strike Sir Walter Scott (who came in 1828) as merely an example of 'the bad taste of James the Ist's reign'. It was finally repainted in 1861, the choice of colours being plausible rather than authentic.

In short, though it served as the main shrine at which Shakespeare pilgrims worshipped for several generations, the monument seems to have impressed none and satisfied few. The problem was not just the Jacobean taste but Janssen's special failings as portraitist. Shakespeare's plump, inexpressive features and fixed stare came as a disappointment to people whose increasingly romantic notions of what a great poet should look like had been encouraged by the elegantly casual figure on view in Westminster Abbey. The bust could feed the imagination only of someone with wits as scattered as Dickens' Mrs Nickleby, who mixes together Janssen and Scheemakers with fine abandon:

After we had seen Shakespeare's tomb . . . we went back to the inn there, where we slept that night, and I recollect that all night long I dreamt of nothing but a black gentleman, at full length, in plaster-of-Paris, with a lay-down collar tied with two tassels, leaning against a post and thinking and when I woke in the morning and described him to Mr Nickleby, he said it was Shakespeare just as he had been when he was alive, which was very curious indeed.

Such feats of fancy were denied the antiquarians, historians and guidebook writers who fostered and served Stratford's growing reputation, and they had on the whole to make do with more modest exercises in interpretation. In 1795 Samuel Ireland offered this dubious assurance: 'In the countenance of the late Mr Thomas Harte, the descendant of Shakspeare's sister . . . I always perceived a strong similitude to the markings of this figure.' But Ireland, as we shall see, enjoys a special place in that large gallery of the credulous who played an essential part in Stratford's rise to fame. Robert Bell Wheler, an altogether more scholarly man, put the best complexion he could on Janssen's achievement. 'Our immortal poet', he instructed readers of the *History and Antiquities of Stratford-upon-Avon*, 'is represented in the attitude of inspiration, with a cushion before him, a pen in his right hand, and his left rested upon a scroll.' Apparently realising that the matter could not be completely laid to rest with this kindly description he was tempted, unwisely, into apology and explanation: 'The air of it is indeed somewhat *thoughtful*, but then it seems to arise from a *chearfulness of thought*, which it must be allowed, SHAKSPEARE, at proper times, was no stranger to.' The main cause of his cheerfulness of thought, we learn, was the uncommon good fortune that allowed Shakespeare to invest in property and so retire to a pleasant town like Stratford at an early age.

Wheler was writing in 1806 and by this time no single monument, however expressive, could have satisfied visitors' appetite for glimpses of Shakespeare's disposition, whether thoughtful or cheerful or some ingenious combination of the two. While Janssen's bust was suffering its various changes and various criticisms, local Shakespearian legends flourished in a fertile soil of curiosity, imagination and commercial advantage. We have no means of knowing if the seventeenth-century vicar carried out his private resolve to instruct himself in Shakespeare's plays but he certainly managed to help a little colourful gossip on its way. To his testimony we owe the now familiar tradition that Shakespeare died as the result of a drinking bout with his fellow poets Michael Drayton and Ben Jonson.

Such mildly scurrilous anecdotes appealed by making the great man seem human, and they became yet more satisfying when they could be attached to specific local landmarks. In 1762, for example, a corre- spondent reported to *The British Magazine* that a Stratford innkeeper had taken him to see a crab tree where the young Shakespeare had spent the night after incautiously testing his drinking capacity against the men of Bidford. Others were eager to follow in the correspondent's footsteps and the Stratford landlords were not slow to oblige; perhaps their trade lent the pilgrimage authority. Samuel Ireland managed to fall into ecstatic reverie before the imagined spectacle of the poet sleeping it off. Others were not so reverential, and in 1824 Wheler recorded the end of the tree: 'For several years previously the Branches

The Shakespeare crab tree at Bidford, which 'spread its shade over him, and sheltered him from the dews of the night'. A woodcut from Samuel Ireland's *Picturesque Views on the Upper, or Warwickshire Avon* (1795).

had entirely vanished from the further depradations of pious votaries; & the stock had mouldered to touchwood, the roots were rotten, & the time worn remains totally useless.'

Another instance of Shakespeare's human weakness proved less ephemeral. Nicholas Rowe's edition of 1709 first described how the young Shakespeare had been arrested for poaching deer in Charlecote Park by its owner, Sir Thomas Lucy. With suitable elaboration, the story quickly gained acceptance and became the most stubbornly enduring addition to the Shakespeare legend. Even the discovery that in his day Charlecote had boasted not a park but a warren, which could at best have sheltered only roe deer, did not prove an insurmountable obstacle to belief. The deer-stealing was simply transferred to nearby Fulbrook and the honour of Shakespeare's arraignment reserved to Charlecote. When Sir Walter Scott found room for the episode in the ample framework of *Kenilworth* he raised it to the status of unassailable historical fact in the public mind. The happy result, of course, was that the pilgrim could expand his itinerary to include a picturesque stretch of the Warwickshire countryside and a charming Tudor mansion.

The pastoral charms of Bidford and Charlecote were only tributaries of the enlarging myth, mere sideshows to the main spectacle of Stratford itself. Apart from the Holy Trinity monument, the most substantial and authentic landmark to survive in the town was New Place, the property Shakespeare bought in 1597 and made his home when he retired from the London stage. In the course of the seventeenth century the house found its way back into the hands of the family who had originally built it, the Cloptons. By this time timber and plaster were starting to look crudely antiquated to fashionable eyes, and so in 1702 New Place was thoroughly renovated. There the matter rested until 1753, when the house was bought by the Rev. Francis Gastrell, Vicar of Frodsham in Cheshire, Canon Residentiary of Chester Cathedral and, by virtue of these appointments, a man of some affluence. He was also the most reluctant character to play his part in Stratford's growing tourist trade.

When he chose New Place as his summer residence Gastrell was apparently unaware of its connection with Shakespeare, but he was shortly enlightened by the steady tramp of feet to his door, the same pilgrim feet regularly making the journey to Holy Trinity and Charlecote. Their goal was not so much the house itself as a tree in its garden. This was hardly surprising for, if we believe the common report, poets in general and Shakespeare in particular have much to do with trees. In

Versions of New Place: 1. The building shown in this aquatint and the claim accompanying it in *Picturesque Views on the Avon* are implausible even by Samuel Ireland's standards: 'The view is copied from an old drawing of one Robert Treswell's, made in 1599, by order of Sir George Carew, afterwards Baron Carew, of Clopton, and Earl of Totness. It was found in the Clopton house in 1786, and was in the possession of the late Mrs Patriche, who was the last of the antient family of the Cloptons. The drawing, I am informed, is lost or destroyed.'

old age, according to local tradition, he had planted a mulberry at New Place. Neither the tradition nor the visitors it provoked were welcome to Gastrell, who had obviously come to Stratford to relax from his clerical duties and not to act as the custodian of a tourist attraction. He chopped the tree down. The result was a small local riot and Gastrell found it wise to keep clear of the town for a while.

He returned, but only to stir up further controversy. This time the dispute was about the monthly assessment of his rates, which went towards the maintenance of the parish poor. Rather uncharitably for a man of the cloth, Gastrell argued that he was entitled to a reduction because he lived at New Place only during the summer months. With the mild but crushing reasonableness which is the hallmark of the determined tax collector, the Corporation retorted that he maintained

Versions of New Place: 2. New Place 'thoroughly repaired and beautified, and a modern front built to it' by the Cloptons in the early eighteenth century. An illustration from Robert Bell Wheler's *History and Antiquities of Stratford-upon-Avon* (1806).

a staff of servants all the year round and so was liable to the full rate. But the Corporation, neglecting to ponder the episode of the mulberry tree, had underrated Gastrell's quickness to anger and his love of the bold expedient. In 1759 he demolished New Place.

He then vanished from the scene, permanently quitting Stratford 'amidst the rage and curses of its inhabitants' and the more lasting abuse of Shakespeare's admirers, whose kindest epithets for him were usually 'sacrilegious' and 'irreverent'. But, however unwittingly, he had helped local commerce. Instead of using the remains of the mulberry tree as firewood, which had apparently been his first intention, he had relented and sold them to a local tradesman, Thomas Sharp. With ready enterprise, Sharp used his purchase to start Stratford's first relics industry: an apparently inexhaustible stream of mulberry trinkets in the form of toothpicks, snuff boxes, spectacle cases, goblets and even pieces of furniture. As the business flourished sceptics, let alone rival entrepreneurs, pointed out that the full range of

Mr Sharp's wares would have depopulated a small forest. He took to providing his knick-knacks with a guarantee of authenticity and was finally driven to swearing an affidavit which traced the history of the tree, described the purchase of its lumber and ended: 'I do hereby declare, & take my solemn oath, upon the four Evangelists, in the presence of Almighty God, that I never had worked, sold, or substituted any other wood, than what came from, & was part of the said tree, as or for Mulberry-wood.' This sonorous declaration was signed in October 1799. A few days later Mr Sharp took his conscience to the grave with him.

Sooner or later the local enterprise of men like Sharp was bound to join hands with the more sophisticated enterprise of the London theatres, where Shakespeare's plays were now a staple of the repertoire. And it was almost inevitable that the man responsible for bringing them together should have been the modern Roscius, David Garrick. Of all the age's actors, it was Garrick whose name and reputation were most closely linked with Shakespeare's work.

Things began modestly enough in 1769, some four years after the bicentenary of Shakespeare's birth had passed without special remark in Stratford, when the Corporation needed a suitable ornament for their new Town Hall. They approached Garrick with the suggestion that he might wish to contribute a statue of Shakespeare. Garrick responded thriftily with a copy of a copy of the Westminster Abbey sculpture and, more generously, with a painting of the poet by Benjamin Wilson and a fine portrait of himself by Gainsborough. It showed him leaning against a bust of Shakespeare in an attitude that neatly combined respectful worship with easy, almost proprietorial familiarity. The Corporation awarded him the freedom of the borough, presented (of course) in a box made of mulberry.

During these civil negotiations Garrick's imagination and business flair were seized by the prospect of using the official opening of the Town Hall to celebrate Shakespeare in his home town on a scale that had not been attempted before. He approached the task with all his age's considerable powers of invention when it came to amusing themselves: their love of music and dancing, masquerades and fireworks, and their delight in alternating between informal conviviality and public ceremony. It is significant that the centrepiece of the Jubilee, the large wooden Rotunda built on the bank of the Avon, should have been modelled on the amphitheatre at Vauxhall Gardens. With the technical expertise of his Drury Lane theatre, Garrick set out to recreate all the amusements, both gaudy and refined, of the eighteenth-century pleasure gardens in a small provincial town. Having such ideas at his command, he was not driven to the barren expedient of staging Shakespeare's work. Instead, he expressed the sensibility of his age at play as perfectly as the Eglinton Tournament did in the nineteenth century or the rock festival does in our own. Understandably, historians waver between calling the occasion the 'Shakespeare Jubilee' and the 'Garrick Jubilee'.

The first day of the Jubilee in September 1769 was a great success. The local inhabitants were awed and the crowds of visitors enchanted by the magnificence of the celebrations. They were wakened at dawn by a volley of cannons and the pealing of bells. Serenading singers and musicians processed through the streets, summoning visitors to a public breakfast in the new Town Hall. This was followed by an oratorio in the church, composed and conducted by Dr Thomas Arne, the age's leading musician. Dinner was held in the Rotunda that afternoon and in the course of the entertainment afterwards a tenor, holding a mulberry goblet in his hand, sang a song by Garrick about the famous tree:

> As a relic I kiss it, and bow at the shrine.
> What comes from thy hand must be ever divine!

The proceedings were rounded off by a ball in the evening.

The second day's programme was even more splendid. It announced a pageant by Drury Lane actors dressed as Shakespearian characters, a performance by Garrick of his ode to Shakespeare, a fireworks display and a costume ball. In obedience to English custom the promise of these delights was accompanied by the qualifying phrase 'if the Weather will permit'. It poured with rain all day. The pageant was cancelled and the fireworks fizzled ingloriously. Garrick managed to rescue the performance of his ode, scoring a remarkable triumph over the leaky Rotunda and the banality of his own verse, but the ball in the evening turned into disaster. Only James Boswell seems to have succeeded in enjoying himself, proudly showing off his Corsican costume to disconsolate fellow guests who had splashed through puddles to reach the Rotunda. By dawn the rising waters had stranded the revellers, who made their messy exit sinking in quagmires and falling in ditches.

In London afterwards Garrick recouped his losses by restaging the Jubilee as a play, a spectacular affair mainly designed as an excuse for the pageant which Stratford's weather had frustrated. On the safer, drier boards of Drury Lane it was a great success. But Garrick was never tempted to return to Stratford, and when its Corporation proposed an annual jubilee he showed them no mercy:

w^d. the Gentlemen do real honour, & show their Love to Shakespeare – Let 'Em decorate ye town (y^e *happiest* & why not y^e *handsomest* in England) let your streets be well pav'd, & kept clean, do Something with ye delightful Meadow, allure Everybody to visit y^e *holy Land*; let it be well lighted, & clean under foot, and let it not be said for y^r. honour, & I hope for y^r. Interest, that the Town, which gave Birth to the first Genius since ye Creation, is the most dirty, unseemly, illpav'd, wretched-looking Town in all Britain.

IV

Neither the laughter of his critics nor Garrick's own recrimination of Stratford could alter the main result of the Jubilee. The town was now more firmly established, more prominently marked on the traveller's map of England than ever before. That indefatigable tourist John Byng came in 1785 and stayed at the White Lion – an obvious choice, since the Henley Street hotel had been made famous on the stage at Drury Lane. In the course of his tour he restrained himself from buying mulberry trinkets, but not out of scepticism, for in his diary he regretted his 'aeconomy and abstinence'. Happily, however, he was able to pick up a genuine relic in a very economical way while the sexton's back was turned at Holy Trinity church: 'I pilfer'd (in common with other collectors) from the Roman pavement, at the head of Shakesperes grave-stone, a tesselated tile, which I hid in my pocket; and which I should suppose will be honor'd and admired by every spectator.'

Samuel Ireland's visit in 1792 has already been mentioned for its display of gullibility. In fact, Ireland threw himself with happy innocence at anything that could possibly be linked with Shakespeare's name. When he left he could take with him not just a sheaf of sketches and the material for a chapter of his travel guide to the river Avon but also a greater prize than Byng could boast. John Jordan, the self-styled Shakespearian expert who often acted as guide to visitors, had directed him to Anne Hathaway's cottage in Shottery – the first published reference we have to that now familiar landmark in the tourist itinerary. Ireland found it still inhabited by Hathaways, who were 'poor and numerous' but possessed of relics. Shakespeare's 'courting chair' and purse were irresistible temptations to a man eager 'to obtain the smallest trifle appertaining to our Shakspeare'. Even his failure to

Stratford, with Holy Trinity (lacking its spire) seen in the distance beyond the medieval Clopton Bridge. In the text accompanying this illustration to *Picturesque Views on the Avon* Samuel Ireland made the best of a rather unexciting prospect: 'The entrance to the town of Stratford across the meadow partakes neither of the beautiful or picturesque; the buildings are mean, and the adjoining scenery flat and uninteresting: but looking to the left, the eye is gratified with a pleasing view of the venerable church of Stratford rising on the margin of our gentle Avon.'

buy the family bed had its bright side: 'Her absolute refusal to part with this bed at any price was one of the circumstances which led to a persuasion that I had not listened with too easy credulity to the tale she told me respecting the articles I had purchased.' After this, it comes as no surprise to learn that William Henry Ireland, who accompanied his father on the trip, soon set up in business as the most daring Shakespearian forger of his time and chose Samuel Ireland as his first victim.

The most striking fact to emerge from Byng's and Ireland's accounts is that a new star had been hoisted in the Stratford firmament. Shakespeare's birthplace was now the first item on the traveller's agenda and would soon overshadow all rival attractions. Indeed, it seems curious in retrospect that the Henley Street house should have lain overlooked for so long. In the course of the seventeenth century it had reverted to the Hart family, descendants of the poet's sister Joan, where it had quietly rotted. The eastern half became the Swan and Maidenhead, an inn whose refreshments were never recommended to the genteel traveller, and had its half-timber frontage bricked over. The western half, on which attention would later focus, became a butcher's shop.

Garrick was apparently the first to spot its possibilities. By an act of faith rather than scholarship, he had declared the front bedroom over the butcher's shop to be the very birthroom itself and draped its window with an illuminated transparency bearing the legend: 'Thus dying clouds contend with growing light'. The fortunes of the place began to flourish, though its physical state for long remained 'humble

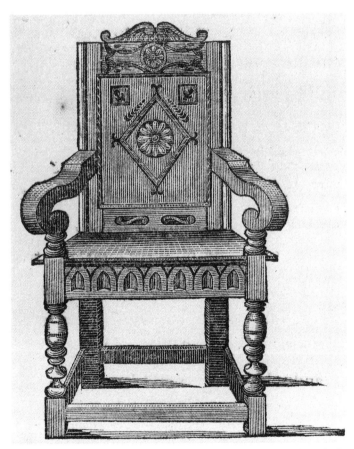

Shakespeare's 'courting chair' (whatever that might be), bought by Samuel Ireland on his visit to the Hathaways' cottage at Shottery and depicted in this woodcut from his *Picturesque Views on the Avon*.

Versions of Shakespeare's Birthplace: 1. The earliest known engraving, published in *The Gentleman's Magazine* for July 1769. From a drawing by Richard Greene, the Lichfield antiquary.

and dilapidated', presenting a 'cheerless appearance' to the street. The phrases come from the first guidebook specifically devoted to the birthplace, written by the local historian Wheler in 1824. He goes on to provide a careful, scholarly account divided between substantiating its claim to authenticity and lamenting the sorry spectacle it then offered to the visitor. One entered past the butcher's counter, over which hung a sign:

WILLIAM SHAKSPEARE WAS BORN IN THIS HOUSE.
    N.B. – A horse and taxed cart to let.

In the back was a kitchen and, upstairs, the birthroom, its walls and windows increasingly scrawled with visitors' signatures.

In themselves these humble accommodations were hardly impressive, but they had been made an Aladdin's cave of treasures. Mrs Hart showed the chief glory to Byng with a fine flow of patter:

Why, there, sr is Shakespears old chair, and I have been often bid a good sum of money for it, It has been carefully handed down on record by our family; but people never thought so much of it till after the jubilee, and now see what pieces they have cut from it, as well as from the old flooring of the bed room!

Byng bought a 'slice of the chair equal to the size of a tobacco stopper' and returned later to bargain successfully for its lower cross bar. Ireland was eager to inspect a relic 'which had for a number of years received nearly as many adorers as the celebrated shrine of the Lady of Loretto' but it had gone. The chair, he learned, had been sold in 1790 for twenty guineas to a Polish princess, who had taken it off in triumph, complete with 'a proper certificate of its authenticity on stamped paper'.

When Washington Irving arrived in 1815 the chair had mysteriously reappeared. It was the custom for visitors to sit in it, and from this comfortable position he could survey the remarkable collection now assembled in the kitchen:

There was the shattered stock of the very matchlock with which Shakespeare shot the deer, on his poaching exploit. There, too, was his tobacco box; which proves that he was a rival smoker of Sir Walter Raleigh; the sword also with which he played Hamlet; and the identical lanthorn with which Friar Laurence discovered Romeo and Juliet at the tomb!

Irving was able to regard these objects with a shrewd but tolerant eye. 'I am always of easy faith in such matters', he confessed engagingly, 'and am ever willing to be deceived, where the deceit is pleasant, and costs nothing.' In this he seems to have been typical of the Americans whom Stratford's fame was beginning to attract in a regular stream. It was the English who alternated between gullibility and indignation.

By the time of Irving's visit the birthplace had changed hands. On the death of old Mr Hart his relatives let the butcher's shop to Mary Hornby. She remained as tenant after the whole property was sold in 1806 to the Court family, who came to live in the Swan and Maidenhead next door. Irving found Mrs Hornby 'a garrulous old lady in a frosty red face, lighted up by a cold blue anxious eye, and garnished with artificial locks of flaxen hair, curling from under an exceedingly dirty cap'. The bizarre collection of relics was largely her creation. She claimed to be a descendant of Shakespeare and set her hand to poetry in support of the claim, starting modestly with an anthology of *Extemporary Verses* drawn from the visitors' book but later rising to two plays, *The Battle of Waterloo* and *The Broken Vow*.

Her guardianship, indeed, could endow even the most prosaic object with the character of fantasy. Apart from extempore verses her visitors' book bore the signatures of the Prince Regent and the Duke of Wellington, dignitaries who had never been near Stratford or Mrs Hornby in their lives. It was left to the stern and scholarly Wheler to point a moral, and incidentally to remind us how little human nature changes over the years: 'entries are made by strangers, if the books be improperly superintended, which serve in too many instances to record, not their real names, nor their admiration of the poet, but their own levity and folly'.

It is sad to record that Mrs Hornby's career ended on a note of anticlimax. From the Swan and Maidenhead next door Mrs Court had been watching her success with a jealous eye, and the two fell into dispute about the rent. Mrs Hornby was evicted in 1820, the same year Irving made her famous in print, and decamped across the road to set up her collection of relics in exile. Mrs Court, meanwhile, installed herself in the butcher's shop and respectfully invited 'the nobility and gentry visiting Stratford-upon-Avon to gratify their own laudable curiosity and honour her by inspecting the house in which the immortal Poet of Nature was born'.

When she died and the two adjoining properties came up for sale in 1847 even the estate agent's gift for superlatives was stretched to its limit: 'THE TRULY HEART-STIRRING RELIC OF A MOST GLORIOUS PERIOD, AND OF ENGLAND'S IMMORTAL BARD ... THE MOST HONOURED MONUMENT OF THE GREATEST GENIUS THAT EVER LIVED'. In answer to rumours of an American plan to buy the house and reconstruct it on the other side of the Atlantic, the Stratford Birthplace Committee was formed to launch a public appeal. It quickly became a national event. Benefit performances, not always of Shakespeare's plays, were staged and Prince Albert donated £250. As a result the Committee, by then acting in concert with its London counterpart, was able to put in the successful bid of £3,000 at the September auction. The occasion did not pass off without a small voice of dissent being raised, though it was quickly smothered amid the crescendo of enthusiasm:

A person here interposed, and called upon Mr Robins to prove that the house he was about to sell was the identical one in which the poet was born. Mr Robins replied that tradition pointed out this house as that of Shakespeare's birth. His father lived in it, and there could be no doubt that the great Poet was born in the house and spent the greater part of his life in it. (Cheers.) They must take it as a matter of course. He wished that those who were sceptical on the point would stay away, instead of starting doubts which had no foundation to rest upon.

The immediate effect of the sale on the Birthplace was not dramatic, although it now seems entitled to the capital letter. Nathaniel Hawthorne paid a visit in 1855, while he was working as American Consul

Poster advertising the auction of Shakespeare's Birthplace.

at Liverpool, and to the reader familiar with previous descriptions the essay in *Our Old Home* is a finely blended mixture of the old and the new. From outside, the house was still not prepossessing. Traces of the butcher's shop still lingered inside, though the rooms were not as dirty as they had been in Mrs Hornby's day: they were 'white-washed and exceedingly clean', in fact. The custodian was cleaner, too. To his surprise Hawthorne found that she had 'the manners and aspect of a gentlewoman, and talked with somewhat formidable and appreciative intelligence about Shakspere'. Mrs Hornby's curios had been replaced by a display of 'various prints, views of houses and scenes connected with Shakspere's memory, together with editions of his works and local publications about his homes and haunts'. The financial side to a visit had not altered, of course, and Hawthorne found that his guide did not share his embarrassment over the matter of a fee. He was moved to pass on advice to his fellow countrymen: 'nobody need fear to hold out half-a-crown to any person with whom he has occasion to speak a word in England'.

Shortly afterwards the Birthplace was restored, or perhaps we should say 'restored'. The site itself was greatly altered by the demolition of neighbouring houses with which the Birthplace had formed a continuous row – to reduce the risk of fire, it was said. When it came to the Birthplace itself, the architect undertook major rebuilding of a property that had barely been maintained for two centuries. Much of the timber needed replacing, and pieces of the old wood were sold as relics to raise funds. The result was a scholarly reconstruction of the building that might once have stood on the site. It was on view by the 1860s and can still be seen today.

Even at the time not all responsible observers approved. The Shakespearian scholar J. O. Halliwell (later Halliwell-Phillipps) said bluntly in the preface to a guide on sale at the Birthplace that it would have been better if 'the premises had simply been protected against the casualties of fire and the weather, and then left in precisely the state in which they had been purchased'. But in terms of tourism the restoration proved no bad thing. At the beginning of the nineteenth century there had been about a thousand visitors a year, or so the auctioneer later claimed. In 1853–4, when more systematic records were being kept, the figure had become nearly three thousand – of whom, incidentally, nearly five hundred were American. It continued to rise sharply for the rest of the century and had reached thirty thousand a year by 1900. As it did, the Birthplace Committee gained in power. In 1866, the year it officially became the Birthplace

Versions of Shakespeare's Birthplace: 2. In 1847, the year it was bought by the Shakespeare Birthplace Committee.

Trust, it took over responsibility for the New Place estate and later acquired Anne Hathaway's Cottage, Mary Arden's House and Hall's Croft, the house once occupied by Shakespeare's daughter and son-in-law. By the 1980s well over a million visits a year were being made to these five properties together, more than half of them to the Birthplace itself.

V

Rendered more imposing by its isolation from neighbouring houses and facelifted to a picturesque splendour it may never before have possessed, the Birthplace that rose from the decayed remains of the old expressed a new, typically Victorian attitude to Shakespeare. Like the text of his plays, his local reputation and its guardian shrines needed bowdlerising. Earlier generations had mixed their admiration with a

Versions of Shakespeare's Birthplace: 3. In 1864, after restoration.

fatal taint of gossip and scandal-mongering; their worship had been negligent and even cavalier. They had relished stories of the poet's drunkenness, whitewashed his bust, pilfered from his grave and demolished or neglected the houses he lived in. In retrospect it was all rather embarrassing. Washington Irving, who could regard Mrs Hornby's relics with knowing good humour, was disturbed by the thought that Shakespeare had been a poacher. One suspects that the new generation guarding Shakespeare's memory heaved a sigh of relief when the plundered remains of the Bidford crab tree were finally carted away in 1824.

The new orthodoxy was firmly established by the time John Wise wrote his guide to Stratford in the early 1860s. Like Washington Irving he could smile tolerantly on the buyers of fake relics as worshippers, however misguided, of the good and the great. But his own manner of worship is altogether more exalted. In Stratford he traces the footsteps of a saint who emerged from obscurity to perform miracles for the benefit of mankind and of a self-made man who worked his way up from humble origins. When he enters the Holy of Holies, the birth-room, his voice drops to hushed ecstasy:

> It is but a platitude to say that this room stands before all palaces. And as we look at it, and remember that probably it was much scantier and smaller, we bethink ourselves how little Nature cares for her greatest children. She flings them by in obscure corners of the world, leaving them to fight their way. In poverty have been born the world's greatest men.

Stratford could now find room even for a sidechapel devoted to a lesser cult. Marie Corelli, immensely popular author of *The Sorrows of Satan* and *The Mighty Atom*, came in 1890. She left with the idea of writing a novel about Shakespeare's son who died in infancy. Or, as she characteristically put it: 'The clouds of my imagination are turning into soft rosy and gold colour, and I see a little figure with wistful eyes and serious baby face advancing towards me, called Hamnet!' The vision proved mercifully fleeting and the book was never written, but Stratford had suggested a more lasting ambition. It had impressed her as the perfect spot for 'the cradle and grave of the divine Shakespeare' and Marie Corelli was always unblushing in her imitation of genius.

It was too late to arrange to be born in Stratford and, besides, she had already made the best she could of her birth by changing her name from Minnie Mackay and claiming Venetian ancestry. But something could still be done about the latter end of life and done, moreover, not in quiet obscurity like Shakespeare but in the pleasant glow of publicity. She moved to Stratford in 1900 and later leased Mason Croft, the building that now houses the Shakespeare Institute of Birmingham University. Her last years were spent worshipping regularly at the church and the Birthplace, feuding with their appointed guardians, fighting a libel suit with the editor of the local newspaper and being propelled along the Avon in a gondola. She became a tourist attraction to rival Shakespeare himself. *Punch* wrily commented:

> The Yankee streaming to the shrine
>   Of our immortal Mummer,
> Forgets the dead and doubtful 'Swan',
> And concentrates his worship on
>   The real and living Hummer.
>
> 'Behold', he cries, 'the actual house
>   That Miss Corelli leases,
> In yonder study's restful shade,

> Accepting none but Heaven's aid,
>   She makes her masterpieces.'

Indeed, some visitors thought she was descended from the poet, a misunderstanding she did not labour to correct.

As it entered the Marie Corelli phase of its history Stratford flourished, like the medieval Catholic Church, on a combination of solemn reverence and blatant hype. And like the Church in the Middle Ages, it could provoke doubts, crises of faith, even heresy. By the middle of the nineteenth century the American Delia Bacon was already haunting Holy Trinity in the belief that the opening of Shakespeare's grave would show his plays had been written by her namesake, Sir Francis. Fear of disappointment stopped her going ahead with the experiment and she died insane in 1859. Two years before, her *Philosophy of the Plays of Shakespere Unfolded* had slipped from the press unnoticed by all except Hawthorne, whose kindly preface managed to stop well short of endorsing her views. Yet at Stratford even he could be troubled by 'ugly doubt', if only about the authenticity of the birthroom. In the years that followed Baconians began to descend regularly on Stratford, citing its history of palpable fraud, the former meanness of the Birthplace and the rumours about the extent of its restoration to support their theories. Vilification of Stratford became as essential a feature of their writing as cryptography and perverse spelling of the poet's name.

Such visits were not necessarily bad for trade; a little controversy helped quicken interest. More serious were the doubts of those who noted that the union of reverence and commercialism did not always breed scholarly accuracy. Mrs Hornby's collection had long since been broken up, of course, though the mulberry trinkets still pursued a ghostly career; two had even been offered for sale at the Birthplace auction in 1847. And was not the acceptance of local legend still too eagerly uncritical, the labelling of certain items in the Birthplace collection too generously optimistic? In 1891 Joseph Skipsey, ex-miner and self-taught poet from Northumberland, resigned his post as custodian, sickened at being required to 'act the part of a common showman'. 'And what made matters a thousand times worse,' he complained, 'we had not held our office more than a few months before we discovered that not a single one of the many so-called relics on exhibition could be proved to be Shakespeare's — nay, that the Birthplace itself is a matter of grave doubt.'

Skipsey's resignation gave Henry James the hint for his story, 'The

Charlecote Park, near Stratford, with descendants of the deer Shakespeare was supposed to have poached. An engraving by W. J. Linton from *The Illustrated London News* for 18 September 1847, one of several views of Stratford and its neighbourhood illustrating an article prompted by the sale of the Birthplace.

Birthplace', a wry little parable of faith and doubt in the nineteenth century. The fictional custodian, Morris Gedge, is reduced to disillusion: 'There was somebody ... But They've killed Him. And, dead as He is, They keep it up, They do it over again, They kill Him every day.' A sympathetic American tourist to whom he confides his doubts reminds him of the need to earn his bread and exhorts him to 'keep it up, keep it up'. Gedge recovers and does not resign as Skipsey had done, but throws himself into the task of entertaining the visitors with histrionic abandon. The takings pick up marvellously.

Hawthorne's moment of doubt in the birthroom was only brief, but at the end of his visit he still had to admit: 'I was conscious of not the slightest emotion while viewing it, nor any quickening of the imagination.' To him, as to so many visitors after him, the Birthplace seemed just a shell, emptied of whatever spirit it might once have harboured.

Before he turned to the troubled conscience of Mr Gedge, James had already published 'In Warwickshire', an essay conspicuous in the travel literature of Stratford for its refusal to take more than an oblique glance at the town itself. The closest he will come is to Charlecote. Here, very sensibly, he does his best to put all thought of deer-stealing poets out of his mind and to settle instead to admiring a park 'whose venerable verdure seems a survival from an earlier England and whose innumerable acres, stretching away, in the early evening, to vaguely seen Tudor walls, lie there like the backward years receding to the age of Elizabeth'.

2

Envious show: the opening of the country house

> As is usually the case with people who go over houses, Mr Guppy and his friend are dead beat before they have well begun. They straggle about in wrong places, look at wrong things, don't care for the right things, gape when more rooms are opened, exhibit profound depression of spirits, and are clearly knocked up ... Thus they pass from room to room, raising the pictured Dedlocks for a few brief minutes as the young gardener admits the light, and reconsigning them to their graves as he shuts it out again. It appears to the afflicted Mr Guppy and his inconsolable friend, that there is no end to the Dedlocks, whose family greatness seems to consist in their never having done anything to distinguish themselves, for seven hundred years.
>
> Dickens, *Bleak House*

I

When Evelyn Waugh looked at English society in the 1940s he saw its traditional structure and values in danger of being swept away, and he found the natural symbol for this maddening, heartbreaking process in the fate of the country house. *Brideshead Revisited* piled on the nostalgia with passionate sincerity, making the home of the Marchmain family a poignant reminder of a glory that was passing from the world, a glory too refined and fragile to survive an age of war, vulgarity and Socialism. Waugh wrote, he later explained, in the conviction that 'the ancestral seats which were our chief national artistic achievement were doomed to decay and spoliation like the monasteries in the sixteenth century'. The parallel might sound melodramatic but it also cropped up in the more sober pages of the Gowers Committee Report in 1950. After considering the social changes, as well as the crippling burden of taxation, that threatened country houses, it warned of an 'impending catastrophe': 'we are faced with a disaster comparable only to that which the country suffered by the dissolution of the monasteries in the sixteenth century'.

Some forty years have passed since gloom and anxiety made such unlikely bedfellows of Evelyn Waugh and a government committee, forty years that have done much to fulfil their prophecies. England has lost about 250 houses, and scarcely a year goes by without news of another case, another emergency, another last-minute appeal to save a major building. 'The Destruction of the Country House', an exhibition held at the Victoria and Albert Museum some years ago, brought the sorry record dramatically to life. It confronted spectators with photograph after photograph of roofless corridors, crumbling plaster and stone, charred and worm-eaten timbers, parkland reverting to wilderness, mere shells of buildings that had once embodied Tudor exuberance or Georgian elegance or Victorian opulence.

Yet this is only half the story; indeed, it is something less than half. When we look at country houses today we are struck, not by the spectacle of bare ruined choirs, but by all the signs of a lively and resilient industry. In 1960, not so long after the publication of *Brideshead Revisited*, Waugh himself admitted in a new preface to the book that he had misread the future. Places like Brideshead had not vanished but instead, disconcertingly, become objects of a growing cult. The Historic Buildings Council (a creation of the Gowers Committee Report) was making grants to help preservation and the National Trust was taking over properties from owners who could not afford to maintain them. At Woburn the Duke of Bedford and at Longleat the Marquis of Bath – *enfants terribles* of the stately homes business – were ushering in a new age of fun-fair attractions. And so Waugh revised his prophecy: 'Brideshead today would be open to trippers, its treasures rearranged by expert hands and the fabric better maintained than it was by Lord Marchmain.' To appreciate the truth of this, and to appreciate how steadily the cult of the country house has kept on growing since 1960, we need look only at the present state of Brideshead's real-life model, Castle Howard. Helped by astute commercial management, and by its starring role in the TV version of Waugh's novel, it is now a major landmark for the tourist. When we add the number of its visitors to all the other visitors at all the other houses so eagerly opening their gates to the public, we arrive at a figure that comfortably passes the 16-million mark each year.

One thing, at least, is clear about this flourishing industry: aesthetic considerations have played only a small part in its rise. Country houses deserve attention for their architecture and for the art objects they contain, and there are heartening signs that, belatedly, we are on our way towards the recognition of 'our chief national artistic achievement' Waugh demanded. But this by itself has not been enough to ensure survival, much less to draw crowds. National Trust properties, where the buildings' original features are preserved with museum-like accuracy, are never as popular as those privately owned houses where eighteenth-century portraits hang next to photos of the present Marquis shaking hands with the Queen, piles of *Country Life* obscure the Regency tables, and safari parks, craft fairs or parachute displays enliven the grounds.

For country-house visitors the pursuit of culture is a less powerful motive than basic human curiosity. We admire the architecture and the paintings, but often just in a cursory way. This duty done, we throw ourselves into the business of envying the people who lived in leisure among all this splendour and of pitying the housemaids who had to dust all that furniture. Nor does our curiosity exhaust itself on the past, for we eagerly snap up all the titbits of information and gossip about the present inhabitants which guides and custodians so adroitly let fall. 'The public', concludes a detailed survey of present tastes, 'like to believe that a visit to a great house affords an inside view of the lives of the owners.'

As tourists we are always aware, to whatever degree, of enjoying the liberties and the powers that democracy has brought. This knowledge makes up much of the pleasure – much, indeed, of the whole point – in country-house visiting. We celebrate our right of entry into places that would once have excluded us, or at best required us to enter humbly through the back door. We enact our victory over élitism. If at times the hordes of fellow visitors or the fun-fair amusements in the park disturb and repel us, we are feeling unease at democracy's tendency to cheapen what it touches. Yet even then we can still take consolation from the reminder that we have shown ourselves less vengeful and barbarous in our triumph than Evelyn Waugh first feared. Instead of sweeping country houses and their owners away, we have agreed to become their communal paymasters.

II

It is always dangerous to suppose that modern tourism is really all that modern and to place the credit – or the blame – for its achievements entirely on the shoulders of our own age. It is certainly mistaken to see the present fate of our country houses as a complete break with tradition, a dramatic shift forced on them by the Second World War and its aftermath. Attracting tourists has always been part of their function, and it has been a major function since the eighteenth century, when so many aspects of modern tourism first began to emerge. But to understand the history of country-house visiting, and to see the current situation in its proper context, we need first to challenge some of our assumptions about country houses themselves.

If they have gone down in popular myth as aloof and exclusive bastions of privilege, it is not hard to see why. One aspect, at least, of the face presented by the country house to the rest of society was always deliberately forbidding. Even in the eighteenth century, when houses had long since lost their strictly defensive character, they still appeared exclusive and, indeed, the fashion of the age was to stress their exclusiveness. Owners moved their houses away from the village where they had once nestled cheek by jowl with the church and the market place or, more drastically, razed the village and rebuilt it at a suitable distance. They closed their entrance drives with wrought-iron gates, surrounded their parkland with walls and guarded their game preserves with mantraps.

These physical changes were symptomatic of changed, and drastically diminished, relations with the surrounding community. Owners spent less time in the country – their love of the fashionable life in London and the spa towns became the most familiar complaint against the landowning classes – and when they did return, their firm control over local politics made sociable relations with tenants and freeholders less necessary. Inside, the household was no longer the rich and complex hierarchy it had been in the Middle Ages and the Renaissance. The gentlemen retainers and gentlemen servants who had once been proud to stand behind the master's chair at table had left – for the world of trade and commerce, the universities and the professions. The household that remained was rigidly stratified into two classes, masters and servants, with the servants increasingly cramped into hidden, out-of-the-way parts of the buildings.

By the eighteenth century, then, the sort of country-house life Ben Jonson had celebrated in 'To Penshurst' had disappeared, if indeed it

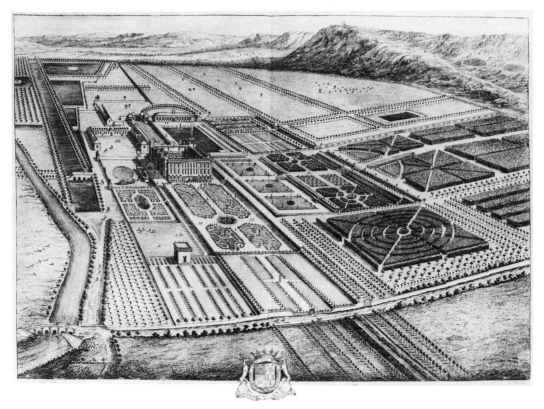

Chatsworth: Three ways of looking at a show house. 1. As real estate.
Engraved by Johannes Kip from a drawing by Leonard Knyff in *Britannia
Illustrata* (1707).

had ever existed in quite those admirable forms the poet alleged. The
vital, free-and-easy sociability epitomised by the communal Great Hall
had gone the way of the Great Hall itself. Only the memory lingered, as
a stick with which critics could beat the present age for its decadence
and modern lords of the manor for their displeasing churlishness. And
yet, despite this seeming impoverishment, the country house was far
from looking like an institution shrivelling into decline. Indeed, it had
taken on new importance as a statement – emphatic, tangible and
permanent – of its owner's position in society. The country house was,
the age agreed, the most effective way of staking a claim on the social
ladder and letting people know where one stood, or wanted to stand. It
could announce that a newly made fortune had arrived or remind that
an established fortune was still to be reckoned with. So buildings grew
in number, in size and in magnificence. Rooms were furnished ever
more sumptuously with painting and sculpture, and parks were landscaped with increasingly artful design. The eighteenth century was, by

common consent of both critics and admirers, the great age of the 'show house'.

Show houses, obviously, were built to be shown – but to whom? Not servants or tenants or local freeholders, who were ceasing to matter. And not just equals, rivals and superiors, given the ways power worked in eighteenth-century society. The monarch was unlikely to be impressed, since the Hanoverians were the least mobile of sovereigns: the grand state apartments which Renaissance aristocrats had built for the Tudors and Stuarts would now wait in vain for a royal guest. Peers and politicians, moreover, transacted their business in the fashionable, metropolitan centres which are so striking a feature of the age. They went to London or Bath for the 'season' – longer, critics alleged – and did their power-broking in Piccadilly clubs or spa assembly rooms rather than country houses.

In fact, show houses owed much of their purpose to the middle classes, those unlanded gentlemen now freed from service in aristocratic households to devote their energy to commerce and the professions. Their achievement lay behind the burgeoning national prosperity which all contemporaries agreed in remarking. It gave new dignity to the professions and new importance to the manufacturing towns. And it made the middle class a force for the landowning class to

Chatsworth: Three ways of looking at a show house. 2. As aesthetic object. An engraving from Colen Campbell's *Vitruvius Britannicus or The British Architect* (1715–25) showing the west front, rebuilt in 1700–3 to make the principal façade.

Chatsworth: Three ways of looking at a show house. 3. As part of a picturesque setting. An engraving from John Preston Neale's *Views of the Seats of Noblemen and Gentlemen, in England, Wales, Scotland and Ireland* (1822–3).

reckon with: aristocratic aloofness could not be afforded and would not be tolerated. At Bath the Master of Ceremonies, Beau Nash, set out to discourage '*Gothic* haughtiness' and establish 'general society among people of rank or fortune'. He achieved a mixture of people at his assemblies that could disgust some observers. The novelist Smollett is speaking here in the voice of Jeremy Melford, the travelling young gentleman in *Humphry Clinker*:

I was extremely diverted, last ball-night, to see the Master of Ceremonies leading, with great solemnity, to the upper end of the room, an antiquated Abigail [lady's maid], dressed in her lady's cast-clothes; whom he (I suppose) mistook for some countess just arrived at the Bath. The ball was opened by a Scotch lord, with a mulatto heiress from St Christopher's; and the gay colonel Tinsel danced all evening with the daughter of an eminent tin-man from the borough of Southwark – Yesterday morning, at the Pump-room, I saw a broken-winded Wapping landlady squeeze through a circle of peers, to salute her brandy-merchant, who stood by the window, propp'd upon crutches; and a paralytic attorney of Shoe-lane, in shuffling up to the bar, kicked the shins of the chancellor of England, while his lordship, in a cut bob [short wig] drank a glass of water at the pump.

Matthew Bramble, the old-fashioned squire in Smollett's novel, thinks these goings-on 'destructive of all order and urbanity': 'plebeians' will be made arrogant and their superiors vulgar. Melford (despite the vividly contemptuous tone of his description) replies with what had become the official doctrine of eighteenth-century society: informal contact between the classes will encourage plebeians to adopt the manners of their superiors. In other words, by abandoning an aloofness that would render them irrelevant to the rest of society or identify them as its snobbish enemy, the aristocracy could become instead a pattern to the middle classes, a benevolent example of how riches could breed refinement and taste. Part of the point could be made by suffering a vulgar dancing partner or a hack on the shins at Bath, but not the best or most eloquent part. That was made on home ground, by opening their country residences to the traveller.

III

And so country houses became a prominent and familiar part of the landscape for the leisured, mobile middle classes — not just imposing spectacles to be glimpsed from a distance but attractions to be entered and viewed in the course of their travels. This is why the weak and sketchy guidebook to England published by George Beaumont and Captain Henry Disney in the 1760s still managed to list country seats exhaustively, often giving them as much prominence as population centres. This is why Daniel Paterson was careful to note the names and owners of country houses in the distance tables making up the first edition of his *Roads* in 1771 and in the strip-maps of his *British Itinerary*, which first appeared in 1785. Edward Mogg continued the practice when he took over the format of 'Paterson's Roads' in the 1820s, and it even survived into the early railway guides of the 1830s and 1840s. When the agriculturist Arthur Young wrote up his detailed reports on English farming at the end of the 1760s, he could see an obvious way to broaden the market for his work: 'The professed design of my sketches is husbandry; but it would have been great stupidity to pass very near a celebrated house without viewing it.' If anything, this is modest. Young is one of our fullest sources of information on the subject, describing and recommending at least as many houses as the modern tourist would expect to find in a modern guidebook.

The writings of Young and his contemporaries give a clear picture of the range and type of houses open to the respectable traveller. At the top end of the scale was a royal palace like Windsor Castle, already the subject of a substantial history by 1749 and a shorter guidebook by 1755. When Carl Moritz, the German visitor, came some thirty years later he found at Windsor something of the stale atmosphere we associate with the tourist trap:

But let me never more suffer the chagrin of being told about such marvels by insensitive timeservers who have learnt their speech by rote and troll it forth unwillingly a hundred times a day. The disgusting boor who showed me round the chapel for a shilling ruined the impression of the place itself by his claptrap.

Opening arrangements at Windsor were still liberal enough during the Regency to allow an American visitor a glimpse of George III making his final descent into madness: 'He was dressed in a plain blue coat – his hat flapped over his eyes – stooped a little – looked thin, and walked fast; talking continually, and with an appearance of earnestness. We could at times distinguish his voice at twenty yards distance – this does not look like recovery.'

At the other end of the scale were the modest gentlemen's houses – 'living houses', as Arthur Young called them when he recommended them as a pleasant alternative to the aristocratic mansions 'commonly hunted out by travellers'. The Hon. John Byng, a dedicated country-house visitor of whom we will hear a great deal more in this chapter, had no qualms about knocking on the door of any house, however small, even when he had no manservant to announce him. At Spalding, for example, 'a very antient house of bay windows, surrounded by yew hedge gardens' took his fancy. He was at first delighted to learn that he and its owner had once served in the same regiment, and then embarrassed to find that the old man was too senile to have the least idea what his unexpected visitor was saying.

Eighteenth-century travellers showed clear preferences among this broad range of houses. For much of the century, at least, anything medieval was despised and, unless it had been substantially renovated, a castle needed royal or important historic connections to attract the visitor. Indeed, it probably needed these connections to have survived in a state fit to be shown. At Alnwick Castle, the Border stronghold of the Percy family, the visitor of antiquarian tastes could find his curiosity well satisfied: 'A Mr Kirk, a favourite old soldier of the present Duke, whom his Grace has appointed superintendent of the Castle, conducts me through the outworks, and shews and explains them to me in the most sensible and satisfactory manner.' At the other end of the kingdom the visitor to Arundel would find a similar reception. Dover was popular enough to make Byng adopt the world-weary tones of the tourist who hates being treated like a tourist:

It seemed necessary to have a cicerone about The Castle, to talk about Julius Caesar, and Queen Elizabeth; to make us Examine the Queen's Pocket Pistol; To fling Stones into The Well; to see the Old Sword, and Keys; and to peep into The Old Church, now a Five's Court.

Then as now, Warwick was among the most popular castles. In the seventeenth century the diarist John Evelyn had come to see its collection of dubious relics, 'Sir Guys greate two-handed Sword, Staff, horse-armes, Pott & other reliques of that famous Knight errant'. Byng found them 'kept in perfect order' a century later and they are still on view today, now in the charge of the Castle's new owners, Madame Tussaud Ltd.

Otherwise, castles and ancient manor houses suffered from the general contempt for Gothic which my next chapter analyses in detail; they were shunned by tourists, just as they were neglected or abandoned by their owners. Among the age's travellers Byng is unusual in his admiration of the past and the enthusiasm with which he sought out old buildings. His diaries often make sorry reading. At Conisbrough Castle he managed to get a key from the local inn but could not find a guide to its history – the history Sir Walter Scott would later make famous to readers of *Ivanhoe*. At Bodiam Castle, a charmingly symmetrical fortress in Sussex, he found that the owner 'has lock'd up the gate leading into the interior of the square; and from a narrowness of possession does not allow a key to any neighbour'. Things were scarcely better at Tattershall in Lincolnshire, which he rightly praised as 'the most perfect, the grandest piece of brick work in the kingdom': he found a poor family living on one floor of the building. A tenant farmer and some cottagers were the only inhabitants of Allington Castle, once home of the Wyatt family which had produced a Renaissance poet and a rebel against Bloody Mary. Wingfield Manor, where the Earl of Shrewsbury had acted as jailer to Mary, Queen of Scots, typified the fate of such buildings, though at least Byng was able to find a concerned and knowledgeable guide:

He deplored the late desertion and destruction of this place: within these ten years it was (in part) genteely inhabited, and since that by a gardener, till within this twelvemonth; but the present owner, Mr Halton, has demolish'd this grandeur to help build his little meanness, having lately torn up the flooring of the fine old vaulted cellars, and strip'd off the lead that roof'd the hall.

The saddest and most poignant example of neglect was at nearby Haddon Hall, probably the most completely satisfying medieval manor house to survive and now rightly seen as one of the best reasons for making a trip to Derbyshire. The Manners family had stopped living there in 1700 – uninhabited houses were exempt from the unpopular window tax – and when Byng came in 1789 he found its emptiness 'awful, and melancholy'. He was not blind to its possibilities and, as usual, he did not mince words: 'As a place it might be made of greater beauty, by the power of water and a romantick country, than cou'd ever be the nasty stare-about Castle of Belvoir.' But, as so often, he was virtually alone in his appreciation. When the artist Edward Dayes came a few years later the visit just confirmed his belief in progress: 'Not anything can show in so strong a point of view, the improved condition of society, as this Hall; the poorest person at present possessing apartments, not only more convenient, but at the same time better secured against the severities of the weather.' Nor was appreciation necessarily helped when Gothic began to come back into fashion near the end of the century, for (as my next chapter will show) that movement of taste drew its inspiration more from abbey ruins than from old houses. Even Horace Walpole thought that Haddon 'could never have composed a tolerable dwelling'.

By these standards of judgement Renaissance houses did not necessarily fare much better, since the vigorous motley of their architecture could look merely disordered to the eighteenth-century eye. Byng, predictably, could praise Hardwick Hall as 'the foremost old manor I ever saw' but to Horace Walpole it was merely the result of an unfortunate hiccup in the history of taste, being 'not Gothic, but of that betweenity, that intervened when Gothic declined and Palladian was creeping in'. Given such criticism, it is hardly surprising that the Smythsons' achievement at Bolsover should have been standing empty when Byng paid a visit in 1790. 'A school wou'd warm it well', he suggested, a prescient remark in light of the various uses our own century has found for so many houses once thought white elephants.

Powerful though it may be as a motive for modern country-house visitors, nostalgia had little hold over their eighteenth-century forerunners. The suspicion that life used to be more happy or humane, more comfortable or kindly is a characteristically modern anxiety. Before the advent of Romanticism people believed confidently in their superiority over their ancestors, especially their superiority when it came to comfort, efficiency and taste. So when they turned tourist and visited country houses, they sought modernity and admired improvements. They were drawn to Baroque palaces and Palladian mansions, houses that had often been built within their lifetimes and, indeed, were sometimes still being built, extended or further improved.

The list of major attractions makes familiar reading, since all its items are still conspicuous on the tourist's itinerary. Blenheim Palace stood at the top, already an object of curiosity before the roof was on, let alone before it had been furnished. It was, after all, built out of public funds in tribute to the Duke of Marlborough, so it was only natural that people should wish to view this monument to what Defoe called their 'generous Temper'. Blenheim, moreover, was conveniently near Oxford and Stratford-upon-Avon. Its popularity overshadowed Vanbrugh's other vast essay in the Baroque at Castle Howard, which suffered the double disadvantage of its remote situation and of local roads which Arthur Young, an expert in bad roads, called 'infamous'. Yet Castle Howard, too, was open to visitors from the time of its building, and its popularity was such that in 1756 wings were added to Vanbrugh's massive arch at the south entrance to create an inn. Chatsworth might also have suffered from its location – Defoe thought the Peak District a 'houling Wilderness' – but it triumphed over apparent difficulty by the sheer scale of the first Duke of Devonshire's rebuilding and by that quickened interest in the geological curiosities of the Peaks which my last chapter will describe.

Wilton House was helped by being near Salisbury and Stonehenge (another curiosity that appealed to the traveller) as well as by Inigo Jones' Double Cube and Single Cube Rooms, for long a yardstick of excellence by which other country-house interiors were judged. The elaborate Baroque state apartments at Burghley House, complete with carvings by Grinling Gibbons and massive frescoes by Verrio, did much the same thing for the fame of a Renaissance mansion that might otherwise have followed Hardwick Hall and Bolsover Castle into contempt and neglect.

Blenheim, Castle Howard, Chatsworth, Wilton and Burghley: all these established their reputation with visitors in the early decades of the eighteenth century. Other houses joined the list once the necessary

improvements had been made. In his tour of England in the 1720s
Defoe had noted both the deficiencies and the possibilities of Woburn
Abbey:

a good old House, but very ancient, spacious and convenient rather than fine,
but exceedingly pleasant by its Situation . . . The very Situation of this House to
promise itself another *Burleigh* or *Chatsworth*, whenever an Heir comes to
enjoy the vast Estate of this Family, who has a Genius for Building.

Fulfilment of the promise began when Flitcroft undertook remodelling
of the west front some twenty years later and was completed by the
landscaping of the park.

Of the age's new buildings, several were particularly sought out by
travellers. Sir Robert Walpole's seat at Houghton and the first Earl of
Leicester's Holkham Hall were the two most splendid achievements of

Cross-section of the hall and dome of Castle Howard, from Colen Campbell's
Vitruvius Britannicus.

Eaton Hall: The making of a show house. 1. The original building of 1675–83, from Colen Campbell's *Vitruvius Britannicus*.

English Palladianism. Baron Scarsdale's Kedleston Hall started by being Palladian on the drawing board but in the hands of Robert Adam became a freer and more sumptuous exercise in the classical style. And at Eaton Hall (the only one of these buildings which no longer stands) the eighteenth-century tradition of the show house adapted itself to the Gothic Revival in a series of gigantic leaps and bounds. The original Hall, a modest gentleman's seat dating back to the seventeenth century, made way for a Gothic mansion in 1803 and this mansion in turn was twice remodelled in the course of the next seventy years. The stages of its elaboration kept pace with its owners' rise through the peerage, from Earl Grosvenor to Marquess of Westminster to Duke of Westminster.

It would be misleading to dwell longer on the architecture of these houses since, beyond the general demonstration of modernity, it did not greatly matter to visitors. The age produced many handsome collections of country-house engravings, from Colen Campbell's *Vitruvius Britannicus* in the early decades of the eighteenth century to Peter Frederick Robinson's new *Vitruvius* a century later, but it had no Pevsner. Most accounts written by travellers or designed for them offer only the briefest and blandest sort of architectural commentary. What drew people to places like Blenheim, Chatsworth and the rest was their size and their cost. Some might complain that this was merely vulgar, like Byng when he rages against the 'foolish glare' of Chatsworth or Horace Walpole when he remarks that Blenheim 'looks like the palace of an auctioneer who had been chosen King of Poland'. But they are exceptional and most visitors were apparently willing to accept the houses in the spirit they were intended, as statements of the owners' power and status. Defoe, for example, approaches them like an estate agent. Blenheim, he tells us, has 'Land and Pensions to the value of above One Hundred Thousand Pounds *Sterl.*'; just one of the bridges in the park alone cost £20,000. Arthur Young is by his own admission 'no connoisseur': he concentrates instead on measuring and comparing the size of rooms.

Yet, as I suggested earlier, the country house was not meant to show just that its owner was rich and powerful. It was meant to show that he had taste as well, that he justified his prominence by offering a pattern of aesthetic, even moral, refinement to the rest of society. Readers of *Pride and Prejudice* will remember Elizabeth Bennet's visit to Mr

Eaton Hall: The making of a show house. 2. Rebuilt in the Gothic style by William Porden in 1803–25. An illustration from J. and J. C. Buckler's *Views of Eaton Hall in Cheshire* (1826). Remodelled twice more in the course of the nineteenth century, the second time by Alfred Waterhouse in 1879–82, the house was largely demolished in 1961.

Eaton Hall: The making of a show house. 3. Attracting tourists. Thomas Rowlandson's illustration to William Combe's *The Second Tour of Doctor Syntax* (1820) shows the hero admiring Porden's building. Syntax makes a speech defending the owners' choice of the Gothic style:

'And if old time's destroying power
Has shaken ancient hall or bower,
The new rais'd structure should dispense
The stile of old magnificence:
The grandeur of a former age
Should still the wond'ring eye engage,
And the last Heir be proud to raise
The mansion as of former days.'

Darcy's seat at Pemberley, a house Jane Austen puts suggestively in Derbyshire and so invites the reader to identify with Chatsworth. Elizabeth goes to Pemberley expecting to find 'a very fine place' and she is not disappointed. But she goes, too, with a strong prejudice against Darcy himself, thinking him guilty of that 'Gothic haughtiness' the age deplored in aristocrats. The visit shakes her opinion and makes her start to see him in a more favourable light. The landscaping of the grounds, the elegant furnishing of the interior, the housekeeper's good opinion of her master: all these factors combine to make Elizabeth, who came to disapprove, feel 'admiration of his taste'.

'Taste' is a word apt to become vague in the mouths of practically everybody except Jane Austen. Though it turns up in the literature of country-house visiting almost as often as the term 'improvement', its meaning is often elusive and its use sometimes slovenly or inappropriate enough to make Jane Austen herself shudder. One simple fact, however, stands out. To most visitors the real proof that a country-house owner had taste as well as wealth and power was his collection of art. The eighteenth century was the great age of the Grand Tour, and country houses quickly became repositories for the magnificent souvenirs their owners brought back from the Continent. A suitable array of painting and sculpture was not merely a prestigious ornament to a great house but an essential requirement.

It was in fact the single most tangible feature to attract and impress visitors. According to Arthur Young, Castle Howard was sought out by the traveller not because of Vanbrugh but 'on account of the great collection of antique busts, statues, and marbles it contains'. Nearby Duncombe Park, which might otherwise have been put entirely in the shade, could offer the lure of 'statues, brought lately from *Italy*'. Wilton owed its place on the shortlist of most popular houses not just to Inigo Jones but to the fame of its contents. Walpole might dismiss them as 'heaps of rubbish' and propose to 'shovel three parts of the marble and pictures into the river', but others agreed in their praise of a collection 'not to be equalled, by any person's in England, or, perhaps, by any subject's in Europe'. And so the travel books and guidebooks of the period, silent or ineloquent when it came to architecture, are usually precise, detailed and enthusiastic in their description of painting and sculpture. Many of them, indeed, regard country houses as museums and offer catalogues. It is a powerful tribute to the most important, and most widely appreciated, service that country houses provided in an age before public galleries and colour reproductions.

IV

These, then, were the houses people went to and the reasons they went there. But how did the practical arrangements for visits work? How were tourists received and how were they expected to behave? In fact, for much of the eighteenth century country-house visiting remained an informal affair by comparison with the modern way of doing it. It was still a matter of etiquette rather than regulation, a social custom rather than an organised system.

Admission procedures and opening times, for example, were usually

The Portrait Gallery at Woburn Abbey, engraved in 1827 by Henry Le Keux for Peter Frederick Robinson's series about country houses, *Vitruvius Britannicus*, a title deliberately borrowed from his great eighteenth-century predecessor Colen Campbell. The detail of Le Keux's engraving and Robinson's accompanying description assert the continuing importance in the nineteenth century of country houses as museums and galleries of art.

loose and flexible. Arthur Young needed a letter of introduction to the Duke of Norfolk to forestall difficulty getting into Worksop Manor, but he mentioned the fact as a special case the unwary traveller should be warned about. When Byng had to give his name to the owner before he could set foot over the threshold of Raby Castle, he took it as a great imposition and made rude comments in his journal about the place being manned like a medieval fortress. Otherwise, houses might limit the rooms open to public inspection when the family was in residence or even, in some cases, bar visitors altogether. In this respect, Byng seems to have been plagued with misadventure, like the time he and his companions found themselves passing near Wroxton Abbey:

I prevail'd upon my party to drive down to it; when unluckily for us Ld G——— was just arrived from London, and denied us admittance. Very rude this, and unlike an old courtly lord! Let him either forbid his place entirely; open it allways; or else fix a day of admission: but, for shame, don't refuse travellers, who may have come 20 miles out of their way for a sight of the place.

On the same tour he found himself fretting outside the closed door of Shirburn Castle, Lord Macclesfield's seat in Oxfordshire, 'after a tedious sultry ride of 16 miles'.

These experiences were not typical, even of Byng's bad luck. His very anger shows how the custom of the times encouraged him to expect a welcome whatever the circumstances, and his diary records many happier occasions than his attempts to get into Wroxton and Shirburn. While the servant was showing him round Bramall Hall, for instance, he came upon the owner's wife unexpectedly and was struck by the 'very civil deportment' with which she greeted him. William Bray is just one of several visitors to praise the Straffords of Wentworth Castle for 'the easy access which strangers have to examine every beauty of the place'. Arthur Young records that Lady Strafford 'retired from her apartment' so that he could view it; the incident reminds us that, even when the family was at home, the traveller could still hope to see not just the state apartments but also the private apartments – the rooms for use, as they were called. The bedrooms and kitchen were included in Byng's tour of Clumber Park, and Young had this advice for visitors to Raynham: 'Ask to see lady *Townshend*'s dressing-room; it is furnished with prints, stuck with much taste on a green paper.'

At Burghley House the Earl of Exeter seems to have made a habit of going out of his way to welcome people even in the most inconvenient circumstances. For Horace Walpole's benefit he 'made every door and every lock fly open, even of his magazines [storehouses], yet unranged. He is going through the house by degrees, furnishing a room every year, and has already made several most sumptuous.' Walpole would have been an obvious candidate for special treatment, since he was a member of fashionable society and had, besides, given advance notice of his call. But a similar reception met Mrs Lybbe Powys, arriving unannounced while repair work was still going on: 'Lord Exeter happened to be overlooking his workmen, and reading, as I suppose, curiosity in our countenances, politely asked if the ladies chose to see it, our reply being in the affirmative, he himself informed us where was the most easy entrance.'

At such moments the distinction between respectable tourist and invited guest seems almost to disappear and the same laws of hospitality to apply to both. Byng and Mrs Powys were both well connected – he the younger brother of a Viscount and she wife to the owner of Hardwick House in Oxfordshire – and so they were particularly favoured. When she visited Holkham Hall the housekeeper served her party a breakfast 'in the genteelest taste' even though the Earl of Leicester was absent from home. At Grimsthorpe Castle the Earl of Ancaster quite overwhelmed Byng and his party, even though he was not formally in residence and did not have his staff of servants to hand:

then his Grace obliged us to see every part, every Closet, of this wretched uninhabited House . . . We were obliged to be drag'd into every Bed Room; and his Grace desired me to fix on that I shou'd chuse to Sleep in when I came there (to which I inwardly replied – 'You need not fear that I shall ever come again').

Byng is, of course, an incurable grumbler (which is one reason why he makes so entertaining a travel writer) and ends by recording annoyance that without servants the Earl could not invite him to dinner. Indeed, Byng always took his appetite with him into country houses. At Ashburnham Park he 'proposed to view the kitchen-garden, from the hope of getting fruit; but here we were most uncivilly disapointed, for tho' in abundance the gardener made no offer, nor wou'd even permit us a handful from the profusion of Morello cherries: so we turn'd out in dudgeon!'

Most visitors, of course, did not expect such generosity; nor did they expect to meet the owners of the houses they viewed. The gardener showed them the grounds and the housekeeper took them through the rooms, an arrangement which had the merit of encouraging a little quiet gossip about their employer. We have already seen how the housekeeper at Pemberley lets fall enough anecdotes to help improve Elizabeth Bennet's opinion of Mr Darcy. In real life, Fanny Burney was distracted from the famous paintings and sculptures by gossip of an opposite tendency when she visited Wilton during the lifetime of Henry Herbert, the notoriously immoral tenth Earl of Pembroke:

'Tis a noble, noble collection: & how might it be enjoyed if – as an arch old rustic Labouring man told us, *fine folks lived as they ought to do*! He had worked on the Grounds, he said, upwards of 30 years, & could not forbear speaking his mind seeing such doings as were going on for thirty years the best of a body's – 'Tis a sad waste of Fortune's Gifts. One must hope better for the next advancing Possessors.

By the eighteenth century the housekeeper had taken over domestic management of the house from the male steward of earlier centuries, and more and more of her duties were absorbed in catering to the needs of tourists. She became the figure most associated in the public mind with the practical side of country-house visiting. And so the house-keeper joined other people in the tourist trade – guides, ostlers, innkeepers and coachmen – as the butt of almost universal complaint and satire. When Boswell described his visit to Kedleston Hall with Dr Johnson he took care to mention that the housekeeper who showed them round was 'well-drest' and 'a most distinct articulator'. He did this to distinguish her from the rest of her breed, or rather from the image her breed had acquired with the travelling public. By common reputation housekeepers were dirty, mumbling, ignorant and sometimes drunk into the bargain. The 'old growling superannuated housekeeper' who showed the relics at Warwick Castle conformed nicely to the stereotype; so did the one Arthur Young found at Temple Newsam, for she was unable to identify any of the paintings in her charge. The lady 'of a very drunken, dawdling appearance' who received Byng at Belvoir Castle was a great source of accidental comedy: 'The mistakes of the Housekeeper were numberless, – pointing to a Picture of the great Duke of Buckingham, she call'd him that Villain Felton; finely confusing the Murder'd with the Murderer!'

However inadequate, the housekeeper's services were not free. Arthur Young reported that in all his travels round the country Wallington in Northumberland was 'the only place I have viewed, as a stranger, where no fees were taken'. Elsewhere, tips were expected. The amount levied seems to have started at a shilling, but the higher a visitor's social rank, the more the housekeeper expected from him. That, at any rate, is one of several inferences to be drawn from the anecdote Horace Walpole gleefully tells about the owner of Longleat's gaffe when he visited Holkham Hall: 'Lord Bath and his Countess and his son have been making a tour: at Lord Leicester's they forgot to give anything to the servants that showed the house; upon recollection – and deliberation, they sent back a man and a horse with – half a crown!'

Obviously the etiquette of country-house visiting was rigidly insisted on. Indeed, etiquette was already beginning to harden into regulation. Contemporaries who remarked on the change had usually encountered it in the form of restrictions or obstacles to their visits. They usually condemned it as a resurgence, or stubborn survival, of that 'Gothic haughtiness' which was the natural tendency of the aristocrat or landowner. Arthur Young is obviously taking this view when he refers darkly, without naming any names, to 'that unpopular and affected dignity in which some great people think proper to cloud their houses'. No doubt this accounted for some cases. There must always have been country-house owners who refused to adapt to the 'general society' of the age. And certainly, in the 1790s, the French Revolution was enough to make at least part of the English upper class recoil from the rest of society in a sort of feudal horror. Mark Girouard has shrewdly pointed to the revival of a castellated style in country-house architecture in the following decades.

Yet that revival was a short-lived and largely symbolic gesture. The English upper class did not retreat behind moats and drawbridges; country houses continued to be open to tourists. If those tourists were increasingly made subject to regulations, then this was mainly because they were starting to come in numbers large enough to require some formal system of management. Not surprisingly, precise statistics are very hard to come by, but the few fragments that have been preserved are themselves eloquent. When Mrs Home, the housekeeper at Warwick and a servant of the Brooke family for more than seventy years, died in 1834 her obituary recorded that she had amassed more than £30,000 from 'the privilege of showing the castle'; £30,000 represents a lot of shilling, or even half-a-crown, tourists. When Mrs Lybbe Powys signed her name in the strangers' book at Wilton in 1776 she noticed that 2,324 other visitors had already been that year.

All the signs suggest that social custom was growing into mass industry. Houses stated and fixed their opening times. By the 1790s Woburn could be seen only on Mondays, and the show houses at the very top of the list had been forced to adopt similar arrangements even earlier. By 1760 the Duke of Devonshire was limiting himself to 'two public days in a week' at Chatsworth. By the 1780s Blenheim – more generous or more eager for trade – was receiving visitors between two o'clock and four o'clock every afternoon except Sundays, public holidays and days when the fair was being held at nearby Woodstock. Some houses introduced a ticket system – not tickets one bought at a turnstile, of course, but notes of permission obtained in advance from the owner. Arthur Young grumbled about it in discreetly general terms; in defending the practice, Horace Walpole pointed out that the Earl of Burlington had been enforcing it at Chiswick House since the 1750s. Formalities could extend even to regulating the conduct of tourists once they had got inside a house. A Regency visitor to Stourhead had a mildly embarrassing experience of a sort the present-day tourist can easily recognise: 'One of the ladies and myself having sat down a moment to look at a picture more conveniently, a young girl who showed the house, told us as civilly as she could, that it was *the rule of the house not to allow visitors to sit down.*'

The appearance of country-house guidebooks also heralds the need to cope with an increased volume of traffic. Of course, country houses had for long been the subject of various types of writing. The commendatory poem dated back at least as far as Ben Jonson's 'To Penshurst', written in the early years of the seventeenth century, though few of the works that maintained the tradition had anything like its claim to literary merit. By the eighteenth century they were regularly being joined by antiquarian treatises which traced the history of a particular house and the genealogy of its owners, sometimes adding a brief description of the building's present appearance and contents at the end. Yet these books were 'chiefly intended for the Closet' and did not answer the purposes of 'a Pocket Companion ... for the present guidance and direction'. The phrases come from an advertisement of 1755 in which the printer and antiquary Joseph Pote announced that he had shortened and simplified his earlier history of Windsor Castle to make a more practical handbook for the visitor. Given the notorious failings of housekeepers when it came to explaining the objects in their care, it is not surprising that the idea should have spread. In the course of the century almost all the major show houses equipped themselves with handbooks on Pote's model: short, pocket-size, locally printed and locally written, usually devoted to listing the paintings and sculptures. The 'half-crown catalogue' Arthur Young found on sale at Wilton in the 1760s is typical.

Organisation, regulation and the provision of special services are all important signs of change, but the rise of a tourist industry is usually signalled by something further: a ground swell of complaint from the travelling public. In particular, we can be sure that tourism in a recognisably modern sense of the term is under way when people start grumbling at how commercialised everything seems to be getting. The two most visited places, Blenheim and Chatsworth, are also the ones that acquired the worst reputation. If it stood by itself Byng's account of the greedy obsequiousness of the Chatsworth servants might be dismissed as part of his general determination to dislike show houses, but it is echoed too often for that. Bray's visit in the 1770s led him to remark in cautiously general terms that 'the manner in which the house is shewn does not much prejudice a person in its favour'. The problems at Chatsworth were notorious enough for William Mavor, editing

Bray's account at the end of the century, to be more specific about the 'surly porter', 'avaricious housekeeper' and 'begging, insolent gardener' who preyed on tourists. Mavor was still careful to stop short of criticising the Duke of Devonshire himself, but his contemporary the Hon. Mrs Murray felt no such delicacy: 'When noblemen have the goodness to permit their fine seats to be seen by travellers, what a pity it is they suffer them to pay their servants' wages.'

Things were even worse at Blenheim, 'the servants of the poor D— of Marlborough being very attentive in gleaning money from the rich travellers'. This is Byng again, and again he is supported by other visitors. He came in the 1780s, but in the previous decade Horace Walpole had already found the gardeners at Blenheim 'ravenous' and Arthur Young's visit in the 1760s had provoked him to an uncharacteristic outburst:

One circumstance I shall not omit, which is, the excessive insolence of the porters at the park-gate, and at that into the court-yard; for I was witness to their abusing a single gentleman in a very scurrilous manner, for not feeing them after giving the house-porter half a crown for seeing it. The person abused complained aloud to several parties of this impudence, and observed that he had seen most of the great houses in the kingdom, but never knew a *park* or *yard* locked up by gentry who formed such a gauntlet. Him in the court, asserted in an insolent manner, that the gate was his living.

Young obviously found it hard to reconcile annoyance with his concern not to be rude about a peer:

I hint these circumstances as a proof, that noblemen of the most amiable character, like the Duke of *Marlborough*, have, unknown to them, the real magnificence of their seats tarnished by the scoundrel insolence of the lowest of their servants. The vile custom of not being able to view a house, without paying for the sight, as if it was exhibited by a *showman*, is detestable; but when it extends to double and quadruple the common fees and impudence; the exorbitancy calls aloud for that public notice to be taken of it, which its meanness so well deserves.

The call fell on deaf ears. When Louis Simond visited Blenheim in 1811 he had to run the gauntlet of outstretched palms belonging to the porter at the entrance, the woman who showed the collection of old china near by, the gardener who showed the park, the woman who showed the theatre, the one who showed the pleasure grounds and, finally, 'a coxcomb of an upper servant, who hurried us through the house'. The fees for all these different guides came to nineteen shillings.

The other side of the coin was that tourists themselves got an equally bad reputation. If common report makes the professionals in the travel business a vulgar, greedy lot, then it also makes their customers a vulgar, ignorant crowd. Horace Walpole wrote with astonished disdain of his experiences as a guide to his father's house, Houghton Hall:

A party arrived ... to see the house, a man and three women in riding-dresses, and they rode post through the apartments – I could not hurry before them fast enough – they were not so long in *seeing* for the first time, as I could have been in one room to examine what I knew by heart. I remember formerly being often diverted with this kind of *seers* – they come, ask what such a room is called, in which Sir Robert lay, write it down, admire a lobster or a cabbage in a market-piece, dispute whether the last room was green or purple, and then hurry to the inn for fear the fish should be overdressed.

We also hear, again from Horace Walpole, about acts of vandalism committed by tourists. There was the experience of the Roman Catholic owner of Wooburn Farm near Chertsey, who 'was forced to shut up his garden, for the savages, who came as conoisseurs, scribbled a thousand brutalities, in the buildings, upon his religion'. And there was the 'beautiful table of Oriental alabaster' he saw at Canons, the mansion built by the first Duke of Chandos, 'split in two by a buck in boots jumping up backwards to sit upon it'.

V

Clearly, Walpole took a certain shuddering pleasure in collecting such horror stories. He had some reason to, just as he had reason for defending the ticket system at places like Chiswick and for taking so lively an interest in the way other houses were shown to the public. Horace Walpole was in the country-house business himself. His experience dealing with 'customers' (his own word) at Strawberry Hill is one of the best examples of the state country-house tourism had reached by the late eighteenth century. Thanks to his love of letter-writing and his habit of keeping records, it is also the best documented.

Of course, Strawberry Hill was not a typical country house – indeed, hardly one at all in some respects. Walpole's experience of Houghton Hall in his youth had given him his fill of ordinary country-house life and convinced him that the provincial beef-and-ale existence his father, Sir Robert, delighted to lead when he was away from London and politics was not to his taste. He wrote *Aedes Walpolianae*, a catalogue of the pictures his father had collected at Houghton, and left in 1747 for the more congenial atmosphere of Twickenham. Twickenham was then still rural, but it was already fashionable ('Dowagers as plenty as flounders', Walpole said) and it was in easy reach of London. Instead of an estate populated with farms and tenantry he chose a few acres which brought him no income – just large enough to cultivate a gentleman's garden. As for his house, that too was utterly unlike the provincial grandeur of Houghton. It had once been a coachman's cottage and still bore the unglamorous name of Chopped-Straw Hall

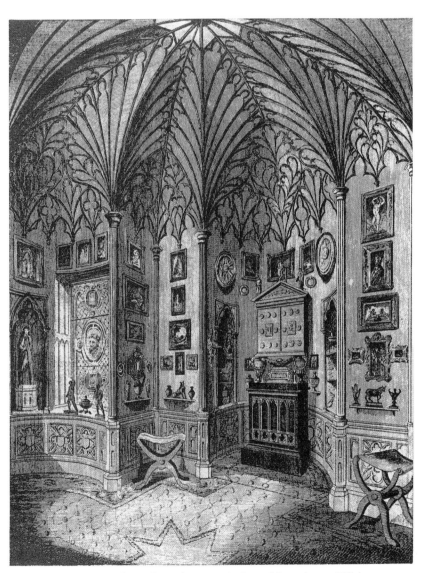

Horace Walpole's Cabinet from the *Description* of Strawberry Hill he published in 1784.

when he took up residence. It was, he said, a 'little play-thing house' and would make 'the prettiest bauble you ever saw'. This is his own characteristically light-hearted description of his plans for Strawberry Hill. In fact, Walpole wrote a major chapter in the history of English taste. Other people rediscovered the Gothic style, and had done so before Walpole. Other people built in the Gothic style, and built more expensively, more extravagantly, more accurately. But nobody else did

The Chapel in the gardens of Strawberry Hill, from Walpole's *Description*.

it with quite his combination of earnestness and grace, obsession and wit.

Small, unlanded, Gothic: Strawberry Hill looks an oddity among country houses. Yet it had the necessary qualification to attract public interest, and its very oddity turned that interest to active curiosity. It was, after all, an expression of taste – indeed, a more genuine and personal expression of its owner's taste than any of the houses this chapter has considered so far. Walpole was unlikely to have been left in the monkish seclusion that might seem fitting to the author of *The Castle of Otranto* even if he had wished to be. But, of course, he did not. His pride in his achievement, his sense of *noblesse oblige*, his large sociability, his endless curiosity about people – all made him more than ready to open the doors of Strawberry Hill to the public. His surburban novelty became a miniature show house.

His letters provide a running commentary on the results. Their prevailing tone is complaint, witty, rueful but unremitting. By 1769 he could write:

The first time a company came to see my house, I felt ... joy. I am now so tired of it, that I shudder when the bell rings at the gate. It is as bad as keeping an inn, and I am often tempted to deny its being shown, if it would not be ill-natured to those that come, and to my housekeeper.

Instead, he kept the small dash of ill nature in his generous temper for his letters and took morbid delight in writing to friends about the 'great inconveniences' and 'many rudenesses' he suffered.

Tourists, of course, were hasty, inappreciative people, and foreign tourists were the worst:

We have swarms of French daily – but they come as if they had laid wagers that there is no such place as England, and only want to verify its existence, or that they had a mind to dance a minuet on English ground; for they turn on their heel the moment after landing. Three came to see this house last week, and walked through it literally while I wrote eight lines of a letter; for I heard them go up the stairs and heard them go down exactly in the time I was finishing no longer a paragraph.

Their ignorance led them into silly blunders, like the man who solemnly removed his hat in the Gothic 'cabinet' or 'chapel' Walpole reserved for his choicest *objets d'art*. Or it made them ask silly questions: 'I heard a gentleman in the Armoury ask the housekeeper as he looked at the bows and arrows, "Pray does Mr Walpole shoot?"' And, of course, Walpole had his own list of breakages to lay beside stories of the damage done at Wooburn Farm and Canons: 'Two companies had been to see my house last week, and one of the parties, as vulgar people always see with the ends of their fingers, had broken off the end of my invaluable eagle's bill, and to conceal their mischief, had pocketed the piece.' (The eagle, incidentally, was a marble sculpture he had brought from Rome.)

Walpole tried to control matters but remained 'so tormented with visitants, and demands for breaches of my rules' that in 1784 he introduced an elaborate ticket system. Prospective visitors had to apply in advance and get a note directed to the Strawberry Hill housekeeper authorising their admission on a particular day. The note was sent with (or sometimes just scribbled on) a printed list of regulations announcing that: the opening season lasted from the first of May until the first of October; opening hours were between twelve and three; only one party would be admitted each day; the maximum number allowed in a party was four; and children were not welcome. It is remarkably comprehensive, and if cameras and ice-cream cones had been invented then no doubt Walpole would have had a word to say about them too. Yet his system never worked as neatly as he intended. People broke appointments without apology, and they turned up without tickets; they came in parties of seven or eight, and they appeared in late October to throw themselves on his 'particular indulgence'.

Not all this information comes from Walpole's letters, where he obviously takes zest in painting as black a picture as he can. His appointment book for the years 1784–96 also survives, giving a factual record of the visitors to Strawberry Hill. Their numbers were strikingly large. Walpole was receiving from 70 to 100 'companies' (as he called groups or parties) each year – an average of somewhere between 250 and 300 people. The figure shows that not all Walpole's complaint about being invaded by crowds is just whimsical exaggeration. Taken together with the figure of over 2,000 people noted by Mrs Lybbe Powys at the grander, better established, more famous Wilton in the 1770s, it demonstrates again that by the end of the eighteenth century country-house visiting was no longer the recreation of a handful of gentry.

The names of those who came to Strawberry Hill bear out the same point. Walpole was himself a celebrity and Strawberry Hill a fashionable curiosity, so it is only natural that his appointment book should list famous people: Dr Johnson's friend James Boswell, the novelist Fanny Burney, the actress Mrs Siddons and her brother John Philip Kemble, as well as artists, architects and the landscape gardener

Humphry Repton. It is natural, too, that Strawberry Hill should have attracted dignitaries like the Duke and Duchess of Marlborough and the Archduke and Archduchess of Austria, whom Walpole showed round himself. Much of the remaining list is taken up by family parties from the respectable middle and upper-middle class: there is a heavy sprinkling of military ranks and clerical titles.

None of these visitors, presumably, is the sort to justify Walpole's nervous fear of damage to his *objets d'art*; none of them, surely, explains the continual insinuation in his letters that showing his house brought him into contact with the vulgar mob. Yet there are suggestive names at, as it were, the bottom of his list. They include a Mr Railton, whom Walpole identifies as a distiller from nearby Hampton, and the lady icily described as 'A Mrs Burton from Richmond, seeming disordered'. 'Deputy Wrench of Thames Street' in the City came in 1796 and, most surprisingly of all, he had been preceded two years before by the Duke of Buccleuch's servants. Their presence at Strawberry Hill implies a 'general society' even broader than could be found in the pump room or the assembly room at Bath.

VI

With its elaborate regulations, the number of its visitors and the cross-section of society it could attract, Strawberry Hill in the 1790s looks uncannily like country-house tourism in its modern phase. To strengthen, if not complete, the resemblance took another fifty years; it needed the coming of the railway and the enterprise of Thomas Cook.

In his way, Thomas Cook was quite as typical of the temper of his age as Horace Walpole had been of his. Where Walpole had been a wit and a connoisseur, Cook was a Victorian idealist. A self-made man, a Baptist lay preacher and Temperance advocate, he regarded himself as both champion and educator of the new, urban working class created by the Industrial Revolution. To Cook the vastly increased opportunities for travel brought by the railway system were not just stimulants to business and to recreation: they were the means for carrying out a social mission. He began his mission modestly enough in 1841, ferrying people from his home town of Leicester to a Temperance meeting at nearby Loughborough. By the beginning of the next decade he was able to offer cut-price excursion tickets to the Great Exhibition, greatly swelling the number of working-class visitors from the provinces who had the chance to inspect that monument to Victorian trade and prosperity. As his business flourished, Cook's activities spread

A poster advertising one of Thomas Cook's early, local excursions. Note the emphasis on access to the grounds of Coleorton Hall, and on the house's connection with Wordsworth.

beyond England to the Continent and America. By the time of his death in 1892 he had founded a dynasty, and could bequeath to his heir the most famous name in the English travel business.

In the late 1840s and the 1850s, when business was just starting to expand, Cook turned his attention to country houses. He organised excursions, usually for about 300 people, to the obvious houses in the Midland area: Chatsworth, Burghley House, Belvoir Castle and Coleorton Hall, home of the Beaumont family near Ashby-de-la-

Zouch. His advertisements for these outings, and his reports on them in the house magazine he issued, invoke Victorian festivity. Brass bands and local dignitaries waited on station platforms to greet Cook's 'excursionists'; the promise of picnics (with non-alcoholic refreshment) and the lure of cricket and archery, as well as the country houses themselves, lay in store.

Yet these outings were also tense occasions. Country-house owners, however obliging, could not look with complete calm on invading groups of working-class people whisked in by train from nearby towns, for they embodied social changes that were only partly understood and were already partly feared. Cook himself acknowledged and even shared these fears. He regarded his excursionists with the nervous anxiety teachers commonly feel when they take their charges on trips outside the school grounds. In the *Hand-Book of Belvoir Castle* he wrote for his excursion in 1848 the 'Hint to Visitors' is dropped like a brick:

It is very seldom indeed that the privileges extended to visitors of the mansions of the nobility are abused; but to the shame of some rude folk from Lincolnshire, there have been just causes of complaint at Belvoir Castle: some large parties have behaved indecorously, and they have to some extent prejudiced the visits of other large companies. Conduct of this sort is abominable, and cannot be too strongly reprobated. We are sure that Leicester visitors will not *knowingly* commit the slightest infraction on the rules of good behaviour, and all we desire of them is to observe the 'notices' which hang in the different apartments of the Castle; and in the promenades through the surrounding walks, to satisfy themselves with observations, and not damage in the slightest degree shrubs or flowers, or deface by writing, seats, walls, statues, or any objects of interest. A word to the wise is enough.

The occasion seems to have passed off smoothly. Certainly the visit to Burghley House in 1857 ended in sighs of relief. The housekeeper, reported a local newspaper, 'assured Mr Cook that she had not witnessed nor heard of a single act of rudeness or indiscretion; and on examining the rooms she could not perceive a trace of dirt, or disarrangement of any article'. Cook was obviously proud of this character reference for his excursionists, since he reprinted it in his house magazine. He added that he had been rewarded by a private interview with the Marquess and Marchioness of Exeter, who expressed their satisfaction and invited him back again next year, 'so admirably did the visitors behave'.

Not all the suspicion attending these visits came from the owners. There is a long tradition of combining flowery compliments to the aristocracy with a covert lecture on their social duties, and for all its apparently vague phrasing Cook's praise of the Duke of Devonshire managed the job rather neatly:

Not more grateful to the sense is that fragrance which arises from the perfume of the varied and accumulated exotics of Chatsworth Gardens, than to the soul is the richer and sweeter influence of aristocratic exaltation which blends its dignity and power with the feelings, the desires, the aspirations and the pleasures of universal humanity. May every visitor to Chatsworth feel the hallowing influence of this sentiment in the coming week, and throughout the season.

If the working class can be tolerated provided it behaves itself and doesn't tread on the flower beds, then the landowning class can be tolerated provided it behaves itself as well and is friendly to the rest of society. Dignity and power are all very well as long as they do not scorn 'the feelings, the desires, the aspirations and the pleasures of universal humanity'.

Cook's praise of country-house owners carries a democratic warning, and his visits to country houses have a missionary zeal. 'What object of human exaltation or benevolence has not his Grace the Duke of Rutland patronized?' asks his *Hand-Book of Belvoir Castle*. 'When did the poor and down-trodden labourer or artizan present to that nobleman a prayer which was unheeded?' It goes on to offer excursionists not just a jolly outing but a glimpse of ideal social harmony:

This liberality on the part of the aristocracy of the country constitutes a pleasing feature of the present times, and is calculated to produce a good moral effect in binding together in one harmonious chain the different sections of society. May God speed the day when the sons of toil shall live happily in the enjoyment of the just rewards of their labor, and the rich shall live at ease in the undisturbed possession of the wealth and greatness to which they have a legitimate claim!

VII

I began this chapter by suggesting that as tourists in country houses today we feel ourself to be enacting a characteristic triumph of democracy, or at least of the particular forms democracy has taken in England. We are right in this feeling, but obviously mistaken if we suppose that the present role of our country houses as tourist attractions is entirely a creation of the years since the Second World War.

Country houses now need tourism for their economic survival to a degree they never did before, but receiving visitors on something approaching a mass scale has long been a part of their function. The opening of the country house, in fact, is one aspect of that larger opening of the élite which has helped England over some of the trickiest stiles in its social and political history.

'*How is the Castle mann'd?*' demanded Byng sarcastically when he came to Raby near the end of the eighteenth century. His question evoked all the age's latent, potentially revolutionary anger against feudalism. Yet he had no need to storm the gates of the Castle, merely to send his name in to the owner and 'ask permission of entrance'. In the 1790s Walpole grumbled at the inconvenience, rudeness and vandalism he suffered from visitors to Strawberry Hill but (as he well knew) he was faring better than his counterparts in France during the Reign of Terror. Thomas Cook brought his excursionists to Belvoir in 1848, a year of unrest in the industrial cities and of revolutions throughout Europe. And so, while crowned heads were being toppled all over the Continent, a typically English compromise was celebrated on the lawns at the Castle. For his part the Duke dropped Gothic haughtiness and acknowledged that he was custodian, even showman, of a public monument. As for Cook and his party, they were demonstrating their readiness to become tourists instead of revolutionaries.

3

A proper state of decay: ruins and ruin-hunters

We are struck with an extensive ruin in a proper state of decay, to shew the depradations of time, without effacing the grandeur of what it once was.

Journal of a Three Weeks Tour, in 1797,
through Derbyshire to the Lakes,
paraphrased in William Mavor,
The British Tourists

Do not let us deceive ourselves in this important matter; it is *impossible*, as impossible as to raise the dead, to restore anything that has ever been great or beautiful in architecture. That which I have ... insisted on as the life of the whole, that spirit which is given only by the hand and eye of the workman can never be recalled ... Do not let us talk then of restoration. The thing is a Lie from beginning to end.

Ruskin, *The Seven Lamps of Architecture*

I

Stonehenge, at a distance, appeared only a diminutive object. Standing on so vast an area as Salisbury Plain, it was lost in the immensity around it. As we approached, it gained more respect: and we could now trace a large ditch round the whole, confined within a gentle mound. But when we arrived on the spot, it appeared astonishing beyond conception. A train of wondering ideas immediately crowded into the mind. Who brought these huge masses of rock together? Whence were they brought? For what purpose? By what machines were they drawn? Or by what mechanic powers erected?

The visitor describing Stonehenge is William Gilpin, one of the most influential English travellers of the eighteenth century, or indeed of any

92

century. His 'Observations on Picturesque Beauty' (as he called the published accounts of his tours through the various regions) had a lasting effect not just on where his fellow tourists chose to go but on what they found to admire or deplore when they got there. In particular, he did much to shape the taste for ruins which I will be describing in this chapter and the appreciation of nature which makes the subject of my final chapter.

For the moment, though, Gilpin matters less than his subject and the train of wondering ideas it provokes. Some of his deliciously teasing questions, to be sure, tease us rather less than they did him. We know, for example, that Stonehenge was built in successive phases beginning about 3100 BC, when the outer ditch and its concentric ring of holes were dug out with antler picks, and continuing until about 1100 BC, when all the several circles were in place. We know that two types of stone were used: sarsen from the Marlborough Downs for the outer circle and the inner horseshoe of trilithons, and bluestones from the Preseli Mountains of South Wales for the rest. Modern archaeology can even provide a convincingly detailed description of how the monument was built, with the upright stones being bedded in chips left over from trimming and carving and the lintels being raised into position on piles of logs and brushwood.

Yet the sense of mystery remains, quite as powerful for us as for earlier visitors like Gilpin. Sooner or later, we all join Byron in asking of Stonehenge: 'what the devil is it?' At this point the professional archaeologists become tight-lipped, gingerly weighing the merits of rival theories that the stone circles had a religious or a scientific function. Amateur conjecture rushes happily in to fill the vacuum left by academic caution, with talk of UFOs or ley lines or gigantic stellar observatories. These fashionable theories regularly come and just as regularly go – each generation needs to rebuild Stonehenge in its own image – but they all serve to whet public appetite for an underlying puzzle. And, of course, its stubbornly enigmatic character is what has given Stonehenge its enduring popularity: it has made it our oldest and most tantalising tourist attraction.

Popular interest stretches back a long way, at least several centuries before William Gilpin. As a convenient starting-point we can take Geoffrey of Monmouth, who recorded in his twelfth-century chronicle that the stones had been whisked from Ireland and put in place by Merlin the magician. Linking ancient sites and puzzling natural phenomena with Merlin or King Arthur or the Devil was common medieval practice; later centuries made the same use of Robin Hood.

The results are often embalmed in folk-names, which stand as reminders not so much of exploded historical theory as of the desire to set a seal of respectability on curiosity about such places. Geoffrey's fable certainly helped make Stonehenge a sight to tempt the traveller across Salisbury Plain out of his way and, from the very beginnings of modern travel, the antiquarians and the casual tourists came. The earliest pictures do not show the stone circles deserted, but with travellers on horseback pausing near by or groups of curious observers pointing at the monument; in one picture of 1588 we can even see a graffiti artist at work, apparently carving his name on one of the uprights.

The seventeenth century was the age of the new science, when the delight in fable and legend which characterised the older tradition of antiquarianism was touched by the beginnings of empirical method. James I commissioned Inigo Jones to compile a professional report on Stonehenge and his notes, written up and published by his architectural pupil John Webb in 1655, made the first book-length study of the monument. Like many observers after him, Jones detected elegance and sophistication in the ruins and, again like many later observers, he took this as proof that Stonehenge could not be native work. The primitive Britons would obviously have been incapable of spacing their stones so regularly and rounding their circles so neatly, let alone of devising the subtle arrangement of equilateral triangles Jones fancied he found in the placing of the inner trilithons. Stonehenge, he concluded, must be Roman: it was a temple to Coelus, the Roman god of the sky, probably built in the time of Agricola.

Although it took a long time to die, Jones' view was never universally accepted. John Aubrey, for example, challenged it in the course of his research for a book on the ancient monuments of Britain – research which marks him as the most important Stonehenge scholar of the seventeenth century. He was the first to identify the ring of holes near the outer ditch (still called the Aubrey Holes) and the first to give proper attention to the remains at nearby Avebury. Yet his achievement was obscured because, in the manner of antiquarians, Aubrey never completed his work on British monuments and never published his notes. The tradition of learning they embodied passed, in the next century, into the hands of William Stukeley.

Of all the long list of people who have investigated Stonehenge, Stukeley remains probably the most influential. His achievement is paradoxical, making him at once the heir to that scientific method towards which the earlier antiquarians had been advancing and the prototype of all the crackpot theorists who still flourish today. His early fieldwork was particularly valuable in recording the position of stones at Avebury even as they were being broken up and carted away. At Stonehenge he performed a useful service in coining the term 'trilithon' before his instinct for scholarship slowly yielded to the promptings of imagination. In Aubrey's notes he found the suggestion that the circles were not Roman, as Jones had argued, but Druidic. The very poverty of his information about Druids encouraged rather than chilled speculation, and by the time he published his conclusions in 1740 Stukeley was the confident master of an entire vision of the ancient British past, with Stonehenge at its centre. It was the temple of a natural religion, whose lineage is tortuously declined from the pages of the Old Testament and whose occult symbols can be deciphered in the very stones themselves.

In fact, Stukeley was so successful in putting the Druids into Stonehenge that it has proved almost impossible to get them out again. However much this achievement may have depressed scientific standards – and it certainly helped distract archaeologists from the straight and narrow path of their discipline for a good hundred years afterwards – it also stimulated, indeed liberated, popular feeling. After Stukeley, visitors came with greater enthusiasm and came in greater numbers. Stonehenge was no longer a dry enigma for antiquarians to fuss over but a richly brooding icon into which the tourist could read all his fantasies and imaginings about the ancient British past. In travellers' diaries the descriptions become less technical and ever more majestically cadenced in echo of Stukeley's own rolling prose. In paintings, drawings and engravings the plains around Stonehenge grow more spacious and sublime, the skies above more fraught with mystery and drama.

In the previous chapter I mentioned Mrs Lybbe Powys among the visitors to nearby Wilton House. She also came to Stonehenge – twice, in fact – including both the mansion and the ruin in a day's outing from Salisbury, a little circuit already popular in the eighteenth century. Her impressions of Stonehenge are as typical of her age as her impressions of Wilton. On her first visit, in 1759, she came armed with Stukeley's book, copied its descriptions into her diary and left 'highly entertained by the sight of what in the same moment gave one sensations pleasingly awful'. This exalted mood did not stop her indulging a common foible of the tourists, 'endeavouring with some tools our servants had, to carry some pieces of it with us, which with great difficulty we at last accomplished, and have since had them polished'. From a second visit

Versions of Stonehenge: 1. A restrained view by the antiquary John Britton, from *The Beauties of Wiltshire* (1801–25).

in 1776 she could carry away a less tangible souvenir in the form of the old wives' tales which local guides still liked to keep in circulation:

Our coachman informed us it was impossible to tell [count] them, and no one ever did, as they would actually die if they attempted it. Our sagacious servant told us 'the Devil brought them there from Ireland, tied up in a withe, which breaking, is the reason they are so scatter'd, and one fell just at the river at Amesbury'. He told us this with the gravest countenance, and seem'd angry at our laughing.

Such popularity soon endowed Stonehenge with the familiar adjuncts which mark the developed tourist attraction. By 1739, the year before Stukeley published his theories, the ruins already boasted a refreshment stall of a sort: 'One Gaffer Hunt of Ambresbury [i.e. Amesbury] built a hut against the upright stone of Mars; and attended there daily with liquors, to entertain the traveller, and shew him the stones: his cellar was under the great stone, next the hut.' In 1822 a more offical custodian appeared on the scene in the person of Henry Browne. He supplemented his income from tips by printing and selling his own guidebook, which offered in rivalry to Stukeley the theory that

Versions of Stonehenge: 2. A romantic view, with the clouds piled
melodramatically behind the rugged, asymmetrical stones, from John Hassell's
Tour of the Isle of Wight (1790).

Stonehenge was the only monument surviving from before the biblical
Flood. Browne was succeeded by his son and then by a William Judd
who, enterprisingly, introduced a camera and a darkroom on wheels.
He in turn was followed by a guide named Smeeth but commonly
nicknamed 'Sikher', who steered clear of archaeological theory and
apparently preferred to entertain tourists with reminiscences of his
days in the Indian Army.

During all this time Stonehenge remained private property, the
stones and their surrounding acres first in the neglectful hands of the
Duke of Queensberry, the notorious 'Old Q', and after 1824 in the
rather more respectful care of the Antrobus family. Yet the influx of
tourists, and the needs of professional archaeologists, raised an
obvious question: had official protection of such monuments and,
perhaps, official power over their fate become necessary? After years of
campaigning Sir John Lubbock (later, fittingly, Lord Avebury)
achieved at least a limited success in 1882 with the passage of his
Ancient Monuments Protection Act, which offered protection to

historic properties and help to their owners, though on a voluntary basis only. Of the twenty-nine English and twenty-one Scottish properties which the Act specified, all were prehistoric and Stonehenge, of course, was by far the most famous.

Sir Edmund Antrobus, owner of the stone circles at the time Lubbock's Bill became law, does not seem to have appreciated this public concern but in 1898 his nephew offered them and some 1,300 acres of the adjoining land to the nation for £125,000. This provoked the inevitable rumours of an American buyer in the offing, ready like Merlin (or the Devil) to transport the stones across the sea, but they did not have the gratifying effect such rumours had done in the case of Shakespeare's Birthplace, for neither the Government nor anyone else met the rather stiff asking price. In 1915, however, Stonehenge did at last come under the auctioneer's hammer – for a mere £6,600 – and three years later the buyer, a local landowner, presented it to the nation.

Since then, responsibility for the care of Stonehenge has passed from government body to government body, from the Ministry of Works to the Department of the Environment to English Heritage, as it calls itself in the present climate of aggressive marketing. During this period the number of visitors each year has steadily mounted. In 1901, when admission had first been formally charged and recorded, the figure stood at 3,770. By the early years of public ownership in the 1920s it had risen to some 20,000. It has now passed the half-million mark, putting Stonehenge comfortably in the same league as Shakespeare's Birthplace and Blenheim Palace, as well as making it the most visited prehistoric monument in England, if not the western world.

II

If I have given only a brief sketch of Stonehenge's history as a tourist attraction, particularly in its later stages, this is partly because I imagine it to be familiar, or at least unsurprising, ground for many readers, and partly because I will be returning several times in this chapter to our changing views of how ancient monuments should be preserved and displayed. My immediate concern is not to obscure the importance of that time, in the middle of the eighteenth century, when Inigo Jones' theory that Stonehenge had been built by the Romans was finally beaten from the field by Stukeley's Druid theory. It was a turning-point, not just in people's view of Stonehenge or its popularity with visitors but in a much larger cultural process. Horace Walpole remarked that after examining Stonehenge people then assign it to whatever period of antiquity they most admire. Viewed in this sensible light, the triumph of Stukeley's Druids over Jones' Romans embodies, in miniature, the triumph of Romanticism over Neo-classicism.

Neo-classicism, of course, is the name we give to the system of values that dominated English culture from, very roughly, the middle of the seventeenth century to the middle of the eighteenth. It cultivated order, regularity and harmony (in social and political affairs as well as aesthetics) by its imitation of the classical world and, particularly, by its determination to recreate Roman civilisation in England. So when a Neo-classicist like Inigo Jones linked Stonehenge with the Romans he was paying it a high compliment, and assigning it special value as a tangible link between the classical world and an England that could too often appear intractably uncouth or hopelessly barbarian. The same motive led seventeenth- and eighteenth-century archaeologists to concentrate their energies on Roman remains elsewhere in England, joyfully unearthing the fragments which confirmed that the great age of Augustus had once had life on English soil and so, perhaps, could live again.

Literally speaking, Stukeley's Druids were the enemies of Jones' Romans. Eighteenth-century antiquaries eagerly developed slender hints in their classical sources to suggest that the priests had led the ancient Britons in resisting the foreign invaders. Figuratively speaking, the Druids were the heroes of a new age disillusioned with Neo-classicism to the point of active rebellion. Shaggily bearded, clothed in animal skins, haunting the groves where mistletoe blooms and living by natural religion rather than by rule, they were the opposite of everything Neo-classicism represented. In this guise they obligingly stalked the pages of English literature until the time of Blake's Prophetic Books and Wordsworth's *The Prelude*.

The ramifications of this shift in cultural values are so large and so numerous that it is as well most of them should lie outside the scope of my present study. Yet, of course, Romanticism had a profound influence on tourism: by changing people's perception of what was admirable or beautiful, it altered and expanded the list of sights people visited on their travels. My next chapter will explore the new appreciation of natural scenery which is the most striking example of this process in action. Yet by altering their attitude to the past, Romanticism also changed people's views of old buildings and monuments in much broader ways than by just making them seek out Stonehenge in a more largely enthusiastic spirit. Medieval architecture, previously

Stonehenge (or a neat pocket version of it) and the Druids. This engraving
from Francis Grose's *The Antiquities of England and Wales* (1773–6) is
accompanied by some lines from William Mason's poem *Caractacus* (1759),
one of many contemporary works which helped widen the influence of
Stukeley's Druid theory:

> These mighty Piles of Magic-planted Rock,
> Thus rang'd in mistic order, mark the Place
> Where but at times of holiest festival
> The DRUID leads his train.

neglected or despised, attracted first new interest and then dawning
admiration. Gothic ruins and, above all, the ruins of the great
monasteries ceased to be merely antiquarian curiosities and became
major features on a redrawn tourist map of England.

III

Whatever the limitations of the modern eye for architecture, at least we
now possess a great deal of scholarly information about the history of
Gothic. The guidebooks we take with us when we go visiting parish
churches, cathedrals and ruined monasteries are rich in technical lore,

dutifully pointing out the differences between Early English lancets and Decorated tracery or between Early English rib-vaulting and Perpendicular fan-vaulting. Yet even this elementary classification of the various phases of Gothic into Early English, Decorated and Perpendicular is a surprisingly recent achievement, pioneered in 1817 by Thomas Rickman (otherwise remembered as the architect of New Court and the Bridge of Sighs at St John's College in Cambridge). Before that date there had been only preliminary forays into the field by Gray's friend Thomas Warton in the 1760s and John Aubrey a century earlier. For most of the seventeenth and eighteenth centuries, in fact, 'Gothic' was applied indiscriminately to any building that was not obviously classical. Sporadic attempts were made to draw the line between Romanesque and Gothic but it was rarely observed: even the antiquarians usually lumped round and pointed arches together. As for the division of Romanesque into Saxon and Norman, that went altogether unnoticed.

To the seventeenth- or eighteenth-century observer, then, a medieval church could pose almost as many puzzles as Stonehenge itself. This, presumably, is why most of the early antiquaries preferred to concentrate on safe, easily datable details like funeral monuments – which appealed, besides, to their fascination with genealogy and their weakness for paying compliments to the local nobility and gentry. Larger questions about the nature and origins of Gothic were answered by theories vague or exotic enough to bear a marked family resemblance to speculations about Stonehenge. Batty Langley, for example, was not being nearly as eccentric as his name might suggest when he argued that most Gothic buildings dated from before the Danish invasions. Even the more approved theories were hardly less crude than use of the term 'Gothic' itself would imply. The Goths, of course, were one of the Germanic tribes commonly blamed for the sacking of Rome, and they had first been brought into architectural history by Henry Wotton in 1624. When Sir Christopher Wren drew up his report on Westminster Abbey in 1713 he found the label unsatisfactory – since 'the Goths were rather Destroyers than Builders' – though 'Saracenic', the alternative he suggested, was equally exotic. After this, the Goths and the Saracens wandered through the pages of architectural writing in a state of tribal confusion. This, for instance, is Bishop Warburton writing in the 1740s:

When the Goths had conquered Spain, and the genial warmth of the climate, and the religion of the old inhabitants had ripened their wits and inflamed their

'History Preserving the Monuments of Antiquity', from Francis Grose's *The Antiquities of England and Wales* (1773–6). Note the uncertain flying buttresses and the classical column on which History sits.

An 'Emblem of Antiquities' from William Hutchinson's *The History of Antiquities of Cumberland* (1794).

mistaken piety, *they struck out a new species of architecture*, unknown to Greece or Rome, upon original principles, and *ideas much older* than what had given birth even to classical magnificence. For this northern people having been accustomed to worship the Deity in groves, when their religion required covered edifices, they ingeniously projected to make them resemble groves as nearly as the distance of architecture would permit; at once indulging their old prejudices, and providing for their present conveniences, by a cool receptacle in a sultry climate.

Clearly, Bishop Warburton's Goths are brothers under the skin to Dr Stukeley's Druids.

Warburton intended his comparison between the favourite shapes of Gothic and the favourite shapes of nature as a compliment. It is by no means an insensitive reaction, and it has occurred to other students in a better state of scholarly information. By the same token, Wren proposed the term 'Saracenic' out of respect, 'for those People wanted neither Arts nor Learning'; and again, the possibility of Arabic or

Moorish influence on the Gothic style cannot be discounted. Yet the handling of such theories usually managed to obscure whatever seed of truth or admiration they might contain. Indeed, the customary purpose of theorising was to justify the prevailing contempt for Gothic. Even the word itself did double work, as the name for a style of building and as the name for anything obviously old-fashioned or, worse, anything hopelessly primitive and barbaric.

Gothic offended on at least two counts. With its complex rhythms, its love of dramatic contrast and its delight in rich decoration, medieval architecture was bound to look 'fantastical and licentious' to people whose eyes were trained in the cool harmonies of Neo-classicism. The phrase I have just quoted is from the diarist John Evelyn, for whom the lovely intricacies of the Henry VII Chapel at Westminster Abbey were just 'sharp *Angles*, *Jetties*, narrow *Lights*, lame *Statues*, *Lace*, and other *Cut-Work* and *Crinkle-Crankle*'. Behind this aesthetic objection that Gothic is irregular and confused lurks another, less coherent and less openly confessed, which we can hear when Evelyn complains more generally of 'Congestions of heavy, dark, melancholy and *Monkish Piles*, without any just Proportion, Use or Beauty'. That word '*Monkish*' expresses more than a strictly visual distaste, and suggests how fatally the style was tainted, for English Protestants, by its connection with Roman Catholicism. If medieval castles and manor

Woodcut from William Hutchinson's *The History of Antiquities of Cumberland* (1794).

houses stirred up memories of feudalism – the 'Gothic haughtiness' which later generations were quick to resent in their aristocracy – then medieval churches awakened memories of the horrors, real or alleged, of the Catholic past from which Englishmen were proud to have freed themselves at the Reformation.

All these various prejudices against Gothic are on parade in a famous passage from Smollett's novel *Humphry Clinker*. When Matthew Bramble and his party come to York in the course of their travels he can find nothing to admire about the Minster. Its style of building, he concludes, is not Gothic but Saracen and made its way to England from Spain. Whatever practical merits it may have had in that country, it is utterly inappropriate to the English climate, being 'vast, narrow, dark, and lofty, impervious to the sunbeams'. This consideration seduces Bramble into a hypochondriac digression about the health hazards of churchgoing in England, but he returns to his main point in a damning summary which combines aesthetic distaste with shuddering memories of past despotism and cruelty:

The external appearance of an old cathedral cannot be but displeasing to the eye of every man, who has any idea of propriety or proportion, even though he may be ignorant of architecture as a science; and the long slender spire puts one in mind of a criminal impaled, with a sharp stake rising up through his shoulder.

After this judgement, it is natural that he should turn with relief from the Minster to York's Assembly Rooms, designed in 1730 by Richard Boyle, third Earl of Burlington, the pioneer and patron of Palladianism in England. There visitors of Bramble's taste could admire an Egyptian Hall with double rows of columns, as declined by Palladio from Vitruvius, and mural paintings of Roman York which endow Constantine the Great with Burlington's own features.

Bramble's view of the social changes witnessed by his age, which I quoted in the previous chapter, marks him as old-fashioned. So does his attitude to Gothic. *Humphry Clinker* appeared in 1771 and by that date the rebellion against Neo-classicism was already well under way, bringing Gothic back into a measure of favour. Indeed, from the 1720s landowners had begun to include neo-Gothic temples or ruins among the buildings with which they liked to decorate their picturesque landscaped gardens. Horace Walpole added his sham battlements to Strawberry Hill and opened his doors to an admiring public before *Humphry Clinker* was published. And in the years after the novel's publication the Gothic Revival would advance from what Kenneth Clark has called its 'Picturesque Phase' into its 'Ethical Phase'. Gothic would be exalted from a novel, agreeable plaything to the very embodiment of architectural purity. First Pugin and then Ruskin would propose the style and the culture that produced it as an ideal to which the nineteenth century should seek to return. In churches, town halls, railway stations, memorials and suburban villas the Victorian love of Gothic would leave its mark on every town in England.

Such changes obviously do not happen overnight, and they do not progress at a steady pace. In fact, they are often urged forward by people whose own attitudes are not all of a piece. Even Horace Walpole, whose home at Strawberry Hill is sometimes used to give a general name to the eighteenth-century Gothic Revival, still paid at least lip service to the superiority of the classical style in architecture. Several of the eighteenth-century travellers whose accounts I will use as evidence of the new interest in Gothic did not see in the style the same qualities we now see and so did not admire it for the same reasons we now do. Arthur Young called it 'vile and barbarous', and passed a judgement on York Minster that sounds like Matthew Bramble: 'I never met with any thing in the proportion of a gothic cathedral, that was either great or pleasing.' Even Byng, whose intense love of the past I have already demonstrated in the previous chapter, could sometimes find cathedrals and churches disappointing: the pillars of the nave tended to be gloomy and too fat, and the subjects of the misericords indelicate. All three men – Walpole, Young and Byng – remain troubled by the Catholic overtones of Gothic, an anxiety that would not be completely exorcised until Ruskin.

In fact, the new interest in Gothic did not necessarily challenge the assumptions on which contempt had earlier depended. Because its rhythms are not of the Neo-classical sort, Gothic was still taken to lack proportion, and because it was built by Catholics, it could still be thought tainted. Yet irregularity and even Catholic corruption can take on a certain picturesque charm if viewed from a remove of several centuries. Gothic buildings still in use did not grant the spectator this necessary distance, but ruined ones did. So the remains of England's great monasteries could be admired not despite their ruination but precisely because of it. William Mason made just this point in his influential poem, *The English Garden*, or at least he made it as clearly as the straitjacket of his poetic diction would allow him:

> In thy fair domain,
> Yes, my lov'd Albion! many a glade is found,
> The haunt of Wood-gods only: where if Art

> E'er dar'd to tread, 'twas with unsandal'd foot,
> Printless, as if the place were holy ground.
> And there are scenes, where, tho' she whilom trod,
> Led by the worst of guides, fell Tyranny,
> And ruthless Superstition, we now trace
> Her footsteps with delight; and pleas'd revere
> What once had rous'd our hatred. But to Time,
> Not her, the praise is due: his gradual touch
> Has moulder'd into beauty many a tower,
> Which, when it frown'd with all its battlements,
> Was only terrible; and many a fane
> Monastic, which, when deck'd with all its spires,
> Serv'd but to feed some pamper'd Abbot's pride,
> And awe th' unletter'd vulgar.

This is, after all, only a roundabout way of saying that time lends objects a charm they did not originally possess, and that monasteries can be very charming so long as they are dead. Sir Uvedale Price, a leading authority on the Picturesque, put it more bluntly: 'The ruins of these once magnificent edifices are the pride and boast of this island; we may well be proud of them, not merely in a picturesque point of view – we may glory that the abodes of tyranny and superstition are in ruin.'

IV

Armed with this cautious licence to take delight in Gothic as a dead style, eighteenth-century travellers set out in quest of suitable ruins to admire. But in what state of decay did England's once great monastic foundations then lie, and how had they fallen into that state? Almost as soon as the question is asked, we run into the same stubborn favourite among English legends which the eighteenth-century travellers themselves encountered. 'Whenever I enquire about ruins I allways get the same answer', Byng reported, 'that it was some papish place, and destroy'd by Oliver Cromwell.'

He was right to complain that Cromwell was made the scapegoat for 'much more devastation than he really committed'. Whatever damage Cromwell or the seventeenth-century Puritans may have done to English parish churches (and, of course, even this has been exaggerated in the popular memory), they had little need to direct their iconoclasm against monastic buildings. These were already defunct, and the main work of their despoliation had been thoroughly carried out in the years 1535–40, when they were officially dissolved by Henry VIII.

At the Dissolution a handful of foundations (like Gloucester) were promoted to cathedral rank. Rather more (like Hexham and Beverley) were downgraded to parish churches, a fate which offered no protection to any of the other buildings around the cloister and, as the cut-down proportions of Malmesbury Abbey and Bolton Priory bear witness, did not even guarantee that the whole of the church itself would survive. The remainder of the monasteries became part of a vast boom in real estate and building materials. Their immediate cash value lay in the ornaments and metal they contained, so the plate, the bells, the lead from the roof and sometimes its timber were appropriated by the Crown. What remained had some value for its stone, and more for the land it stood on and the estates it had once controlled. These were granted or, more commonly, sold into private hands to suffer all the various adaptations and humiliations that private enterprise could devise for them. In towns a use might be found for some of the buildings as houses, schools, even factories: at Thorney in Cambridgeshire the cloister has given its shape to the charming village green. The rest would be plundered for their fabric and vanish beneath later development. In rural areas a monastery might make the nucleus for a country house – though it would usually be adapted beyond recognition as the centuries passed, until (as at Woburn) only the name hinted at its origin – or simply left to moulder unnoticed in a corner of the estate. The result has been that about one-third of England's monasteries have left no visible mark above the soil.

So the ruin-hunter, as Byng cheerfully called himself, did not always have an easy task, and the problems he ran into at Swineshead in the Lincolnshire Fens were not unusual:

here I made enquiries after the old abbey of Swineshead, (by all the names of enquiry) of a young man; to whom, at last, I said, 'Are there any ruins?' Who answer'd, 'I know of no brewings'. – An old man did assist me: 'Why it is to the left, not a chain mile out of town'. So I found the scite thereof, and a good farm house upon it: — where long I did call and halloo, as I saw a cap at a window, seemingly of a woman; at last came out an old fat farmer in his nt [i.e. night] cap, who was very civil, begg'd me to alight, and drink rum and water, or what I chose; and explain'd to me where he believ'd the old priory stood.

At Jervaulx in Yorkshire he had 'to climb over walls, and force my way thro' nettles, and brambles', and at Neath in South Wales he found the old abbey buildings 'inhabited at odd corners ... by nests of copper-workers': 'Pillars, and stone work go hourly to wreck; and many curious carvings and images have been lately pull'd down.' When he came to Neath nearly seventy years later George Borrow saw the abbey sunk even further in industrial degradation.

This was ruination too extreme to please even an age half in love with decay. If not the most poignant example, the fate of Margam Abbey near Neath was noted in particular detail and with particular outrage by eighteenth-century visitors. The abbey church, or most of its nave, had become the parish church, and the other buildings belonged to Lord Talbot's estate of Margam Castle. Interest concentrated on the lovely chapter house, unusual for a Cistercian chapter house in being polygonal rather than rectangular, with its roof supported by a central column. Byng found a stag stabled in it when he came in 1787. He could not resist one of the tickings-off he liked to administer to country-house owners in the privacy of his journal:

Probably Mr T., a travell'd gentleman, knows not of, or esteems this treasure; but puts more store in some (unpack'd) boxes of *statues*, (as the maid call'd them) he has brought from Italy. – This is one of the advantages of travell, to come home with a vamp'd Correggio, and some shabby marbles, and then neglect the real antiquities, and old pictures at your family seat!

In 1791 another visitor noted that the roof, already beginning to give way, was protected from the elements only by a covering of oiled paper. The next witness was Sir Richard Colt Hoare, owner of Stourhead, with its picturesque gardens, grotto and delightful Gothic follies, as well as the patron of excavations at Stonehenge. He reported in 1793 that two arches of the chapter house had collapsed but that 'even then, with a little care and trifling expense it might have been saved from the ruin which daily impended over it'. The care was not taken nor the expense outlaid, and on a return visit in 1802 Sir Richard found the central column had fallen: 'That chef d'œuvre of elegant Gothic architecture is now, alas, no more, and every passing traveller will weep over its sad relicts.'

By a fast and quite natural process the ruin-hunter becomes an advocate, if not exactly of preservation, then at least of measures to ensure that something survives of the ruin and is properly displayed to those capable of appreciating it. Byng, so quick to demand that country-house visiting be placed on an organised footing, was eager to extend his argument to abbeys. 'I must, at every such place', he wrote after visiting Ulverscroft Priory in Charnwood Forest, 'express my sorrow, and astonishment, that the owners will not guard, and preserve such ruins; and not allways give them up to the mischief of changing farmers, who destroy wantonly, and for repairs.' (It is not hard to guess what Byng would have felt about the 'Keep Out' notices which barred my own attempt to visit Ulverscroft a few years ago.) Only a few miles further on, near Castle Donington, his imagination had leaped ahead to the possibilities that abbey tourism might hold in store: 'Where is the expence of placing an honest, indigent family upon the spot? who wou'd be highly benefited by strangers; and I shou'd add to their advantage, by writing, and printing the history of the place, and of the anchorite who dwelt therein.'

V

The Cistercian abbeys had been among the grandest and the loveliest of all the monasteries in England and Wales. Formed in the twelfth century, the order had broken away from the Benedictines in an attempt to return to the original austerity of their rule. This spiritual purpose gave their buildings great simplicity, for the Cistercians avoided ornate decoration as a matter of principle. It also led them to seek out remote locations, in valleys fringed by woods and fertilised by water, which saved their abbeys from the worst of fates after the Dissolution. Surrounding communities were few and far between and, anyway, had little need to plunder the monastic fabric when local stone was so easily available. The story of what happened to the buildings of the two greatest and most famous abbeys, Fountains in North York-shire and Tintern in the Wye valley, in particular what happened when the popular attitude changed from neglectful indifference to admiring curiosity, makes a revealing case study. It shows more clearly than any general summary what the eighteenth century found to admire in Gothic ruins, and it shows, too, the difficulties of reconciling this admiration with the demand that ruins also be monuments properly maintained and displayed to tourists.

On its dissolution in 1537 Fountains Abbey was stripped of its furnishings, the lead and timber from its roofs, and presumably its glass too, for neither here nor at any other ruin do we find traces of this then valuable and prestigious commodity. The remaining shell and its surrounding estate were sold first to Sir Richard Gresham and then, some sixty years later, to Sir Stephen Procter, courtier to James I, who proceeded to build Fountains Hall near by with 'stone got at hand out the abbey wall'. This must refer to the monastic outbuildings (quite

Versions of Fountains Abbey: 1. Before eighteenth-century improvement, with lollipop trees growing in the nave. A woodcut from Thomas Gent's *The Antient and Modern History of the Loyal Town of Rippon* (1733).

probably to the abbot's house), since the stone of the church itself shows no sign of such large-scale plundering. In fact, Sir Stephen's heirs, the Messenger family, were Catholics and they seem to have protected the buildings from downright vandalism. Such measures, of course, did not extend to protection from natural decay and a visitor in the 1680s reported finding the abbey 'full of trees in the very body of it'.

So it might have remained had it not been for the energy and ambition of the Aislabie family who owned the neighbouring estate of Studley Royal. John Aislabie, their eighteenth-century representative, was a man of some note and, indeed, notoriety. Elected Member of Parliament for Ripon by virtue of his local standing, he rose to become Chancellor of the Exchequer and used his office to promote the South Sea Bubble, the Watergate of early eighteenth-century politics. After the Bubble burst in 1720 the House of Commons passed a resolution proclaiming him guilty of 'dangerous, and infamous corruption' and Aislabie retired from public life in disgrace. In our own age discredited politicians occupy themselves penning self-justifying memoirs and appearing on television chat shows. In the eighteenth century they landscaped their parks.

Aislabie started work at Studley Royal in the 1720s and made its gardens his consuming passion until his death. He marshalled wood and water in a bold, formal geometry, placing statues and temples to mark the grand vistas he had created. Rooted in the Dutch style of gardening, Aislabie's taste was already a little dated when he began; it soon looked unfashionably stiff to a younger generation of visitors educated in the Picturesque taste, who preferred their waters to wind and their views to beckon intriguingly. Yet even they could not withhold praise from Studley Royal, if only because of its scale:

The place is full of lofty hedges, nicely trimmed: strait lines possess every part. The waters are numerous, and kept tame within nice borders, bounded by angular inclosures. The streams, too, that must necessarily escape, drop precisely down very artificial cascades. Still there is an admirable greatness, even in this faulty style of improvement.

Versions of Fountains Abbey: 2. This engraving, dated 1773, from Francis Grose's *The Antiquities of England and Wales* shows the ruins still surrounded by trees even after Aislablie's rash improvements, but makes the genteel visitors admiring the scene more prominent than the two tiny figures just discernible at the bottom centre of Gent's view.

Despite his straight lines, Aislabie was not completely untouched by the new taste. The focal point of his effects was not (as one might have expected) his own house, which was left in a modest state by comparison with the grandeur of his park. The honour was reserved for the overgrown ruins of Fountains, lying in the neighbouring valley and seen in striking prospect from a hilltop boundary of Studley Royal. Since it was in his character to wish to own what he surveyed, Aislabie tried several times to buy the ruins, but without success. They still lay outside the estate when he died in 1742. His son William continued the attempt, no doubt encouraged by the example of nearby Rievaulx, where the terraces of Duncombe Park were being extended to make them overlook the ruined Cistercian abbey in the dale below. In 1767 William Aislabie at last succeeded, though one source tells us that the Messenger who agreed to sell 'most painfully and ceaselessly regretted' the decision until his death. By then it was too late: Fountains Abbey was fully incorporated into the landscaping of Studley Royal.

Arthur Young saw the work in progress during his northern tour in 1768:

The extent of the building was prodigiously great, and many parts of it perfectly complete. The rubbish is at present clearing away, and all parts of it undergoing a search that no pavements or other remains of it may continue hid ... When all the discoveries are made that are expected, and the building left in that proper state, which a gentleman of Mr. *Aslabie*'s [sic] taste will undoubtedly order, it certainly will remain a very noble ruin.

From a man often so uncritically eager to pronounce any change a landowner chooses to make to his estate an 'improvement', there is a marked reticence about that last phrase. Ruins, apparently, do not lend themselves to 'improvement' in the way that houses and parks do; Young can merely hope, a little doubtfully, that after the work has been done they will still 'remain' noble.

When he came to Fountains four years later, in 1772, William Gilpin had no doubts. He did not like the landscaped park of Studley Royal, of course, thinking it 'a vain ostentation of expence; a mere *Timon's villa*; decorated by a taste debauched in it's conceptions, and puerile in it's execution'. But he offered this criticism merely by way of warming up to his opinion of what Aislabie had done to Fountains. It was, Gilpin said, something 'which every lover of picturesque beauty must lament': '*his improvements* have had no bounds. He has pared away all the bold roughness, and freedom of the scene, and given every part a trim polish'.

In this general indictment Gilpin is presumably reacting to the way Aislabie had canalised into straightness the river that flows through the abbey and perhaps smoothed out the flanking hillsides, too – alterations that survive today and still create an oddly formal framework for the ruins. Gilpin's specific points of complaint give a detailed picture of Fountains during the sorriest years of its long history. The monks' garden had been turned into 'a trim parterre, and planted with flowering shrubs'. The buildings themselves bore 'the *recent* marks of human industry' in the form of attempts to reconstruct broken columns, reassemble tiles and repair the shattered tracery of the windows: 'But in vain; for the friability of the edges of every fracture makes any restoration of parts an awkward patchwork.' It may have been necessary to clear the inside of the abbey church and turf over its floor, concedes Gilpin, since 'we see ruins sometimes so choaked, that no view of them can be obtained', and it would have been possible to do the work with propriety. Aislabie, however, had chosen to decorate the nave with 'a mutilated heathen statue' and, crowning sacrilege, to make the great east window a frame for a view of 'some ridiculous figure, (I know not what; Ann Bolein, I think, they called it) that is placed in the valley'.

I have not managed to discover exactly what the statue of Anne Boleyn was; perhaps it is best not to know. The mutilated heathen statue was apparently a stray Arundel marble from the Aislabies' London home, uncovered again by excavations in the middle of the nineteenth century. These excavations showed that the damage Aislabie had inflicted on Fountains went deeper than a visitor's eye could detect. In clearing the church, he had obliterated important evidence by removing the fallen remains of groining and the top courses of the walls. In his eagerness to make a level surface he had torn down the pillars of the arcade in the choir. Once it was laid, the neat turf not only obscured pavement tiles and the foundations showing where the chantry chapels had stood but greatly distorted the building's proportions by covering the bases of the columns to a depth of about eighteen inches.

Although he came to Fountains in 1772 Gilpin did not publish the book that contained his strictures on its treatment until 1786, several years after William Aislabie's death. Gilpin commanded great force; once published, his views were bound to have effect. Aislabie's daughter, a Mrs Allanson, began to remove what a later antiquary tactfully called the 'chief extravagancies' her father had introduced, and began clearing the chapter house, the first of a series of cautious

and responsible excavations which continued until the middle of the
next century. At any rate, when Byng came in 1792 he found a changed
building whose charms he could admire almost wholeheartedly. The
monks' garden was still 'infinitely too spruce' for his taste but he could
take a 'long walk of pious, melancholy reflexion' in the cloisters, and
admire the mosaic pavement and abbots' graves in the newly cleared
chapter house. Oddly enough, Byng was ignorant of the ruin's recent
history – he obviously had not read his Gilpin – and so imagined that
these signs of care had been 'wonderfully done' by Aislabie. It is ironic
to hear a traveller normally so quick to denounce landowners for their
arrogance and bad taste offering praise where it was not deserved.

Byng's confusion should not distract us from the credit Gilpin

Visitors among the ruins of Fountains Abbey. This illustration by Moses
Griffiths to Thomas Pennant's *A Tour from Alston-Moor to Harrowgate and
Brimham-Crags* (1804) looks from the south transept towards the north
transept and the base of the Perpendicular tower added shortly before the
Dissolution.

deserves. What he said about Aislabie and Fountains went far beyond
his anger at the idiocies of one particular man and the desecration of
one particular ruin. Indeed, his very anger at what he saw impelled him
beyond the specific scene to an important general point. Owners might
have a perfect right in law to mess their ruins about, but they are also
answerable to what he called 'the court of taste':

> The refined code of this court does not consider an elegant ruin as a man's
> *property*, on which he may exercise at will the irregular sallies of a wanton
> imagination: but as a deposit, of which he is only the guardian, for the
> amusement and admiration of posterity. – A ruin is a sacred thing. Rooted for
> ages in the soil; assimilated to it; and become, as it were, a part of it; we
> consider it as a work of nature, rather than of art.

By looking beyond the question of individual ownership and by
looking beyond the present generation, Gilpin is preparing the ground
for those laws which would eventually enforce preservation, however
inadequately framed and ineffectively enforced they would sometimes
prove.

VI

To say that Gothic ruins should be protected, whether from the decay
into which Margam chapter house was allowed to sink or from the
foolish 'improvements' which Aislabie made at Fountains, opens
rather than closes debate. It raises the question of what people take the
essential character of such places to be. In the phrase 'Gothic ruin' does
emphasis fall on the adjective or the noun? Do people want to admire a
Gothic abbey as best they can, even though it survives only in a
damaged state? Or do they seek to admire the ruin it has become, with
all the accidental features time has added to it? The modern attitude is
to value ruins as historical and architectural evidence: we strip, clean
and label sites to make them instructive exhibits. The history of Tintern
Abbey – the most popular of all monastic ruins with early tourists –
shows how differently these questions were answered in the closing
years of the eighteenth century.

Tintern was dissolved in 1535. Its bells and lead were melted down
and then sold to Henry, Earl of Worcester, to whom the rest of the
buildings were also granted. He or one of his immediate heirs may
actually have wanted to live at Tintern, for the ruins show vestiges of
an attempt to convert them to secular use. It was obviously short-lived,

and the abbey fell quickly into decay. By the time Lord Herbert of Cherbury came in the 1640s to inspect the grave of his ancestor Sir William Herbert, the first Earl of Pembroke, he found both the tomb and the abbey 'wholly defaced and ruined'.

Part of Tintern's great charm is its remote and lovely situation in the Wye valley. Yet wood and water, the very features which had brought the Cistercians to the spot, could also attract industry and there was, besides, a long tradition of iron-working in the nearby Forest of Dean. An iron forge and a wire-manufacturing plant were set up at Tintern in the seventeenth century, the forge at the river's edge only a few hundred yards from the abbey church. They flourished and spawned a huddle of cottages, no doubt built from abbey stone, around the old buildings.

The villagers found a use for the church. In the early eighteenth century it served as fives' court and a place to play quoits, with the stone effigy of a knight making a handy backstop. The knight was presumably Sir William Herbert and he, poor man, was not fated to rest in peace. In about 1760 a local barge builder, William Sparks, attacked the effigy 'with savage fury and indecency' and managed to chop off the head with his adze. The record does not say whether his vandalism was the result of Protestant ardour or a Saturday night spree, but it does show that the Duke of Beaufort, who had inherited Tintern from the Worcesters, cared enough about his property to take out a warrant for Sparks' arrest – too late, since the man had disappeared from the neighbourhood.

In fact, the Duke of Beaufort was proud of Tintern. It was certainly time to do something about the condition it had sunk to, for (said a local historian) 'the interior was choaked up with rubbish, several feet above the present surface, and overspread with ashlings, elders, and other trees, the growth of such situations, to a very considerable height'. In 1756 or thereabouts a contractor from Chepstow was engaged and over a hundred men put to work cleaning away the mess. They did not touch the abbey's outbuildings, which were left so overgrown that it still took the antiquary Francis Grose a second visit to notice that any survived at all. Nor did the labourers observe anything like the standards of an archaeological dig. The Duke's steward carried off two effigies, and a stone mason sold a brass gauntlet and spear he had found to a stranger for half a guinea. The pavement tiles which afterwards turned up in local houses were presumably filched at this time, too. However, the abbey church itself was cleared and its floor neatly grassed over. As a finishing touch doors and locks were added, making it apparently the only ruin to boast even this rudimentary sign of its proprietor's concern for its safety.

In this state Tintern was seen by Turner, Wordsworth and the other tourists who came in the second half of the eighteenth century. They usually took the boat excursion down the Wye from Ross to Chepstow, being allowed two hours at the ruins before embarking again to catch the tide. The local roads were bad enough to discourage other ways of approach: Coleridge and his party got lost when they walked from Chepstow, and a hardy traveller who came overland from Monmouth reported 'hollow and uncouth tracks, seldom attempted by any carriage but those of the natives'. By 1793 the ruins had become popular enough for a Monmouth printer to devote a pamphlet to them in his series describing beauty spots of the Wye. When he reissued the handbook in 1801 he could add that Mr Gethern, landlord of the neighbouring Beaufort Arms, had become the unofficial custodian of the abbey. His inn could offer 'a clean room, and frugal fare, with every requisite attention', while Mrs Gethern would undertake to 'arrange the repast, which the Visitors often bring with them'.

Gilpin came in 1770, putting himself in the vanguard of this new tourism, though his modesty delayed publication of his Wye valley tour until twelve years later. In the general setting of the abbey he found exactly that air of 'chearful solitude' which Aislabie's garish alterations had destroyed at Fountains:

A more pleasing retreat could not easily be found. The woods, and glades intermixed; the winding of the river; the variety of the ground; the splendid ruin, contrasted with the objects of nature; and the elegant line formed by the summits of the hills, which include the whole; make all together a very inchanting piece of scenery.

This comes very close to fulfilling the picturesque ideal of nature which I will examine in my next chapter. There I will argue that this ideal, so precisely and demandingly imagined by writers on aesthetics, proves incapable of fulfilment by any actual scene. And, indeed, though he finds nothing to provoke anger or demand action as he had done at Fountains, Gilpin is at least mildly disappointed when he starts to inspect Tintern more closely.

The first problem his eye encountered was the ironworks, still smoking busily away within sight of the abbey church. Even more objectionable were the 'shabby houses' of its workers which had grown up near by, for they intruded even on that first, otherwise

Versions of Tintern Abbey: 1. The Picturesque viewpoint adopted by William Gilpin, showing the ruins from the opposite bank of the Wye and deliberately flattering the details of the scene. An aquatint etched by William Sawrey Gilpin, the traveller's nephew, for *Observations on the River Wye* (1782).

delightful, view of the ruins from the river. The solution, Gilpin proposed, was for the visitor to choose his vantage point with care, leaving the river for the road on the opposite bank. There, if he squinted a little, he could manage to exclude the ironworks from the scene, and he could allow his brush to ignore the presence of the shabby houses. In fact, not all contemporaries were willing to follow Gilpin to this extreme: some readers complained that they had difficulty in recognising the Wye valley from his idealised aquatints, and, though they usually followed him in his choice of viewpoint, other artists record the disappointing details rather more frankly.

A more stubbornly discordant note was struck by other evidences of life at Tintern. The forge and its cottages were merely survivals from the days when the beauty of ruins had not properly been appreciated: the rise of tourism would eventually sweep them away, expunging them from reality as they had first been expunged from Gilpin's sketchbook. The down-and-outs were a different matter. I have not been able to find any record of when or why they first came to Tintern,

Versions of Tintern Abbey: 2. A less selective view including some of the near-by buildings and a boatload of tourists protected by a canopy from the fierce heat of the Welsh sun. From Samuel Ireland's *Picturesque Views on the River Wye* (1797).

though it is fair to assume that they were attracted simply because the ruined outbuildings offered primitive shelter; but it must surely have been the influx of tourists, with the promise of tips and charity, that encouraged them to stay. They clustered around, openly begging or making some show of selling their services as guides.

Gilpin's attention was caught in particular by one poor woman who offered to show him the monks' library:

She could scarce crawl; shuffling along her palsied limbs, and meagre, contracted body, by the help of two sticks. She led us, through an old gate, into a place overspread with nettles, and briars; and pointing to the remnants of a shattered cloister, told us, that was her place. It was her own mansion. All indeed she meant to tell us, was the story of her own wretchedness; and all she had to shew us, was her own miserable habitation. We did not expect to be interested: but we found we were. I never saw so loathsome a human dwelling. It was a cavity, loftily vaulted, between two ruined walls; which streamed with various-coloured stains of unwholsome dews. The floor was earth; yielding, through moisture, to the tread. Not the merest utensil, or furniture of any kind, appeared, but a wretched bedstead, spread with a few rags, and drawn into the middle of the cell, to prevent its receiving the damp, which trickled down the walls. At one end was an aperture; which served just to let in light enough to discover the wretchedness within.

'We did not expect to be interested: but we found we were.' It says much for Gilpin's humanity that he allowed himself to be distracted from picturesque appraisal into giving this compelling vignette. And this is one respect in which he did not influence later writers, for it is the nature of the tourist to resent and ignore social problems, particularly those to which tourism itself may be contributing. Byng notes that 'many cripples' were produced for his charity in the 1780s, the guidebook of 1801 coyly admits that the ruins still housed '*temporary inhabitants*' and after that, so far as I can discover, the record of this community of destitutes lapses into silence.

Even when contemplation of the ruin was limited just to its aesthetic character, Tintern could still disappoint. Gilpin criticised its external appearance in a famous passage, still sometimes mockingly remembered by modern guidebooks:

Though the parts are beautiful, the whole is ill-shaped. No ruins of the tower

Versions of Tintern Abbey: 3. A 'General View' engraved from a drawing by Sir Richard Colt Hoare, showing the surroundings of the ruins rather more honestly than Gilpin or Ireland do. From William Coxe's *An Historical Tour in Monmouthshire* (1801).

are left, which might give form, and contrast to the walls, and buttresses, and other inferior parts. Instead of this, a number of gabel-ends hurt the eye with their regularity; and disgust it by the vulgarity of their shape. A mallet judiciously used (but who durst use it?) might be of service in fracturing some of them; particularly those of the cross isles, which are not only disagreeable in themselves, but confound the perspective.

It is disconcerting to find the observer who had adopted so firmly protective an attitude to Fountains now wielding his mallet at Tintern, if only in imagination. We can find a similar contradiction in *The Seven Lamps of Architecture* where, alongside Ruskin's passionate pleas for us to respect old buildings, we can also read his offer to improve the proportions of King's College Chapel by knocking off a couple of pinnacles at either end. Nor was Gilpin being eccentric by the standards of his time, for other travel writers followed him explicitly in condemning the offending gable ends and implicitly in preferring the interior of the church to its exterior.

The key word, of course, is 'regularity'. In Gilpin's eyes Gothic is attractive because it offers an alternative to the outmoded harmonies of Neo-classicism. That much is already apparent in his demand for dramatic contrasts between horizontals and verticals in opposition to the coolly rectangular façades of, say, a Gibbs or a Kent. But the gable ends stubbornly challenge his assumptions, by their specific reminder of the church's cruciform plan and by their unwelcome hint that Gothic had not, after all, been a matter of unregulated profusion but a system of building principles. Eighteenth-century tourists had already chosen, on the whole, to prefer ruins to intact buildings like cathedrals or parish churches partly because time and decay had created irregularities the builders had not intended; sometimes, they were still forced to admit that not all Gothic ruins were Gothic enough.

If the 'formal appearance' of the exterior made visitors prefer the inside of the church, they could still find problems even here. The neat turf that the Duke of Beaufort had thoughtfully laid down caused no dramatic outcry of the sort Aislabie's ill-conceived improvements to Fountains had done. Yet it became an aesthetic battleground on which the age could fight out its attitude to Gothic and to ruin, making clear its deepest assumptions in the process.

Gilpin opened the issue moderately enough. Even at Fountains he had been willing to admit that Aislabie could have done some cleaning-up with propriety, if only so that visitors could get in the door. At Tintern, faced with the smooth lawn and the fragments of stone

Inside Tintern Abbey, engraved from a drawing by Sir Richard Colt Hoare,
published in William Coxe's *An Historical Tour in Monmouthshire* (1801).

organised into piles against the walls, he confessed to a sense of loss:

More picturesque it certainly would have been, if the area, unadorned, had been left with all the rough fragments of ruin scattered round; and bold was the hand that removed them; yet as the outside of the ruin, which is the chief object of *picturesque curiosity*, is still left in all its wild, and native rudeness; we excuse – perhaps we approve – the neatness, that is introduced within. It *may* add to the *beauty* of the scene – to its *novelty* it undoubtedly *does*.

When the usual spokesman for the court of taste offered so cautious a ruling, contemporaries were left ample scope to develop their own judgement.

Some approved. Henry Wyndham, for example, praised the Duke of Beaufort's work on the grounds it allowed visitors to inspect and admire the details of the carvings. Yet he was in the minority, and most visitors echoed Gilpin's doubts in louder key. Samuel Ireland thought the effect of 'tameness and uniformity' out of keeping with the 'brokenness and irregularity' which were otherwise the leading features of the place. Byng called for evergreens and cypresses to be planted, exactly what he hoped the owner of Fountains would go on to do there. The antiquary Francis Grose was particularly violent in condemning the turf, which he thought looked like a 'Bowling-Green' and gave the place 'more the air of an artificial Ruin in a Garden, than that of an ancient decayed Abbey'.

By its very violence, Grose's opinion is also the clearest expression of at least one element in the age's attitude to Gothic. Once a ruin is cleared, it becomes 'undoubtedly light and elegant ... nothing being left for the Spectator to guess or explore'. It has lost the atmosphere of mystery and even horror proper to a monument of the Catholic past, and the spectator has been deprived of the opportunity for a pleasurable frisson. Grose complains of being left quite unthrilled by Tintern: 'it wants that gloomy solemnity so essential to religious ruins; those yawning vaults and dreary recesses which strike the beholder with a religious awe, and make him almost shudder at entering them, calling into his mind all the tales of the nursery'. These phrases closely resemble Arthur Young's thoughts on 'the just stile for a ruin to appear in', stimulated but not satisfied by his visit to Fountains. Ruins are best seen from a distance, he believed, and access to the inside should not be made too easy, lest the visitor be denied the chance to exercise his imagination:

Looking, as it were, by stealth through passages that cannot be passed, heaps of rubbish stopping you in one place, broken steps preventing both ascent and descent in another; in a word, some parts that cannot be seen at all, others that are half seen; and those fully viewed, broken, rugged, and terrible. – In such the imagination has a free space to range in, and sketches ruins in idea beyond the boldest limits of reality.

Young concludes with the practical recommendation that a ruin should be left 'in the wildest and most melancholy state the ravaging hand of time can have thrown it into', but the emotions he describes are more likely to be inspired by the pages of a Gothic novel than by real stone and ivy. I know of no account which claims that any actual abbey fully met these romantic requirements: they are usually listed, as here by Grose and Young, to mark the disappointing gap between the imagined and the real-life experience of Gothic. In practice, the best that tourists could do to work up the sublimity of the occasion was to make their visits at night, when darkness and moonlight combined to give the ruins an appearance of mystery that daylight dispelled. This is Joseph Cottle's description of how Coleridge and his party saw Tintern in the 1790s:

At the instant the huge doors unfolded, the horned moon appeared between the opening clouds, and shining through the grand window in the distance. It was a delectable moment; not a little augmented by the unexpected green sward that covered the whole of the floor, and the long-forgotten tombs beneath; whilst the gigantic ivies, in their rivalry, almost concealed the projecting and dark turrets and eminences, reflecting back the lustre of the torch below.

Mr Gethern and his successors at the Beaufort Arms must have done a brisk trade in torches; the tradition is kept up by the floodlit concerts and the *son et lumière* spectacles staged at old buildings. As Ruskin remarked, a 'Sentimental Admiration' of Gothic is 'excitable in nearly all persons, by a certain amount of darkness and slow music in a minor key'.

Not all those who objected to the Duke of Beaufort's treatment of Tintern took refuge in such expedients. They sought not so much the thrill of the Sublime as the gentler pleasures of the Picturesque at Tintern, and they indulged them by turning away from the smooth grass, ignoring the architectural details it had helped lay bare and concentrating on those parts of the building where age and decay still held sway. The literature of Tintern Abbey at the end of the eighteenth century is lavish in its descriptions of wild flowers growing out of the old stones and verdant tendrils of ivy creeping round the columns. In this respect Wordsworth, who came armed with his copy of Gilpin in 1793 and again in 1798, was merely carrying the picturesque approach

This engraving from Francis Grose's *The Antiquities of England and Wales* (1773–6) shows how easily the love of tombs mingled with the love of Gothic ruins. Note the broken classical column at the bottom right and the broken trefoil defying gravity behind the tomb.

a step further when he used the surrounding scenery rather than the ruin as setting for his poem – not 'Lines Composed at Tintern Abbey' but 'Lines Composed a Few Miles above Tintern Abbey'.

The early visitors cherished ruins, but not for the culture which had produced them or the communities which had lived in them, and hardly at all for their architecture: none of these aspects could yet be viewed without prejudice. Ruins were admired as witnesses to the triumph of time and nature over man's handiwork. The pleasant, pensive melancholy they provoked – we have already seen Byng indulging it in his walk round the cloister at Fountains – has a great deal in common with Addison's mood among the monuments of Westminster Abbey, quoted in my first chapter, and the sentiments of Gray's 'Elegy Written in a Country Churchyard'. The cults of the tomb, the churchyard and the ruin, all characteristic of late eighteenth-century culture, blend easily and at times indistinguishably with one another. At the ruin, however, the distinctive and triumphant presence of nature can leaven melancholy with a visual delight lacking from

The ruin as part of nature. In 1810 John Sell Cotman recorded much the same scene at Rievaulx Abbey that Dorothy Wordsworth had found in the 1790s: 'thrushes were singing, cattle feeding among green grown hillocks among the Ruins'. Cotman's etching appeared in his *Architectural Remains* (1838).

Furness Abbey in the nineteenth century, when tourists enjoying a picnic have replaced animals as the natural complement to the ruins. This engraving (by Thomas or Edward Gilks), which appeared in more than one book in the 1840s, is here reproduced from Charles Mackay's *The Scenery and Poetry of the English Lakes* (1846). By this time the tranquillity of the scene had been threatened by the building of the Furness Railway, though Wordsworth, who found navvies resting from their work among the ruins on his visit in the summer of 1845, recorded their reverential manner in a sonnet: 'All seem to feel the spirit of the place.'

Addison's rather chilly and abstracted account of Westminster Abbey. At times – in the work of William Gilpin – this can break through the hackneyed phrases into which it so readily moulds itself and speak, however frailly, as a living language to our ear:

Ivy, in masses uncommonly large, has taken possession of many parts of the wall; and gives a happy contrast to the grey-coloured stone, of which the building is composed. Nor is this undecorated. Mosses of various hues, with lychens, maidenhair, penny-leaf, and other humble plants, overspread the surface; or hang from every joint, and crevice. Some of them were in flower, others only in leaf; but, all together, they give those full-blown tints, which add the richest finishing to a ruin.

4

Rash assault: nature and the nature of tourism

> Following complaints, the owner of a fast power boat was asked to leave
> Esthwaite Water, where power boats of any kind are not permitted. He
> remarked 'What a pity. I was enjoying myself here. It's such a quiet lake.'
>
> John Wyatt, *The Lake District*

I

In the course of his travels the anonymous military gentleman who made what he called a *Short Survey* of England in the 1630s came to a region 'like a solitary wildernes', its scenery 'nothing but hideous, hanging Hills, and great Pooles, that, what in respect of the murmuring noyse of those great waters, and those high mountanous, tumbling, rocky Hills, a man would thinke he were in another world'. It probably takes us a minute to recognise the Lake District in this description, though not because it is inaccurate: for all his brevity, the seventeenth-century traveller notes the salient contours of lake and fell graphically enough. What disconcerts is his tone, in which wonderment finds no room for superlatives of praise and is dominated instead by that word 'hideous', an adjective which modern travel writers apply to the works of humanity (particularly of nineteenth- and twentieth-century architects) but never to the works of nature.

Our present admiration for untouched nature, increasingly tinged with guilt about our neglectful stewardship of its dwindling reserves, is a luxury belonging to a fairly advanced stage of social development. Before this had been achieved, nature struck people, if not as an enemy, at least as a challenge: civilisation started by clearing the wilderness.

130

Whatever resisted subjugation stood as an inconvenience or a threat: the moor and the fell as unproductive land to frustrate the farmer, the ocean and the lake as hindrances to the traveller and the merchant, the cave and the forest as refuges for wild beasts and bandits. The most stubbornly uncooperative outposts could also create philosophical unease in a culture which saw creation as divinely ordered, with man at the centre and the natural world as his willing servant. Renaissance and seventeenth-century theology still yearned after the vision of a perfectly smooth and regular world, and sought to explain its actual state in much the same terms it accounted for the presence of evil in human nature, by viewing the earth's 'deformities' as a result of the Fall or the biblical Flood.

Such considerations have not vanished completely. When it tackles the problem of evil, theology still starts by addressing itself to floods, earthquakes and volcanic eruptions. And even in an age of agro-chemicals and EC surpluses, it is still hard to shake off the King of Brobdingnag's belief that people can do nothing nobler than to make two ears of corn grow where one grew before. Yet the older attitude to nature has been slackening its grip ever since society had cleared enough of the wilderness to serve the most immediate needs and remove the most immediate threats, a state English society had achieved by the eighteenth century. Living in a country where agricultural improvements were putting so much of the landscape under the plough or inside the fence encouraged people to look on the uncultivated remnants with something other than a farmer's eye and see that 'uncultivated' might in fact mean 'unspoiled'. Leading increasingly safe and ordered lives made people suspect that the wilderness might hold pleasure as well as danger, and that even danger might offer vicarious excitement. Finally, as urban life took firmer hold, people would long for nature as a necessary refuge, a source of spiritual renewal. Indeed, these changes have occupied much of our cultural energy for the last two hundred years, leaving hardly an aspect of our thought and behaviour unaltered. The tourist, often the publicist, populariser or merely bastardiser of such wide-reaching transformations, has in this case also been among the leaders of the experiment.

II

Of all English regions, the Peak District was best suited for testing out the first stages in this long process, since its complex geological formation gave it a freakish abundance of precisely those deformities that could, initially, appear ugly or frightening. The layers of millstone grit and limestone which make up the Derbyshire Dome had created both a high, barren landscape of stony moorland in the Dark Peak and a jagged, though more fertile, landscape of hill and dale in the White Peak. What lay just beneath the surface suggested even more dramatically the convulsive force rather than the smooth design of natural creation: a strange, disordered world of rivers which emerged unexpectedly as wells and springs, and of cave systems whose tunnels and chambers held stalactites, stalagmites and curious mineral deposits like the famous Blue John. And, unlike the Lake District, the Peak District was not tucked away in a forgotten corner of England: it stood squarely in the Midlands near provincial centres like Derby and Sheffield, and its growing industries appealed to the early generation of travellers whose eclectic interests always made them ready to break the journey with a visit to a porcelain factory, a lead mine, a cotton mill or a cutlery workshop.

By the late seventeenth century the major sights had been organised, with the help of Thomas Hobbes and Charles Cotton, into a shortlist of seven 'wonders': 'Two Fonts, two Caves, one Pallace, Mount, and Pit'. The two fonts are the ebbing and flowing well at Tideswell and St Ann's Well, the source of Buxton's original fame as a goal of pilgrimage and its later prosperity as a spa town. The two caves are Poole's Hole near Buxton and the Peak Cavern near Castleton. The mount is Mam Tor, the so-called 'shivering mountain' near Castleton, and the pit is Eldon Hole, on the way from Buxton to Castleton. The palace is the Duke of Devonshire's seat at Chatsworth, a man-made wonder added to the list by way of civilised contrast to the six 'shames and Ills' of nature. These are wonders in the sense that they provoke not admiration but astonishment or even disgust, reactions pungently summed up in the traditional folk name for the Peak Cavern that still lingered on to embarrass genteel travellers in the eighteenth century: the Devil's Arse. Yet this epithet, like the abuse Cotton hurls at the 'Warts', 'Wens' and 'imposthumated boyles' of nature on his list, strikes a jocular note; it even concedes its object a certain grotesque interest. In the parlance of the age, one man's deformity is another man's natural curiosity, particularly if the other man has an antiquarian, scientific or philosophical turn of mind.

Enough people were drawn to the region in the late seventeenth and early eighteenth centuries to make Defoe, after duly characterising it as a 'houling Wilderness', adopt a deliberately blasé tone to dismiss the

'*Wonderless* Wonders of the Peak' as overrated attractions. The history of tourism shows that such dismissals often fuel rather than quench popularity: people still flock to sights labelled disappointing by the guidebooks, if only to show that they are sophisticated enough to agree when they get there. Defoe's criticism certainly did no damage, for later travellers continued to record all the unpleasing signs of a developed yet still expanding tourist industry. From the start, for example, specimens of Blue John and the other local fluorspars had made tempting additions to the visitor's cabinet of curiosities. Hewn from a source less suspect and less easily exhaustible than Shakespeare's mulberry tree, they became widely distributed souvenirs in the eighteenth century, available at the mines and caves themselves or from a shop at Matlock, either in their natural state or 'ingeniously manufactured into vases, cups, seals and all varieties of furniture'. Further afield, Byng found the 'pedantic puppy' of a guide running a similar shop in Derby cathedral. By the early years of the nineteenth century, when Jane Austen's Elizabeth Bennet would immediately include the chance of picking up 'a few petrified spars' among the attractions of a visit to the Peaks, at least one writer judged it necessary to warn visitors against the fraudulent devices sometimes used to enhance the colour of Blue John.

As this would suggest, the caves were by far the most popular sights. Poole's Hole and, in particular, the Peak Cavern overshadowed the other natural wonders, continued to flourish when fewer tourists were following the original itinerary in a systematic fashion, and helped along the fame of other caverns, natural or artificial, not included in the list. In the 1680s Cotton had mentioned the old woman who kept the key to Poole's Hole, 'that it may keep her'. By the 1750s visitors found the entrance surrounded by a handful of 'straggling cottages … inhabited by poor people, whose livelihood is gain'd by shewing Strangers the Place'. Castleton, convenient for Mam Tor as well as the Peak Cavern, presented a similar aspect: 'a Town of Beggars, whose chief dependence for Subsistence is on every curious Traveller who comes to visit'. Defoe had noted the 'little Town' which had grown up in the mouth of the Cavern itself, like the community which had found refuge among the ruins of Tintern Abbey. Its inhabitants lived by spinning pack-thread, showing the underground marvels and begging. Visitors often took a lively interest in the spinning work, but when they found themselves besieged with guides in groups of 'near a hundred, with lighted Candles and wretched Countenances', all of them demanding payment or pleading for alms when the tour was over, they

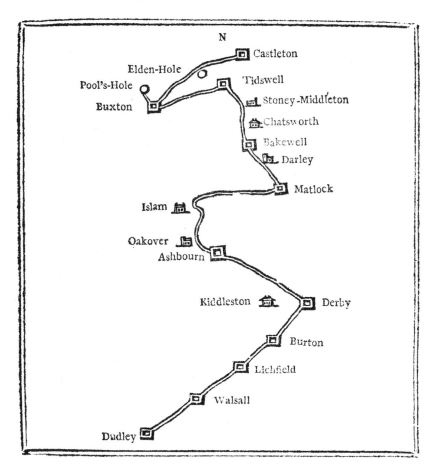

Richard Warner's itinerary for the Peak District in *A Tour through the Northern Counties of England, and the Borders of Scotland* (1802), following a route loosely inspired by the seven Wonders of the Peak.

commonly hardened their hearts in the manner of tourists the world over and told themselves that there 'was not one true object of commiseration among the whole'.

The disgust they felt for guides, beggars and all the accompanying signs of commercialisation strikes a wholly familiar note in eighteenth-century travel literature. In the case of the Peak Cavern, visitors sometimes recorded it more fully than they described the Cavern itself. William Bray, however, outlined the main features of the underground journey, which took about two hours:

At the distance of one hundred and fifty yards from the entrance, you come to the first stream, the roof gradually sloping to within two yards of the surface. This water is to be crossed by lying down in a boat, which is pushed forward by the guide. You then come to an apartment of great extent, with several apertures atop. After crossing the water a second time, on the guide's back,

The Devils Arfe near Castleton.

A the Devils Arse. B. Houses within the Arch where many poor peo
-ple live. C. the first Water. D. the second Water. E. the third and last
Water. where the Rock and the Water Closes and you can pass no
farther.

An early, unromantic view of the Devil's Arse, engraved by Michael van der
Gucht for *The Genuine Works of Charles Cotton* (1715). It is based on an
engraving which had appeared in Charles Leigh's *The Natural History of
Lancashire, Cheshire, and the Peak in Derbyshire* (1700) – a source, also, for
illustrations to some editions of Defoe's *Tour*.

you enter Roger Rain's House, so called from the continual dropping of the roof. Here you are entertained by a company of singers, who, having taken a different route, are stationed in a place, called the Chancel.

Bray was an antiquary, and his dry, prosaic account does little to convey the excitements this tour might have offered. That it required a spirit of adventure is made clear by the Honourable Mrs Murray (also known as Sarah Aust), an energetic traveller who came near the end of the century and wrote an account as full of sensible, daunting advice as a modern potholers' handbook:

Those who dare venture into the cave, should provide a change of dress, and they need not fear getting cold or rheumatism. If Females, dry shoes, stockings and petticoats will be requisite: carry also your night-caps, and a yard of coarse flannel, to pin on the head, so as to let it hang loose over the shoulders; it will prevent the dripping from the rocks in the cave from wetting and spoiling your habits, or gowns; also take an old pair of gloves, for the tallow candle, necessary to be carried in the hand, will make an end to all gloves worn in the cavern. Take some snuff and tobacco, which will be grateful offerings to the old witch-looking beings, spinning in the dark mouth of the cave.

A gentleman from Oxford, who came with his party in 1797, expands Bray's tantalisingly brief treatment of the singing performance which exploited the underground echoes to provide a climax to the visit:

They sung, in parts, a slow piece of music, that had a grand effect, for the discordant tones and wild appearances harmonized with the rugged rocks and the inscrutable darkness. One figure of an old hag, the leader of the band, reminded us of Tisiphone, calling together her confederate furies.

This is significant, not just in providing extra information but in hinting at a sensibility we have not so far encountered, either in my previous quotations or in my explanation of why their authors visited the Cavern. 'Discordant', 'wild', 'rugged' and 'inscrutable' are all adjectives which sit well with the idea of the Cavern as a deformity or natural curiosity; so does calling the leading singer an 'old hag' and, even, comparing the group to Tisiphone and her 'confederate furies'. Yet it is new to suggest that all these ingredients together make a 'grand effect'. The Oxford gentleman confirms it when he writes more generally of his reaction to the Cavern: 'The mind, overpowered sometimes shrinks within itself, but as others rises to the sublime conception of the power, that tore the rock asunder.' The convulsive force of nature and the apparent chaos it can leave behind has ceased to be just offensive to the eye or troubling to the mind: it has become a 'sublime conception'.

I shall be returning to this word 'sublime' several times in the course
of this chapter, since it is the age's favourite term for describing how
what once merely displeased or frightened can also impress. For the
moment, it is worth noting that the sublimity of the Peak Cavern
depends as much on its human occupants as on its natural scenery. To
the Oxford gentleman the singers play a vital part in the grand effect,
and the imagery of hags and furies he applies to them is a common
feature in other accounts as well. Though everywhere abused as greedy
and disgusting, the guides and singers are at the same time clothed in
allusions to myth, legend and literature which give them a sinister
grandeur. The Hon. Mrs Murray's description of the old women at the
cave mouth as 'witch-looking' slips past almost unnoticed because it
had become a conditioned reflex among travel writers to call them
'Infernal Hags, and Imps of Darkness' or compare them explicitly with
the witches in *Macbeth*. Crossing the underground stream is, to
anyone even slightly more imaginative than William Bray, 'like crossing the Styx'. Carl Moritz, the German pastor who toured England in
the 1780s, embellishes the classical reference in describing his reaction
to the guide who offered to carry him over: 'His stringy black hair,
dirty ragged clothes, his harsh voice and the question he asked were so
fitting to the character of Charon that I could not shake off the uncanny
feeling that the sight of this cave had begun to inspire.' The very people
who make a visit to the Peak Cavern a distasteful commercial trans-
action can, from another point of view which the visitors also cultivate
enthusiastically, give it the atmosphere of a Fuseli painting.

Of all these visitors, the Oxford gentleman is the greatest virtuoso in
uncanny feeling. Here he is, in one of the other local caves or, as he puts
it, in another 'abode of silent horror':

Such a place as might of old, have been the unsuspected den of banditti, or the
residence of restless spirits, that only stalked abroad at the solemn noon of
night ... A little stretch of fancy might have supposed the guide, lurking with
the light behind a rock, to have been some nocturnal villain, skulking from the
avengers of murder.

Safe on his sixpenny conducted visit, the eighteenth-century tourist is
happily at play among ancestral fears which have lost their sting. After
enjoying themselves so hugely, the Oxford gentleman and his party
probably went back to their inn and slept like tops but convention – the
new sensibility of the Sublime – demands that the charade be played to
the end: 'Yesterday was a day of horror, and sleep at night was a
stranger to our eyes.'

III

The new appetite prompted travellers to seek out curious natural phenomena elsewhere; no doubt the commercial atmosphere at places like the Peak Cavern gave them an additional incentive to look further afield. Their interest concentrated on the Lake District, of course, though not as exclusively as its later popularity might suggest. The Wye valley, for example, could offer scenery as well as the ruins of Tintern Abbey, Chepstow Castle and Goodrich Castle. Visitors, including several whose names we now primarily associate with the discovery of the Lakes, also began to explore the Pennine Dales and, particularly, the Craven region between Settle and Wharfedale, where geological faults break the Mountain Limestone into dramatic effects. Eighteenth-century travel books about Craven show the developing cult of nature and the Sublime beginning to emerge above ground, adapting itself to spectacles other than the subterranean marvels of the Peak Cavern.

Yet, to start with, the chief appeal of Craven was that it offered curiosities similar to the Wonders of the Peak. Thomas West's account of his tour, published in 1780 as an 'appendix' to his better-known book about the Lakes, gives an itinerary which would have sounded familiar to anyone who had made the tour of Derbyshire: it includes Yordas Cave, Hurtle Pot, Weathercoat Cave, the ebbing and flowing well near Giggleswick, Malham Cove, Gordale Scar and Kilnsey Crag. Even West's sub-title shows that these sights could still inspire the same sort of geological-cum-theological speculation about nature's deformities which had helped put the Wonders of the Peak on the tourist map in the seventeenth century, promising *Some Philosophical Conjectures on the Deluge, and the Alterations on the Surface and Interior Parts of the Earth Occasioned by This Great Revolution of Nature.*

In practice, however, the travel writers usually record a mixture of shabbiness and sublimity reminiscent of Poole's Hole or the Peak Cavern. West complains that tourists had already covered the walls of Yordas Cave with graffiti and broken off many of its stalactites as souvenirs. The vandalism was not bad enough to impede the familiar flow of classical allusion: 'Several passages out of *Ovid's Metamorphosis, Virgil,* and other classics crowded into my mind together.' John Housman, writing in 1800, can use the prehistoric past of Yordas and its ghost legends to conjure up the same sort of fantasy that the Oxford gentleman enjoyed in the Peak Cavern: 'No cave in romance, no den of lions, giants or serpents, nor any haunts of ghosts or fairies, were ever described more frightfully gloomy and dismal than this now before us.'

Housman is still following West's route through Craven. His account, however, confirms that subterranean marvels like Yordas and Hurtle Pot had yielded pride of place to Malham Cove and, particularly, Gordale Scar – originally a cave too, though the collapse of its roof had long since made it a limestone amphitheatre open to the sky. The poet Gray had admired it, 'not without shuddering', in 1769 and West himself had thought it 'awful, great, and grand'. The Hon. Mrs Murray had praised it as 'one of the most astonishing, as well as one of the most terrific effects, that can be produced by rocks and falling

Yordas Cave, looking towards the entrance, drawn and engraved by William Westall for *Views of the Caves near Ingleton, Gordale Scar, and Malham Cove, in Yorkshire* (1818). The accompanying description compares the stalactites and walls to 'a stall in a cathedral, with Gothic ornaments above'.

Gordale Scar, drawn and engraved by William Westall.

water'. Gray had found the alehouse at nearby Malham a regular nest
of artists, and Gordale would remain a favourite spot with landscape
painters of later generations. In 1811 William Ward began the painting
(now hanging in the Tate Gallery) which represents one of the most
doggedly ambitious attempts by an English artist to capture the
Sublime on canvas; in 1818 William Westall published the view which
prompted Wordsworth's sonnet.

Housman himself is a valuable witness, particularly in his description of how Gordale struck him as he first approached it:

We perceive ourselves just entering the apparent ruins of a huge castle, whose walls are mostly entire to the height of about 120 feet. The gloomy mansion strikes us with horror; and a lively fancy would readily place before us the massy form and surly looks of its ancient gigantic inhabitants. What greatly adds to the sensations of fear and amazement, which everyone must feel, in some degree, on his first entering herein, are the rushing cataracts at the farther end, and the hanging walls, particularly that on the right, which projects considerably over its base, and threatens to crush the trembling visitant.

This shows how the various emotions we have so far seen only in the claustrophobic world of the cave can be put to work in the open air. Part of the point, of course, is that since the Sublime feeds on oppressiveness Housman makes as little concession to the open air as he can. He emphasises the size and the scale of Gordale (making it sound rather more than 120 feet high) but only in order to emphasise its confining mass. The enclosed tunnels and echoing vaults of the cave system are replaced by hanging walls which threaten to crush. We will see later that overhanging crags and boulders poised to fall on trembling visitants become a standard element in the landscape of the Sublime – as common as the waterfalls which are usually promoted, as Housman promotes the rather modest one at Gordale, to the grandeur of rushing or roaring cataracts.

Housman binds these elements together with a revealing conceit, revealing not because of its originality but because of its conventionality. He describes Gordale Scar as a ruined castle. In its immediate context, this allows his fantasy about its 'ancient gigantic inhabitants' to play the same part in melodramatising the scene as the Oxford gentleman's fantasy about his guide being a bandit or a murderer. In a larger context, Housman's conceit clinches the resemblance between the sublime experience of nature I have been describing in this chapter and the love of Gothic as wild, gloomy and threatening I described in my previous chapter. The nocturnal visitor to Tintern, using the flickering light of his torch to admire yawning vaults and gloomy recesses, is obviously cousin to the Oxford gentleman exploring the Derbyshire caves. For that matter, we have already seen how the Peak Cavern provided visitors with precisely the combination of darkness and slow music that Ruskin cynically recommended as an aid to the sentimental appreciation of Gothic.

The parallel between Gothic and nature is deeply embedded in the eighteenth-century mind. We have seen Bishop Warburton approaching it from one direction by his suggestion that Gothic architecture borrowed the shapes of nature. Now we can see tourists approaching it from the other by their discovery that natural curiosities resemble Gothic ruins. In fact, this reading of nature had by then as long and respectable a history as Warburton's reading of Gothic. Most pertinently, it derived from the seventeenth-century theologian Thomas Burnet, whose *Sacred Theory of the Earth* tackled the problem of reconciling the disordered and untameable aspects of nature with the notion of a divine order. Burnet's argument that the world fell from its original state of physical perfection, smooth and oviform, when the waters of the biblical Flood burst forth from inside and wrecked its surface still lingered in the scholarly mind a century later, as the sub-title of West's book about Craven shows. Yet it also left an imaginative legacy that was far longer lasting and far more potent: a grand, melancholy vision of nature displaying the 'Ruins of a broken world'.

'What can have more the Figure and Mien of a Ruin, than Crags, and Rocks, and Cliffs?' Burnet had asked. Eighteenth-century travellers agreed, even when they were no longer consciously remembering Burnet's name or debating his theory. As they entered the mouth of the Peak Cavern they noted that 'the sweep of the Arch is not altogether irregular but something in the Gothic taste' and (as William Bray has already testified) they called the underground chamber where the singers entertained them the 'Chancel'. The curious limestone formations of Dovedale, they discovered, looked from a distance 'like a ruined castle'; indeed, one is still known as Dovedale Castle and another as Tissington Spires. At St John's Vale in the Lake District, Castle Rock became a favourite spot for tracing the similarities between nature and Gothic, and for reviving folk tales which gave fanciful support to the idea, long before Sir Walter Scott set the seal on the custom with *The Bridal of Triermain*.

Travellers did not usually draw the analogy in order to theorise about the history of Gothic or the history of natural creation, but simply because it encouraged them to bring a larger stock of ready-made emotions and adjectives to either spectacle. The cult of Gothic and the cult of the Sublime could advance together, borrowing from a common pool of language and feeling which helped people find something appropriately exciting, gloomy or frightening about even the neatest ruin or the smallest crag. Yet the analogy with Gothic also showed the visitor to the Peak Cavern or Gordale Scar how to transcend the cruder symptoms of fear, and so pass beyond the stagey melodrama of the Oxford gentleman in his cave; ideally, he achieved an exalted state of religious awe, a more excited and febrile version of that mood of contemplative melancholy which the ruin could inspire. According to one writer, at least, this is how Gordale Scar could strike the spectator: 'Struck with indescribable Terror and Astonishment, the natural apprehensions of instant destruction being over, a man must have been dead to rationality and reflection, whose mind was not elated with immediate gratitude to the Supreme Architect and Preserver of the Universe.' Far from raising doubts about the divine plan, the natural curiosity now leads the mind to contemplate a supreme architect who works, not according to the principles of Vitruvius or Palladio, but in the Gothic style.

IV

This compact account of the sequence of emotions making up the sublime experience comes from Thomas Hurtley's interesting little guidebook about Craven, published in 1786. Hurtley was apparently a local man; at any rate, he criticises the superficial approach of earlier writers like Gray and the antiquary Thomas Pennant, 'that desultory Tourist', whose carelessness or ignorance had led him to follow the wrong itinerary. And he takes a local pride in his subject that tempts him to top other men's superlatives, always a tricky task in the literature of the Sublime, and sum up his admiration of Gordale Scar with a bold claim: here, he promises the prospective visitor, 'you have *Beauty*, *Horror*, and *Immensity* united'.

It is bold in another sense too, since even by the standards of a literature crowded with quotation, borrowing and downright plagiarism it is a particularly impudent theft. For all his local pride in Craven, Hurtley could not forget or ignore the language of a famous letter written by Dr John Brown to Lord Lyttelton in 1767 to assert the claims of the Lake District and, particularly, of the Vale of Keswick, whose 'full perfection ... consists of three circumstances, beauty, horror and immensity united'. In fact, Brown's letter is seminal, the first important sign of a fascination with the Lakes which would come to overshadow the interest travellers took in other regions. He himself dismissed the natural curiosities of the Peaks as but 'poor miniatures' of the sights awaiting the visitor farther north; by the opening decades of the nineteenth century Elizabeth Bennet, in *Pride and Prejudice*, would be 'excessively disappointed' at having to settle for a visit to

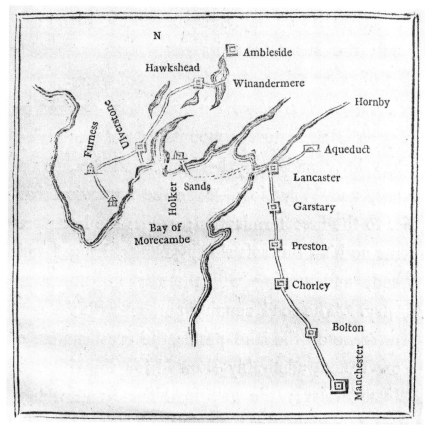

Richard Warner's itinerary for the southern Lake District in *A Tour through the Northern Counties of England, and the Borders of Scotland* (1802). For the most part it follows a route familiar to the modern tourist, though one interesting curiosity is the 'road' across the sands of Morecambe Bay at low tide – an approach to the Lakes recommended by Thomas West and Wordsworth in their guidebooks.

Derbyshire rather than the Lakes.

Historians have many times charted the intervening stages in the Lake District's rise to popularity. The poet Gray came in 1767 and again in 1769, Arthur Young in 1768, and Gilpin – a native of Carlisle who had been taught drawing by Dr Brown – in 1772. The letters which Gray wrote describing his second visit, published in William Mason's posthumous edition of his work in 1775, helped establish the main stopping-points on a fashionable tour: he visited Ullswater from Penrith, used Keswick as a centre for exploring Derwentwater, Borrowdale, Bassenthwaite and the 'Druid' circle at Castlerigg, then continued past the foot of Helvellyn to Grasmere, Ambleside and Windermere, and finished at Kendal. In 1778 Thomas West organised

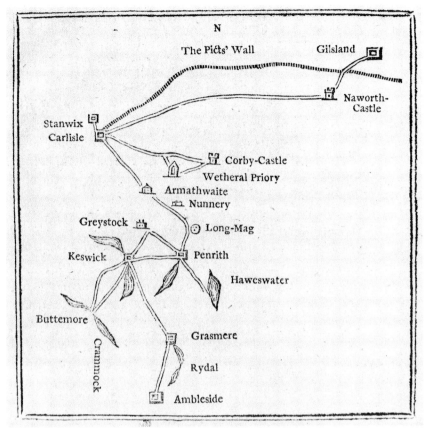

Richard Warner's itinerary for the northern Lake District, with Carlisle and
Hadrian's Wall. Gilsland, so prominently marked, enjoyed a brief popularity
as a spa patronised by Border gentry – including Sir Walter Scott, who met his
future wife there. The spelling of placenames here and by the travellers I quote
elsewhere is wayward, since they are taken down 'from the ear', as Arthur
Young put it when rendering Bowness as 'Bonus'.

the chief sights into a guidebook, the first devoted to the Lakes, which
set the pattern for later tours and all their attendant literature, a
rushing cataract in itself of journeys, excursions, rambles, surveys,
picturesque observations, companions, descriptive sketches, concise
descriptions, guides, useful guides, complete guides and new guides.
Wordsworth's *Guide through the District of the Lakes*, the most
important of these later works, grew from an anonymous text
accompanying a volume of weak engravings by Joseph Wilkinson in
1810 into an appendix to his *River Duddon* sonnets in 1820 and then
into a book in its own right by 1822; further revised and expanded, it
ran through several more editions in the 1830s and 1840s. By this time
Wordsworth could look on the change in attitude which first led

tourists 'to wander over this island in search of sequestered spots' as a process virtually complete, a phenomenon whose history could now be traced and whose larger, often disquieting consequences needed assessing. Yet this change, and its effect on the Lake District, had been wrought in the lifetime of just two generations. In the 1840s, when the proposed Kendal and Windermere Railway again forced him to take urgent stock of what popularity with tourists had done to his native region, Wordsworth could still remember the words of an old woman he had known in his youth: 'Bless me! folk are always talking about prospects: when I was young there was never sic a thing neamed!'

Before Thomas Hurtley had taken it off to Gordale Scar, Dr Brown's 'beauty, horror and immensity united' had already been put hard to work in descriptions of the Lake District, making the round of Derwentwater and Borrowdale with special regularity. There, for example, a Mr Avison of Newcastle whom Gilpin quoted in his book about the Lakes had found '*Beauty lying in the lap of Horrour!*'; and there the Oxford gentleman, fresh from the abodes of silent horror in the Peak District, had found 'an indescribable scene where Nature reigns in primeval horror'. As I have already intimated, the cult of the Sublime concentrates not just on particular scenes or effects in nature but brings a stock, highly stylised vocabulary to their description. Smooth fells and high moorland are 'barren', 'gloomy' and 'desolate'; crags and valleys are 'wild', 'chaotic', 'confused' and 'primeval'. Adjectives like 'hideous' survive but are supplemented and largely replaced by ones which shift the emphasis more decisively from the ugliness of the object described to the fear inspired in the spectator: 'frightful', 'dreadful', 'awful'. These in turn are joined by a particularly suggestive group, 'terrific', 'tremendous' and 'stupendous', which connects the spectator's fear with the scale and size of the object contemplated. All of them soon combine as a fashionable slang of all-purpose intensifiers, used to convey a state of exalted, enthusiastic wonderment.

Some of this language and all its accompanying emotional machinery are invoked when Gray writes about his journey from the southern end of Derwentwater into Borrowdale. It takes him through what the Ordnance Survey maps prosaically label the Gates of Borrowdale, though they are still sometimes known more romantically as the Jaws of Borrowdale:

The whole way down, and the road on both sides is strewed with piles of the fragments strangely thrown across each other, and of a dreadful bulk; the place reminds me of those passes in the Alps, where the guides tell you to move on with speed, and say nothing, lest the agitation of the air should loosen the snows above, and bring down a mass that would overwhelm a caravan.

The passage is a good example of a description by an early traveller which, as well as helping to put a particular spot firmly on the tourist itinerary, itself became a *locus classicus*, quoted, adapted and elaborated often enough to assure that later travellers came prepared to see the Jaws of Borrowdale through Gray's eyes and re-enact his own trembling pleasure. Not all of them could manage to recognise the reality from the heated descriptions in the guidebooks:

They told us of tracts of horrible barrenness, of terrific precipices, rocks rioting upon rocks, and mountains tost together in chaotic confusion; of stone avalanches rendering the ways impassable, the fear of some travellers who had shrunk back from this dreadful entrance into Borrodale, and the heroism of others who had dared to penetrate into these impenetrable regions: – into these regions, however, we found no difficulty in walking along a good road, which coaches of the light English make travel every summer's day.

This is Robert Southey, adopting the fictional persona of a visiting Spaniard for his entertaining and unfairly neglected travel book, *Letters from England*. He is perhaps not the ideal person to rebuke previous writers for their exaggeration, since his own rapturous poem about nearby Lodore Falls led many travellers to be disappointed at the mild trickle which usually greeted them. Yet Southey published *Letters from England* in 1807, when the first ecstasies of the Sublime were beginning to pass their peak.

Gilpin spoke for the earlier generation of travellers by providing a more complex account of sublime expectation and its possible disappointment at Borrowdale. He approached the scene in high hopes:

As we proceeded in our rout along the lake, the road grew wilder, and more romantic. There is not an idea more tremendous, than that of riding along the edge of a precipice, unguarded by any parapet, under impending rocks, which threaten above; while the surges of a flood, or the whirlpools of a rapid river, terrify below.

The prospect leads him into a lengthy digression about similar roads in Scandinavia, which make their way along narrow precipices flanked by roaring cataracts until they dwindle into nothing: 'The appalled traveller arriving at the spot, surveys it with dismay. – Return, he dare not – for he knows what a variety of terrors he has already passed. – Yet if his foot slip, or the plank, on which he rests, give way; he will find his death, and his grave together; and never more be heard of.'

Although he proffers this vignette in the same spirit as Gray did his recollection of Alpine avalanches, it does not produce quite the same effect, for Gilpin returns to the present scene with a bump of a rather different sort from the one he has been so busy imagining: 'But here we had not even the miniature of these dreadful ideas, at least on the side of the lake: for in the steepest part, we were scarce raised thirty or forty feet above the water.'

In context, however, these disappointing technical specifications have virtually no impact. They take up very little space by comparison to the lengthy anticipations I have already quoted, and they are further reduced to the status of a parenthesis rather than a final judgement by what follows: Gilpin still goes on, undeterred, to speak of precipices and dangers for several more pages. There is nothing surprising in this, because Gilpin has already made it abundantly plain that it is the 'idea' of perils on a Scandinavian scale which excites him rather than the actuality, just as Gray's language made it clear that it was the idea of an Alpine avalanche which stimulated him rather than any closer approach to the real thing. Tourists don't cross mountain passes if they really think they are going to fall off them or get buried by avalanches, any more than they go down caves if they really think that murderous banditti lurk in wait for them. What they want (as Burke pointed out) are scenes which hint at the possibility of such perils without actually presenting them. And if Gilpin finds Borrowdale too tame even to serve as a 'miniature' for prompting such imaginings, then he will conjure them up for himself.

Naturally enough, those spectacles were most satisfying which offered some 'miniature' from which the experience of the Sublime could be aggrandised. If the basic contours of hill and valley were not suggestive enough in ordinary conditions, then a good storm could make up for their deficiencies by supplying the necessary cue for 'high-colouring'. William Hutchinson's description of the storm his party encountered on Skiddaw in 1773 became, like Gray's description of the Jaws of Borrowdale, a classic text to nourish later travellers and travel writers: 'to our astonishment and confusion, a violent burst of thunder engendered in the vapour below us stunned our sense, being repeated from every rock, and down every dell, in the most horrid uproar'. Just as the appearance of the guides in the Peak Cavern could be made to heighten the atmosphere of a visit, so Hutchinson ingeniously used the behaviour of the guide accompanying his party up Skiddaw to provide extra melodrama. 'Our guide', he records, 'laid

The 'Laker' eager to capture the scenery in his sketchbook was already a familiar figure, ripe for satire, by the time William Combe wrote and Thomas Rowlandson illustrated *The Tour of Doctor Syntax in Search of the Picturesque* (1809). Syntax welcomes the prospect of a thunderstorm:

> 'I love', he cry'd, 'to hear the rattle,
> When elements contend in battle;
> For I insist, tho' some may flout it,
> Who write about it and about it,
> That we the *picturesque* may find
> In thunder loud or whistling wind:
> And, as often as I fully ween,
> It may be heard as well as seen;
> For, tho' a pencil cannot trace
> A sound as it can paint a place,
> The pen, in its poetic rage,
> Can make it figure on the page.'

upon the earth terrified and amazed, in his ejaculations accusing us of presumption and impiety.' This touch, daring even by the standards of the Sublime, may have troubled later visitors whose guides did not fall about so obligingly. At any rate, when William Mavor came to paraphrase Hutchinson for his multi-volume collection, *The British Tourists*, at the beginning of the nineteenth century, he struggled without much success to spell out the guide's behaviour in more plausible terms: 'Their guide lay on the earth, terrified and amazed at their fortitude, or rather impiety, as he thought, in contemplating, with pleasure, this awful scene.' Yet even without faint-hearted guides the storm could still be safely admired as a pantomime of the earth's first convulsions or its final destruction. The Oxford gentleman, who meditated on 'the sublime conception of the power, that tore the rock asunder' in the Peak Cavern, returns to the theme during a storm in the Lakes, 'the most awful' he ever witnessed:

The peals seemed to rend the mountains. The first burst was, as it were, the tumbling down of immense rocks, shivered in ten thousand pieces; opposite cavities then received the sounds in their deep bosom, and rebellowed them to opposite cavities with added din. It was like the wreck of nature and the crush of worlds.

Not all visitors could hope to enjoy bad weather, even in the Lake District. However, the singers in the Peak Cavern had already demonstrated artificial ways of unleashing echoes, and on the same trip which gratifyingly exposed him to the thunderstorm over Skiddaw, Hutchinson could also sample its man-made equivalent. From an inn near Pooley he took a trip on Ullswater in a pleasure barge belonging to the Duke of Portland, equipped with six brass cannon mounted on swivels. His description of the effect produced by 'a general discharge of the guns' became a set-piece of Lake District travel writing every bit as influential as his account of the real thunder, still quoted or paraphrased in other books well into the nineteenth century:

on every hand the sounds were reverberated and returned from side to side, so as to give us the semblance of that confusion and horrid uproar, which the falling of these stupendous rocks would occasion, if by some internal combustion they were rent to pieces, and hurled into the Lake.

Gilpin, who had come the year before Hutchinson, had noted the same entertainment and its likeness to the thunderstorm in making it seem as if 'the whole scene, from some strange convulsion, were falling into general ruin'. Such effects, he thought, were 'suited chiefly to scenes of grandeur during some moments of wildness, when the lake is under the agitation of a storm', and, being primarily a lover of tranquillity, he yearned for a gentler music:

Instead of cannon, let a few French-horns, and clarionets be introduced . . . The sound of a cannon is heard in bursts. It is the music only of thunder. But the *continuation* of *musical sounds* forms a *continuation* of *musical ecchoes*; which reverberating around the lake, are exquisitely melodious in several gradations; and form a thousand symphonies . . .

By the 1780s travellers were offered a combination of these effects on Ullswater, where the boat on hire from the local landlord was outshone by the Earl of Surrey's much grander craft, politely made available 'to accommodate any gentleman who desires it'. This boasted eight uniformed rowers, twelve brass cannon and French horns. The 'savage uproar' of the cannon and the 'ten thousand varied tones' of the music produced 'a mixture of wildness and harmony as is beyond the reach of art'.

The softer strains of the French horn continued to be heard in the Lake District but the cannon carried the day. Discharged over Derwentwater and Windermere as well as Ullswater, from boats or from the inns along the lake shores, they gave the Lakes all the rustic calm of a battlefield; indeed, mock naval encounters were a central feature of the noisy regattas held on Derwentwater from the 1780s. The fashion also spread to other regions. By 1780 Thomas West was already hearing from his guide of the effect a pistol shot would produce in Yordas Cave, though his reaction was faint-hearted: 'not being desirous to carry our experimental philosophy so far as to endanger or give pain to the organs of hearing, we were not disappointed in having no apparatus for the purpose'. By the beginning of the nineteenth century the Peak Cavern, then under the more professional management of a guide named Dekin, was catering for visitors of sterner metal:

Our entertainment also was varied by a *blast*, as it is termed – the discharge of a small quantity of gunpowder thrust into the rock, occasioning an explosion only to be compared to that sound which the imagination would conceive might be produced, if universal nature were at once to tumble into ruins.

In the Lake District, visitors delighted in comparing the echoes in a spirit of connoisseurship. Those at Derwentwater were usually the most highly admired and the lakeside cannon outside the Lodore inn (conveniently near Lodore Falls and the Jaws of Borrowdale) became a particular favourite: pointed towards Blea Crag and loaded with half a pound of gunpowder, it could stun the senses with nine different echoes. The travel books continue to quote Hutchinson and evoke the customary vision of nature convulsed by its first or last cataclysm, but the experience of the Sublime has clearly begun its descent to the thrills of the fairground. A nineteenth-century traveller describes the loading of the Lodore cannon: 'Mrs Annabella and Matilda were so much alarmed by the preparations, that they ran to a distance of fifty or sixty yards, whilst Miss H—n stood calmly near the piece, like a soldier's daughter.' By this time, the visitors were comparing the prices too. In 1799 James Plumptre, struck by inflation in the Lake District since his previous visit only two years before, noted that the Lodore cannon cost one shilling and sixpence. By the next decade the prices for the two different strengths of gunpowder then available had gone up to half a crown and four shillings, making Southey's visiting Spaniard remark that 'English echoes appear to be the most expensive luxuries in which a traveller can indulge.' Four shillings remained a stiff enough price for one guidebook, published in 1819, to warn visitors to be sure they got their money's worth: 'it is necessary to see that the full charge of gunpowder is put in, and properly rammed down; otherwise, much of the sublime effect, produced by the rolling thunder, will be lost'. Yet Southey's Spaniard did not doubt that the more expensive bang was worth the money, just as Southey himself obviously did not doubt that the customary hyperbole of the Sublime had by then joined forces with the hyperbole of advertising: 'when one buys an echo, who would be content for the sake of saving eighteen pence, to put up with the second best instead of ordering at once the super-extra-double-superfine?'

V

In his *Guide* Wordsworth distinguished two phases in the formation of the landscape, each contributing a different element to the scenery: 'Sublimity is the result of Nature's first great dealings with the superficies of the earth; but the general tendency of her subsequent operations is towards the production of beauty; by a multiplicity of symmetrical parts uniting in a consistent whole.' Preoccupied with nature's first great dealings, the cult of the Sublime concentrated on the masses of rock, hill and lake to solicit from their wildness and immensity an answering violence, even extravagance, of feeling in the spectator. The cult of the Picturesque, on the other hand, delighted in the softer effects which stem from nature's subsequent operations; all the variegation and harmony expressed by the meandering curve of a river or lake shore, the grouping of the rocks and trees which flank it, the interplay of light and shade over these different features, and the subtle gradations of colour which blend the scene together.

This, of course, is only a crude and preliminary way of defining the two movements which together dominated taste in the later decades of the eighteenth century and the early decades of the nineteenth. Each elaborated its own aesthetic in far more sophisticated terms, analysing the mechanics and psychology of the Sublime along lines established by

Waterfalls became a favourite subject with lovers of the Picturesque and the Sublime; one traveller coined the word 'cataractist' to describe himself. Yet they can defeat the eye concerned to seek out symmetry, as in this attempt by Moses Griffiths to illustrate Aysgarth Falls in Yorkshire for Thomas Pennant's *A Tour in Scotland, and Voyage to the Hebrides; 1772* (1774). Later artists showed increasing fluency in combining the pretty with the perilous in their depiction of waterfalls.

Burke's great *Enquiry*, unravelling definitions of the Picturesque from the controversy between Sir Uvedale Price and Richard Payne Knight. In practice, however, most of the tourists we are dealing with in this chapter started, and many of them finished, no more precisely than I have done. If anything, my opening definitions are too nice and differentiate the Sublime and the Picturesque too sharply. 'What pleases the eye', the first meaning of 'picturesque' given by the 1801 supplement to Johnson's *Dictionary*, shows how broad it had become in popular usage, broad enough to overlap with 'sublime'. Even the theorists disagreed (or remained uncertain) whether the Sublime and the Picturesque were categories distinct from each other or from the traditional concept of Beauty; while Gilpin, apostle of the Picturesque as well as the tidiest-minded writer I quote in this chapter, could rest content with a mongrel term like 'Picturesque Beauty' which turns out on inspection to embrace much of the ruggedness associated with the Sublime. Other writers use 'sublime' and 'picturesque' almost interchangeably to describe any landscape of mountain, rock and water which cannot be appreciated by referring to the symmetries of Neoclassicism. At best, they apply the labels to different aspects of the same scene, or different ways of taking pleasure from it. We have already seen this in action, with the same generation of visitors – and even the same people – relishing both the sublime grandeur of Tintern by night and its picturesque appeal by day, or rousing the echoes on Ullswater with both the violent uproar of cannon and the softer music of French horns.

In one respect, though, the term 'picturesque' keeps a certain precision: however loosely it might be applied and however far it might stray from its roots, it never lost touch entirely with the fact it meant, at its simplest, 'that kind of beauty which *would look well in a picture*'. The Sublime, too, has its connection with the visual arts: the storms, caves and banditti we have already met in the travel literature of the Peaks and the Lakes owe a great deal of their atmosphere to the rich chiaroscuro of Salvator Rosa. Indeed, Dr Brown's letter of 1767 nominated Salvator as the best painter to 'dash out the horror of the rugged cliffs, the steeps, the hanging woods; and foaming waterfalls' around Derwentwater. This phrase is sandwiched between praise of two other painters Brown thought better equipped for other aspects of the scene: Claude, who could 'throw his delicate sunshine over the cultivated vales, the scattered cots, the groves, the Lake, and wooded islands' and Gaspar Poussin, whose 'grand pencil . . . should crown the whole with the majesty of the impending mountains'. Long after the cult of the Sublime had shown it could sustain itself through the sheer hyperbole of its own language with only passing reference to Salvator, the Picturesque clung insistently to the example of Claude and Poussin and, more generally, to the principle of appreciating landscape in a spirit of painterly appraisal. Indeed, the very word 'landscape', which the Picturesque movement did so much to make current in the language, was originally a painters' term for the pictorial representation of scenery, whether as the main subject or the background to a portrait, slowly broadening its meaning during the seventeenth and eighteenth centuries to encompass the scene itself, viewed pictorially and from a fixed vantage point, and finally to mean a whole tract of countryside, regarded in visual terms.

Gray's excitement at finding a landscape painting in the actual landscape when he walked out from Keswick one evening could surprise him into speaking the language of the auctioneer: 'I got to the Parsonage a little before sunset, and saw in my glass a picture, that if I could transmit to you, and fix it in all the softness of its living colours, would fairly sell for a thousand pounds.' Like the word 'landscape', the glass he mentions is another legacy of the artist's studio: a convex mirror, usually about four inches in diameter, originally used for painting landscapes. In tribute to Gray's use of it, Lake District tourists called it a Gray's glass or, remembering its origins, a Claude glass. Gray's editor William Mason enthusiastically recommended its use and West's influential *Guide* agreed that it provided 'much amusement among the mountains'. Thereafter it became standard equipment for the tourist during the rest of the eighteenth century, and was still being recommended by guidebooks in the early decades of the nineteenth century. A Claude glass was found on the body of Charles Gough, the tourist whose death on Helvellyn in 1805 prompted poems by Wordsworth and Sir Walter Scott.

The spectator stood with his back to the scene and viewed it in the glass, at one remove and already framed as if it were a picture. The scene itself was distorted and recomposed, to a degree depending on the convexity of the glass, in the same way it is by modern camera lenses: 'Where the objects are great and near, it removes them to a due distance, and shews them in the soft colours of nature, and the most regular prespective the eye can perceive, art teach, or science demonstrate.' The soft colours were achieved by using different backing foils – the equivalent of camera filters – designed to reproduce the much-admired mellow tones and golden light which bathes the landscape in Claude's paintings. Gray favoured black foil, which reduced the glare of sunshine, but in the less than Italian conditions of the Lake District later travellers also used silver foil to relieve the dull light on cloudy days.

Even with the aid of a Claude glass, suitable pictures were not always found in nature as easily as Gray had happened on the one worth a thousand pounds near Keswick. 'With all this magnificence and beauty', Gilpin warned readers of his book on the Lakes, 'it cannot be supposed, that every scene, which these countries present, is *correctly picturesque*.' We have already seen him objecting to the proportions of Tintern Abbey, lopping off an offending gable end in imagination. Elsewhere in his book about the Wye valley he extended the same critical spirit to nature itself, finding it 'always great in design; but unequal in composition'. Clergyman that he was, Gilpin managed to stop short of criticising God's artistry. He explained the apparent blemishes of nature by adapting for the purpose of his aesthetic a familiar explanation of the problem of evil: nature worked, no doubt harmoniously, but on too vast a scale for the human eye to comprehend. In the meantime, however, the artist 'is confined to a *span*. He lays down his little rules therefore, which he calls the *principles of picturesque beauty*, merely to adapt such diminutive parts of nature's surface to his own eye, as come within its scope.' The Picturesque, then, has this in common with the Sublime: it treats nature as the raw material from which suitable effects may be created. But where the Sublime works by hyperbole towards extravagance of feeling, the Picturesque devises rules of correctness to satisfy a more detached spirit of connoisseurship.

What were the correctly picturesque views for the tourist to admire and transfer, with suitable modifications of nature's blemishes, into the sketchbook? The modern preference is for looking at the countryside from hilltops: we embellish them with orientation tables, parking places, litter bins and rustic seats, and we mark their locations with asterisks in our guidebooks and maps. This has a precedent in the tradition of eighteenth-century topographical poetry stemming from James Thomson's *The Seasons*, where the spectator occupies the highest vantage-point the countryside offers to command a wide prospect and a view stretching for miles to the distant horizon. Yet, given how mountainous the Lake District is, rapturous descriptions of bird's-eye views are notably rare in its early travel literature. Indeed, tourists usually disliked the high vantage-point because it flattened the landscape beneath and, said Gray of Keswick Vale, made 'its parts, which are not large, look poor and diminutive'. Adding his footnote to this remark, William Mason surrendered to the Picturesque movement's love of formulating rules: 'The *Picturesque Point* is always thus low in all prospects.'

In practice, contemporaries never agreed exactly how low this low viewpoint should be, and travel writers often debate whether a given scene is best admired from the surface of the lake or from a slightly raised position on the shore or the slopes of the surrounding hills. Purists like Gilpin rejected the 'levelled' for the 'elevated' eye, showing the scene from gently rising ground. This, of course, is the viewpoint that Claude had favoured; though Gilpin might criticise Claude for faults of composition, he could no more escape his influence than any other English artist of the eighteenth century could. So he organised his landscapes in a simplified version of the Claudian manner, as a series of planes receding towards the horizon in alternating light and shade. Whereas the view from the lake surface could lack features to vary the foreground or frame the picture, the properly chosen viewpoint should offer 'a great choice of objects – *broken ground* – *trees* – *rocks* – *cascades* – and – *vallies*'. Usually lit from the back or the side, this foreground is sometimes seen mainly in silhouette. The light falls on the lake, shining in the middle distance. In composing this part of the scene, particular attention should be given to the lake's shape and its margins: 'I have known many a good landscape injured by a bad water boundary', warns Gilpin. By his criteria, any islands should not be round, or in the centre of a round lake, or too heavily forested; when they are irregular, and irregularly positioned, and lightly ornamented with trees, they are picturesque. The distance is filled by sky and fells, their bold masses softened into majesty by the play of light and shadow, and rendered especially pleasing to the picturesque eye when disposed, mountain behind mountain and rock behind rock, in the shape of an irregular amphitheatre.

We have already seen how popular Derwentwater proved with early tourists. As described in West's *Guide*, the view of the lake from the low eminence of Cockshott Hill on its north-eastern shore came close to fulfilling the ideal requirements of the Picturesque:

On the floor of a spacious amphitheatre, of the most picturesque mountains imaginable, an elegant sheet of water is spread out before you, shining like a mirror, and transparent as chrystal; variegated with islands, that rise in the most pleasing forms above the watery plane, dressed in wood, or clothed with forest verdure, the water shining round them.

We would call Cockshott Hill a viewpoint or 'beauty spot'; West and his contemporaries called it a 'station'. His guidebook consists almost entirely of stations, selected, described and even numbered with the same passion for correctness which Gilpin brought to the rules of the Picturesque. It is not enough, for example, to agree in general terms with Gray's account of the road from Lancaster: Gray's chosen viewpoint needs censuring as 'a quarter of a mile too low, and somewhat too much to the left' of the proper station from which to appreciate the scenery. West guides the tourist to all his stations with the same minute, insistent precision. These are his directions for reaching the first station on Windermere, which he helped make one of the most admired views in the Lake District:

Near the isthmus of the ferry point, observe two small oak trees that inclose the road, these will guide you to this celebrated station. Behind the tree on the western side ascend to the top of the nearest rock, and from thence in two views command all the beauties of this magnificent lake.

The first station on Coniston sounds even trickier to find:

A little above the village of NIBTHWAITE the lake opens in full view. From the rock, on the left of the road, you have a general view of the lake upward. This station is found by observing an ash tree on the west side of the road, and passing that till you are in a line with the peninsula, the rock is then at your feet.

No subsequent writer about the Lake District achieves the relentless purity of West's approach, and none follows the canon he had established with complete fidelity. Yet his influence is everywhere apparent. The maps which Peter Crosthwaite of Keswick issued from 1783 onwards mark all West's stations, with some additional ones of Crosthwaite's own. In 1799 James Plumptre found a summer house, 'too finished and artificial' for its surroundings, marking the first Windermere station, 'with a window each way commanding the delightful prospects described in West's guide'. As late as 1823 Jonathan Otley could cite the case of 'a gentleman, who "would not give a farthing for a station, except it was one of West's" – in order, I suppose, that he might borrow Mr West's language in describing the place to his friends'. The cynical tone shows that West's canon was beginning to look old-fashioned: like the term 'station' itself, the Claude glass and Gilpin's exacting rules of correct landscape, it would eventually fade from the popular memory. Before that happened, however, Wordsworth's *Guide* would hand at least part of West's legacy on to subsequent generations, commending a number of his stations and on occasion even quoting him, like the gentleman in Otley.

In a larger sense, the fashions which replaced the Picturesque subsumed much of its approach, though in a looser form. Tourists need more than the literal guidance of maps and itineraries which show them how to plot their way through a particular region. By interpreting the Lake District as a series of static, approved pictures and by providing a language in which these pictures could be admired, West and his contemporaries set a pattern which tourism still follows, and not just in the Lake District. It still reduces landscape to a sequence of conveniently spaced, well-advertised stopping-points where we can get out of the car for a moment to admire and take a photograph, just as picturesque travellers consulted West's list of stations, stopped their carriages and pointed their Claude glasses. If we do not always choose the same places, our reason is often simply that the technical resources of the car and the camera are different from those of the carriage and the Claude glass. And, in fact, our itinerary for the Lake District still includes some of West's stations, just as the word 'picturesque' still lingers in the tourist literature which recommends them to us. The view of Derwentwater from Cockshott Hill praised by West stands very near what we now know as Friar's Crag, which the National Trust acquired as one of its early properties in the region and which tourists still use for taking their first, and sometimes their only, view of the lake.

VI

When Thomas Gray looked down into the Vale of Grasmere in 1769, he described the view by abandoning the formal language of the picturesque station and offering, more evocatively, a vision of almost pre-lapsarian innocence: 'Not a single red tile, no flaring gentleman's house, or garden-walls, break in upon the repose of this little unsuspected paradise; but all is peace, rusticity, and happy poverty in its neatest most becoming attire.' If the passage, like Gray's description of the Jaws of Borrowdale or Hutchinson's account of the echoes at Ullswater, became a text for later writers to quote and paraphrase, it was remembered in a slightly different spirit: not as a guide to the proper way of viewing Grasmere but as a yardstick to measure the changes overtaking the unspoiled landscape and its unspoiled inhabitants.

Tourism made change inevitable, of course. Its seeds were already latent in the attitudes to landscape I have been describing. Nature, Gilpin taught, was promising raw material rather than satisfying finished product. He instructed his readers how to modify views for their sketchbooks in full awareness that he was applying to travel and landscape art the same principles gardeners were putting into practice at gentlemen's estates and parks throughout the country. So, even when the picturesque tourist does not have his sketchbook in his hand, he often appraises the scenery by playing property owner and redesigning it in his imagination. This is James Plumptre at Ennerdale:

An island rises in this broad part of the Lake, in a very nice point of view, but it is only a small bare rock. It might however be easily enlarged, by bringing the loose stones from the side of the Lake, which would be improved in many places by their being removed. It should be both enlarged and raised, and with a little soil to set the trees growing, it might be planted and would soon form a pleasing feature in the scene. If a stone hut were added for the accommodation of fishers, it would form a delightful retreat.

Views of Windermere: 1. An aquatint etched by John Warwick Smith for
Gilpin's *Observations, Relative Chiefly to Picturesque Beauty, Made in the
Year 1772, on Several Parts of England; Particularly the Mountains, and
Lakes of Cumberland, and Westmoreland* (1786). It generalises the scene in
his customary manner, though the dome of Belle Isle can just be made out.

Despite poking fun at the Picturesque in his comic opera *The Lakers*,
Plumptre here shows himself a remarkably conscientious follower of
the movement. 'Mr Price's Essays on the Picturesque would furnish
some useful hints on this head', he concludes, with a respectful bow
towards one of its leading theorists, though, of course, we have already
seen that Gilpin also had plenty of advice to offer about the proper
treatment of islands.

Islands, indeed, were always a great temptation, making visitors
positively itch to remove nature's blemishes. Arthur Young thought
the largest of Windermere's islands, now called Belle Isle, 'the sweetest
spot, and full of the greatest capabilities, of any forty acres in the king's
dominions'. Clearly, the 'and' in Young's phrase is almost a 'because':
for him, the sweetness of Belle Isle is largely a matter of its having
'capabilities' in the Lancelot Brown sense of the word. Gilpin agreed
with Young that a 'more sequestered spot cannot easily be conceived'
than Belle Isle, and proceeded to make suggestions for its improvement:

Views of Windermere: 2. An engraving from a drawing by Joseph Farington,
looking north from below Bowness, belatedly published in T. H. Horne's *The
Lakes of Lancashire, Westmorland, and Cumberland* (1816). Gilpin praised
Farington's prints for rendering 'any other *portraits* of the lakes unnecessary.
They are by far, in the author's opinion, the most accurate, and beautiful
views of that romantic country, which he hath seen.'

He who should take upon him to ornament such a scene as this, would have
only to conduct his walk and plantations, so as to take advantage of the grand
parts of the continent around him; – to hide what is offensive – and, amidst a
choice of great and picturesque scenes, to avoid shewing too much.

Young saw the island in 1768 and Gilpin saw it in 1772, when it still
boasted only an old house falling into disuse and perhaps an additional
cottage. Gilpin remarked that the house stood 'too formally in the
middle of the island' and that the surrounding woods were too scanty,
but West's *Guide*, published only a few years later, would grow lyrical
in remembering these features as 'the sweet secreted cottage, and the
sycamore grove'. His exaggerated nostalgia was provoked by the
changes that had overtaken Belle Isle since Thomas English had bought
it and begun improvements, apparently in 1773. He laid the grounds
out in a formal style and replaced the old building by the round Neo-
classical house with a domed roof that still stands there today, a little

Claudian temple among the northern Lakes. Wordsworth's first public letter opposing the Kendal and Windermere Railway records that English had travelled in Italy, which helps explain where he got his ideas for Belle Isle, but Wordsworth notes the fact for another purpose: to identify him as the vanguard of gentrification and his creation on Belle Isle as the prototype of the weekend cottage, 'the first house that was built in the Lake district for the sake of the beauty of the country'.

It seemed that man, in the Lake District at least, was no better than nature at fulfilling the picturesque ideal. Gilpin, when he finally came to publish his book about the Lakes in 1786, added a footnote to his original description of Belle Isle deploring that its new owner had 'contrived to do almost everything, that one would wish had been left undone'. This is mild by comparison to the attacks which English's work had been provoking ever since it was undertaken. Hutchinson, who saw it before it was complete, had led the way by dismissing the house as a 'Dutch Burgomaster's palace' and deploring the regularity of the grounds. Later critics were much less harsh on the house and concentrated their energy on spelling out the deficiencies of English's taste in landscape gardening: the straight lines of fir trees, the prominent garden wall, the square kitchen garden and the artificially embanked shoreline with its white-sanded footpath. On so romantic a site the mere presence of a kitchen garden full of cabbages was

Belle Isle, distantly seen in Gilpin and Farington's views of Windermere, here shown in a detail from the 1788 edition of Peter Crosthwaite's map of the lake.

condemned by purists of the Picturesque with enough violence to provoke some visitors into reasserting the old-fashioned claims of utility and convenience against the new craze for judging gentlemen's estates by the painter's eye alone. Was English's cook, asked James Clarke, 'to fetch every handful of parsley, or other thing of that kind, cross the Lake, perhaps in a high wind?'

In the event, English's experiment was short-lived. In 1781 he sold Belle Isle to Isabella Curwen, heiress to the Curwens of Workington Hall. With her husband John Christian (who adopted her surname) she set about replanting the island in the picturesque manner. Gilpin could end his footnote recording its ups and downs on a hopeful note and, as George Romney depicts it in the background to his portrait of Isabella Curwen, Belle Isle certainly looks charming enough. On the whole it pleased later travel writers, who made it the occasion for courtly compliment rather than criticism or controversy. According to John Housman writing in 1800, for example, the Curwens' work at Belle Isle 'joined every assistance of Art to the fine dispositions of Nature, in rendering it a most delightful retreat. Sweet groves, pleasant walks, and verdant lawns, with a neat house, in a proper situation, and without one formal or direct line to offend the eye: all contribute towards its beauties.'

Later writers, like Wordsworth in his *Guide* and his letters about the Kendal and Windermere Railway, remembered English's ill-judged improvements to cite them as the first example of a troubling – because growing – phenomenon in the Lake District. But by the 1780s, when Belle Isle was being reclaimed for taste, the real ground of their concern had shifted to another island, this time on Derwentwater, where they could contemplate a second example of the dangers posed by the new class of settler. The invader here was Joseph Pocklington, identified by Wordsworth as 'a native of Nottinghamshire' to make a graver version of the same innuendo he intended by remarking that English had travelled in Italy: Pocklington was not a local man and, worse, he came from a county already associated with the making of vulgar business fortunes. In 1778 he bought what is now called Derwent Isle, originally known as Vicar's Isle since it had once belonged to Fountains Abbey. In the closing decades of the eighteenth century and the opening decades of the nineteenth, however, it was usually called Pocklington's Island in grudging tribute to the determination with which the new owner had stamped his personality on its appearance, making it a far more flagrant example of what James Plumptre called '*tea-garden taste*' than English's regimented firs and cabbages.

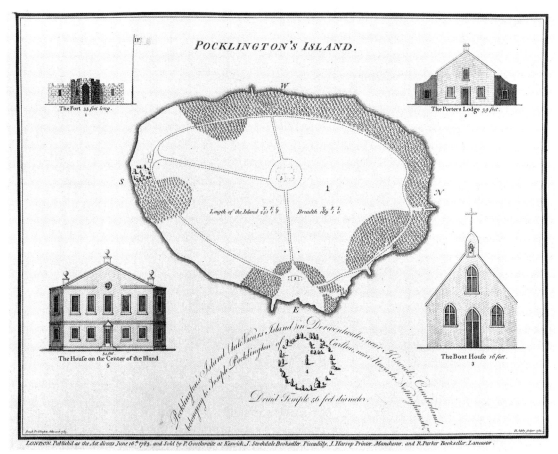

LONDON. Publish'd as the Act directs June 16.th 1783, and Sold by P. Crosthwaite at Keswick, J. Stockdale Bookseller. Piccadilly, J. Harrop Printer. Manchester, and R. Parker Bookseller. Lancaster.

Pocklington's Island (now called Derwent Isle) on Derwentwater, engraved by Ashby from a drawing by Joseph Pocklington and published in 1783. Later editions also show the mock church which Pocklington added to his kingdom. Peter Crosthwaite sold this plan with his maps of the lakes.

Like English, Pocklington built himself a house in the middle of the island and added plantations of fir trees, a 'grievous eye-sore' already beginning to oust native trees in several parts of the region. But his ambition did not stop there, for he proceeded to surround himself with a remarkable assembly of garden buildings: a druids' stone, a druids' circle, a mock church, a battery or fort (complete with cannon, of course), and a boat house in the style of a Nonconformist chapel. They were intended, as Wordsworth explained in shuddering retrospect, to typify 'the state and strength of a kingdom, and its religion as it had been, and was' – a conceit Pocklington carried a stage further in the regattas and mock naval battles he organised on the lake. It sounds as if the general effect lay somewhere between the eighteenth-century craze for follies at its most grandiosely eccentric and the modern theme park.

Pocklington did not enjoy sovereignty over his kingdom for much longer than English had been owner of Belle Isle: he began building work in 1779 and in 1796 he sold his island to a Lieutenant-Colonel (later General) Peachy, who proceeded to rid the spot of its 'puerilities' in much the same fashion that the Curwens had redeveloped Belle Isle: converting the church into a toolshed, dismantling the other garden buildings and replanting the gardens. Contemporaries duly record Peachy's achievement in creating 'beautiful pleasure-grounds' and his 'extraordinary degree of fine taste in the management of the trees upon his island', despite the sinister addition of larches to the already offensive firs. Yet their praise often sounds lukewarm by comparison to the compliments showered on the Curwens. Peachy's work may have taken longer to complete, and he was not as well-connected with the powerful local gentry as the new owners of Belle Isle. Above all, the memory of Pocklington's extravagances proved more vivid than the present reality of Peachy's repairs.

Besides, 'King Pocky' had not left the region, and he was still determined to leave his mark on whatever he owned. He retired from his island kingdom to the south-eastern shore of Derwentwater, where he built Barrow Hall, a 'spruce, white-washed house' of a sort becoming all too common in the Lake District, and diverted the water in his grounds to make Barrow Cascade into a rival of nearby Lodore Falls. What most caught the attention of James Plumptre, when he passed this way in 1799, was that 'in addition to his former mis-demeanours against taste' Pocklington had 'painted the latches and hinges of his gates, the nail heads and tops of the rails, scarlet, and put a large brown J.P. on each gate'.

Worse still, his property included the Bowder Stone, the perilously balanced chunk of metamorphic rock in nearby Borrowdale. 'I sup-pose he will next paint it white and scarlet', snorted Plumptre in contempt. It is just as well Plumptre never published the journal of his tour, since Pocklington might have been quite taken by the suggestion if he had encountered it. What he did do, in fact, was to turn his natural curiosity into the Lake District's first fully developed tourist trap. Southey described how Pocklington, in a campaign of development recalling his earlier flights of fancy, had

built a little mock hermitage, set up a new druidical stone, erected an ugly house for an old woman to live in who is to show the rock, for fear travellers

Barrow Cascade, etched from his own drawing by William Green for *Seventy Eight Studies from Nature* (1809). The cascade is viewed from the house Joseph Pocklington built for himself when he retired from his island. Green's description adds: 'The course of the water has been diverted from its original channel, by Mr Pocklington; who had previously excavated the rock, and who has given the whole to the public eye in its present beauty.'

should pass under it without seeing it, cleared away all the fragments round it, and as it rests upon a narrow base, like a ship upon its keel, dug a hole underneath through which the curious may gratify themselves by shaking hands with the old woman.

This was written in 1807. If anything, the atmosphere had degenerated by the time William Green published his *Tourist's New Guide* in 1819. The old woman had been succeeded by an old man named John Raven, 'who, on the traveller's appearance, commences an exordium preparatory to the presentation of a written paper, specifying the weight and dimensions of the stone, of which, in some seasons, he makes a profitable trade'. He is metaphorically blind – 'blind to all the images of surrounding nature, and to all nature's images' – and literally deaf, but he responds well enough to pantomime gesture: 'The movement of the hand towards the pocket, is an act John understands as well as any member of the fraternity to which he belongs.'

VII

'The fraternity to which he belongs': Raven's profession and Green's contempt for it sound a note heard many times before, in writers' birthplaces, country houses, even the Peak District, but not in the Lake District until now. It reminds us that all the various changes to its physical environment – the cannon sprouting from lake shores, the summer houses marking picturesque stations, the new settlers adding tasteless improvements for visitors to criticise – imply changes to its human environment too. Tourism had subjected the people as well as the landscape to an inevitable process since travellers first fled the grubby outstretched palms that greeted them in the Peaks for the 'unsuspected paradise' Gray thought he espied when he looked down into the Vale of Grasmere: a place of untouched human nature, of 'peace, rusticity, and happy poverty'.

If Gray's language sounds unconvincing in its vague generality, then that is because the attitudes to nature I have been describing tend to dehumanise the people who actually live there. The cult of the Sublime usually reduces local inhabitants to stage extras whose job is to make the drama which the tourist creates for himself more piquant: the old women in the cave mouth are cast as witches, the singers as furies and the guide as a bandit. The cult of the Picturesque uses the familiar pastoral stereotypes of shepherds and fishermen merely as alternatives to rocks or broken ground for providing variety in the foreground. So it is hardly surprising that much of the travel literature which follows immediately in Gray's footsteps should just repeat his generalised praise, making it more precise only by adding practical observations about the inns being rudimentary but cheap and the food simple but wholesome. The few local people mentioned individually are not allowed to step outside their assigned roles of rustic simplicity, mountain hospitality and so forth. West, for example, tells of the man who offered to act as his guide in Borrowdale but 'blushed at the offer of a reward'. 'Such', West comments, 'is the power of virtue on the minds of those that are least acquainted with society.' Almost twenty years later, near the end of the century, the novelist Ann Radcliffe could still meet a descendant of the Borrowdale man on the road from Shap to Bampton, in the form of a boy who opened several gates for her carriage but 'blushed when we called him to have some halfpence'. And this boy's sister took the Oxford gentleman and his party to see the waterfalls near Ambleside:

Our guide hither was Jane Dawson, one of the most beautiful and innocent little girls I ever saw; she was only ten years old, clean in her Sunday dress, glowing as the rose, and pure as the lily. She had never been from this, her place of happy birth, but twice, when she was carried to Hawkeshead, on account of illness.

By the 1790s, however, the locals who make a profession of catering to the needs of tourists have begun to emerge from the pastoral generalisations as a more distinct breed. In Captain Joseph Budworth's *Fortnight's Ramble to the Lakes*, first published in 1792, we see one of them more or less literally detaching himself from the rural backdrop and coming into focus. Budworth and his companion are proposing to climb Coniston Old Man: 'Whilst we were making observations, a man in his harvest dress, with a pair of handsome spectacles on, (an unusual sight for one in his station) seated himself by us, and we were soon convinced, by certain shrewd remarks, he wished to officiate as guide.' How could anyone turn down so artfully casual a salesman? Budworth accepts the offer, and we learn a little more about the guide as the party makes its way up the fell: 'Chreighton ... is a self-taught scholar, and will want few wants to give you a copious account of every thing in his neighbourhood; he said something about his being a descendant of a noble family in Scotland, and seemed inclined to be very *diffuse* in speaking of great people.' Budworth may sound condescending and Chreighton may sound both canny and tiresome, yet even these qualities help make the episode a more human encounter than those brief glimpses of blushing natives which are usually all that other writers have shown us of the local people.

Budworth's condescension is also milder and more tempered by curiosity than we might expect, given the contempt tourists usually feel for their guides. Even when they are no longer just stereotypes of pastoral innocence, the locals who show visitors around the Lakes are treated much more sympathetically than their counterparts elsewhere. In fact, they are commonly mentioned by way of recommendation rather than criticism. Mrs Radcliffe, for example, notes: 'We have reason to think, that whoever employs, at Keswick, a guide of the name of Doncaster, will assist him in supporting an aged parent.' Nobody ever said anything like that about the guides in the Peak Cavern, even though they might well have been supporting aged parents too. And nobody ever called them 'in general intelligent and well informed', which is how James Denholm described the Keswick guides at the beginning of the nineteenth century.

I have not come across any reference to Doncaster elsewhere in the travel books I have read, but two other Keswick men, Hutton and Crosthwaite, stand out as local celebrities. Both were active from the 1780s onwards as guides and keepers of their own small museums, a rivalry which (claimed Plumptre) made them 'bitter enemies'. A long-lived man who served the tourist industry for over fifty years, Hutton took visitors on boat trips to test the echoes from the lake (their effect at night being particularly admired, though not presumably by the local residents) and on tours of West's stations around Derwentwater. Peter Crosthwaite was notably industrious and many-sided. He acted as Admiral at Pocklington's regattas, refusing out of loyalty to sell travel books which criticised Pocklington's Island – a policy which must have reduced his stock quite considerably. Grandly calling himself 'Geographer & Hydrographer', he issued wonderfully detailed maps of all the lakes from 1783 onwards. His map of Derwentwater includes two stations he devised himself in addition to West's: one half-way up Latrigg, which he made easy for visitors by cutting a flight of steps and scoring a cross on the ground, and one at the observatory conveniently near his museum. He also advertised the museum by beating a gong which could be heard several miles away and by publishing the names of his customers in the local weekly newspaper; the total for 1793 ran to '1540 persons of rank and fashion'.

These persons of rank and fashion usually describe Crosthwaite as an entertaining curiosity, rather like the distinctly miscellaneous contents of his museum:

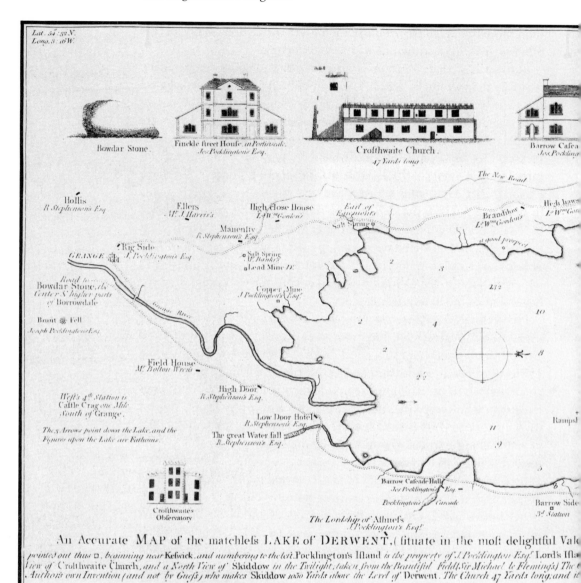

An Accurate MAP of the matchless LAKE of DERWENT, (situate in the most delightful Vale

One of the first and most active local people to make a profession of catering to the Lake District tourist industry, Peter Crosthwaite was also the first to supply detailed maps of the area. This is Derwentwater, from the 1788 edition of the map he first issued in 1783.

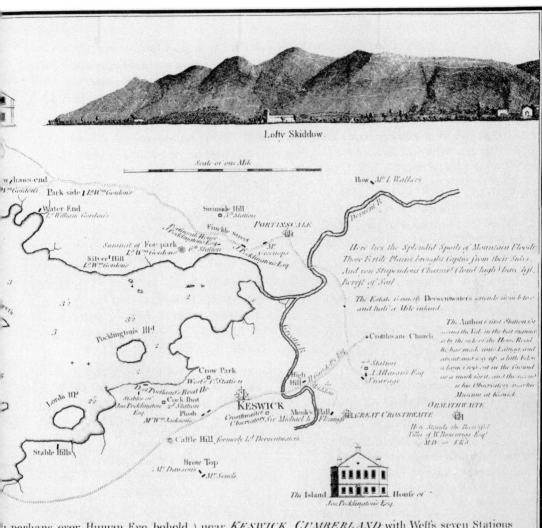

Lofty Skiddow.

Scale of one Mile

w haws end
Wᵐ Gordon's · Park side Lᵈ Wᵐ Gordon's
Water End
Lᵗ William Gordon's
Swinside Hill
5ᵗʰ Station
Finckle Street PORTINSCALE
Derwent R
Derwood House
Pocklington Esqʳ
Summat of Foe park
Lᵈ Wᵐ Gordon's 6ᵗʰ Station
Silver Hill
Lᵈ Wᵐ Gordon's
Mʳ Greenope
J. Pocklington's Esqʳ

How Mʳ J. Wallers

Here lies the Splendid Spoils of Mountain Floods;
These Fertile Plains brought Captive from their Sides;
And you Stupendous Chasms! Cloud high! have left
Bereft of Soil.

The Estate formerly Derwentwaters extends from b to c
and half a Mile inland.

Pocklington's Iᵈ

Crow Park
West's 1ˢᵗ Station
Duke Portland's Boat Hᵒ
Stables of
Jos. Pocklington 2ᵈ Station
Esqʳ   Plosh
Mʳ Wᵐ Jackson's

Lords Iᵈᵉ

Stable Hills

Crosthwaite Church
5ᵗʰ Station
J. Allason's Esqʳ
Vicarage

High Hᴶ Gale's Esqʳ
Hill   to
Skiddow

KESWICK
Crosthwaites
Observatory Sir Michael le Fleming
Monk's Hall

The Author's first Station (by
seeing the Vale in the best manner,
is by the side of the Hoss Road
he has made into Latrigg, and
about mid way up, a little below
a Lime Croft cut in the Ground
as a mark for it, and the ascent
is his Observatory, now his
Museum at Keswick

ORMATHWAITE

GREAT CROSTHWAITE
Here Stands the Beautiful
Villa of Wᵐ Brownrigg Esqʳ
M D — F R S.

Castle Hill formerly Lᵈ Derwentwaters

Brow Top
Mʳ Dawson's Mʳ Sewels

The Island House of
Jos. Pocklington Esqʳ

n perhaps ever Human Eye beheld) near *KESWICK, CUMBERLAND,* with West's seven Stations
erly Lᵈ Derwentwater's Rampsholm Island, dᵒ dᵒ Sᵗ Herbert's Island, Sir Gilfred Lawson's. Above is a S.W. View of Bowdar Stone, a North
nd Stone, are taken from one Scale; being 20 of an Inch to one Yard; and Skidow ¼ of an Inch to 100 Yards; by a Quadrant of the
Pinnacle, 20 Yards: Bowdar Stone 21 Yards long, and 11 high.
Geographer & Hydrographer to the Nobility and Gentry, who make the Tour of the Lakes.

He has all the views of the Lakes, his own plans of them, sells West's Guide, &c. The coins, spars, specimens of wood &c &c, musical stones and the Chinese Gong are very fine; but he has many things which are trifling, such as 6lb of lead swimming in 4lb of quicksilver, a collection of tobacco pipes of all nations – 16 different ways of speaking the proper name of Braithwaite – and 11 different names for a small stream all in common use in Cumberland.

Though a far cry from the churlish greed of the servants at Blenheim or the innkeepers at Stratford, this obviously still leaves something to be desired from the genteel traveller's point of view. Shortly after giving the description of Crosthwaite's museum I have just quoted, James Plumptre goes on to regret that 'no persons of confined circumstances but of liberal manners and information have undertaken the office of Guides of the Lakes' and to project a scheme for using young artists, who would have the chance to study landscape and exhibit their drawings. The suggestion sounds rather like one of Byng's proposals for installing respectable families as custodians in ruined abbeys. Yet in a sense it was brought to life by the career of William Green, the most local of the many artists attracted to the Lakes during these years. Born in Manchester, Green toured the district several times before settling at Ambleside in 1800. He exhibited his drawings there and at Keswick, issuing many soft-ground etchings and aquatints notable for their sensitivity to the style and texture of local buildings. In 1819 he published the *Tourist's New Guide*, which I have already quoted several times in this chapter. Wordsworth, his friend and near-neighbour, paid tribute in his *Guide* to Green's book as a 'complete Magazine of minute and accurate information' and remembered him on his tombstone for his 'skill and industry' in producing 'faithful representations of his country'.

Even as the inns were getting more crowded, the prices higher and the guides and other servants of the tourist industry more numerous, the visitors who recorded these changes directed their abuse not at local people but at each other. Most of the writers I have been quoting in this chapter pause at some point in recording their exalted feelings or refined taste to remark that not all their fellow tourists are capable of exalted feelings or refined taste. In fact, many are frivolous and vulgar. Gilpin, for example, deplores that the Lakes

are too often the resort of gay company . . . who have no ideas, but of extending the sphere of their amusements – or, of varying a life of dissipation. The grandeur of the country is not taken into the question: or, at least it is no otherwise considered, than as affording some new mode of pleasurable enjoyment.

Captain Budworth, a self-described 'rambler', mocks the way other visitors dash past the recommended stations 'with an exclamation or two of "Oh! how fine," &c.; or ... the day after we were upon Windermere, "Good God! how delightful! – how charming! – I could live here for ever! Row on, row on, row on".'

It is in the nature of tourists to wince at the sight of other tourists. Yet the anxiety this implies goes unusually deep in the case of the Lake District. It is not just that other, vulgar tourists will crowd the landscape, spoil the view and get tourism a bad name; they also threaten to destroy the very things they have supposedly come to admire, the rural innocence as well as the landscape. Gray, looking down at the 'peace, rusticity, and happy poverty' of Grasmere, might yet prove to have been more like Milton's Satan than he could ever have guessed. Perhaps because the image of the garden destroyed by the invasion of evil from outside is so potent in the pastoral imagination, the visitors who most admire rural innocence can never contemplate it without also fearing for its corruption or destruction:

Much have those travellers to answer for, whose casual intercourse with this innocent, and simple people tends to corrupt them; disseminating among them ideas of extravagance, and dissipation – giving them a taste for pleasures, and gratifications, of which they had no ideas – inspiring them with discontent at home – and tainting their rough, industrious manners with idleness, and a thirst after dishonest means.

This is Gilpin, writing in his capacity as clergyman as well as devotee of the Picturesque, and locating himself squarely within the eighteenth-century tradition of moral warning against the effects of luxury. Yet he firmly disassociates himself from responsibility: it is not he but those other travellers who do the damage. Plumptre brings the matter much closer to home when he comes to Wasdale Head nearly thirty years later and finds his enjoyment of even so remote a scene overshadowed: 'At the same time that I would recommend this spot to the curious traveller, as well worthy his notice, I cannot forbear adding a *caution* backed by *entreaty*, that he do not introduce luxury, extravagance and vice into these retreats of pastoral simplicity.' Warning has now grown into entreaty, sternness into something very like desperation. Plumptre's mood is guilty as well as anxious since he appears to concede that, however innocent his own motives and behaviour might be, mere praise of the scene could contribute to its destruction. His words contain their own acknowledgement, hapless and unresolved,

The Fish Inn, where the Beauty of Buttermere lived, drawn and etched by
William Green for his *Seventy Eight Studies from Nature* (1809).

of the special responsibilities that the author of the travel book or
guidebook now bears.

Guilt helps explain the fascination which tourists felt for the case of
Mary Robinson, daughter of the landlord at the Buttermere inn and
better known to the world as the 'Beauty of Buttermere' or, from the
passage where Wordsworth praises her in *The Prelude*, the 'Maid of
Buttermere'. By the 1790s Buttermere was just beginning to be
included in the traveller's itinerary – Turner painted it during his tour
in 1797, about the same time that Peter Crosthwaite persuaded Mary
Robinson's father to cut steps up to nearby Scale Force – yet it
remained untouched by comparison with Derwentwater, Ullswater or
Windermere. Mary's mother, it was said, 'had never seen but one
chaise in the valley' and 'spoke of it as a phenomenon'. The inn offered
such humble accommodation it hardly deserved the name. 'Few people
will like to sleep at the Buttermere alehouse', warned the Hon. Mrs
Murray, while demonstrating her own hardihood: 'but, with the help
of my own sheets, blankets, pillows, and counterpane, I lodged there a
week very comfortably'.

Mary Robinson herself first attracted the notice of Captain Budworth in his rambles in 1792, when she was not yet fifteen. His praise identified her as the very type of rural innocence at its most appealing:

Her hair was thick and long, of a dark brown, and though unadorned with ringlets, did not seem to want them; her face was a fine contour, with full eyes, and lips as red as vermilion; her cheeks had more of the lily than the rose; and although she had never been out of the village, (and, I hope, will have no ambition to wish it) she had a manner about her which seemed better calculated to set off dress, than dress her. She was a very Lavinia,

> 'seeming when unadorn'd, adorn'd the most.'

When we first saw her at her distaff, after she had got the better of her first fears, she looked an angel, and I doubt not but she is the *reigning lily* of the valley.

This panegyric made her an attraction to tempt tourists out of their way. Visitors came to appraise her beauty in the same spirit of connoisseurship they brought to West's stations. Some professed themselves disappointed, though most admired the modesty she maintained under this glare of publicity. The Oxford gentleman, for example, found her 'certainly handsome' but not 'singularly beautiful', and reported that she had thought a pair of stockings left as a gift by a previous visitor were just lost property and had put them by against his return.

Budworth himself returned in the winter of 1797–8, partly to visit Scale Force and partly to see if the fame he had brought his lily of the valley was going to her head. The walls of the room where he ate dinner were scrawled with compliments to her beauty in Greek, Latin and French as well as English, but Mary Robinson herself remained unspoilt enough to blush (yes, that again) when they were pointed out to her. Relief did not prevent him ending his visit with a warning:

You may remember, I advised you, in that Book, never to leave your native valley. Your age and station require the utmost care. Strangers WILL come, and have come purposely to see you; and some of them with very bad intentions. We hope you will never suffer from them; but never cease to be upon your guard.

Strangers contined to come, and those with bad intentions included John Hatfield, a criminal adventurer who made a career of forgery and imposture. He arrived in the Lake District in 1801, posing as the Honourable Alexander Augustus Hope, Member of Parliament and brother of the Earl of Hopetoun. His first victims included William Crump, the Liverpool lawyer who later became Wordsworth's landlord at Allan Bank in Grasmere. Hatfield then stayed at the Buttermere inn, paid court to Mary Robinson and married her in 1802, still in his grandly assumed identity. The deceit was soon uncovered and Hatfield, after fleeing the Lake District, was arrested on charges of forgery and brought back for trial and execution at Carlisle in the autumn of 1803.

The scandal is usually remembered for catching the attention of Wordsworth, Coleridge and their circle, but it also became the focus of much wider popular interest, provoking the melodramas, pamphlets and ballads which a juicy criminal case involving sex and a hanging could always call forth in the nineteenth century. If anything, the Maid of Buttermere as the type of innocence seduced and betrayed was an even greater tourist attraction than the Maid of Buttermere as a type of innocence unspoiled. Visitors like James Denholm came to admire a beauty 'rendered still more engaging, from that air of melancholy and grief which appeared in her features, the consequence of her sad fate'. Others, more level-headedly, saluted the fortitude with which she bore her tragedy, what Wordsworth called

> Her patience, and retiredness of mind
> Unsoil'd by commendation, and the excess
> Of public notice.

Interest in Mary Robinson herself dwindled after her second marriage, to a local farmer, and we catch a last unromantic glimpse of her in the pages of Green's *Tourist's New Guide* of 1819 as 'the bulky wife of a farmer, blessed with much good humour, and a ready utterance'.

Her story was not forgotten, however. Fleshed out (like Mary Robinson herself) it remained a staple of the guidebooks for much of the nineteenth century. The spectacle of rural innocence seduced and betrayed by an invading outsider had a lasting appeal to a nineteenth-century public which would later weep for Hetty Sorrel in *Adam Bede* and take Hardy's Tess to their hearts. Moreover, it had special poignancy in the context of the Lake District, as the fulfilment of fears that tourism could contaminate what it sought out, and as the living proof that even an innocent, sentimentally minded tourist and travel writer like Captain Budworth could share some of the guilt with 'a bold bad Man' like Hatfield. Budworth was not a subtle moralist – he was condescending towards Mary Robinson and determined to think her corrupted in ways which a more sympathetic observer like Wordsworth could not detect – yet his part in her fate made him in some ways the most fitting person to point the chief lesson. He did so in a note to the third edition of his *Fortnight's Ramble*, where he accepted responsibility for having introduced the serpent into Eden and took the

opportunity of deploring that he ever wrote in commendation of any young living creature, as vanity, alas, is the most intoxicating of human plants! and too apt to spread, when unfortunately introduced to public approval. Indeed, few minds are proof against it; and happy would it be for many a flower, were they

   'Born to blush unseen!'

VIII

As well as spotting the picturesque capabilities of Belle Isle on his visit in 1768, Arthur Young had been emphatic in recommending that nature be helped by art for more practical purpose of 'enabling the spectator to command, with greater ease, the luxuriant beauties and striking views which to so many travellers are hitherto quite unknown'. There were, he reported enthusiastically,

a vast many edges of precipices, bold projections of rock, pendent clifts, and wild romantic spots, which command the most delicious scenes, but which cannot be reached without the most perilous difficulty: To such points of view, winding paths should be cut in the rock, and resting-places made for the weary traveller: Many of these paths must necessarily lead through the hanging woods, openings might be made to let in views of the lake, where the objects, such as islands, &c. were peculiarly beautiful. At the bottoms of the rocks also, something of the same nature should be executed for the better viewing the romantic cascades, which might be exhibited with a little art, in a variety that would astonish.

By the turn of the nineteenth century most of his suggestions for opening up the landscape to visitors had been carried out: paths had been cut to the waterfalls and the picturesque stations, even resting places for the weary traveller provided in the form of summer houses like the one at the Windermere station. And the results had made Young's tone sound hopelessly, absurdly naïve. If tourism destroys what it comes to admire, then Mr English's fir trees and cabbages, the gimcrack follies on Pocklington's Island, greedy old John Raven at the Bowder Stone and the fate of Mary Robinson all suggested that the Lake District, its human population as well as its natural scenery, was proving a particularly fragile victim of its popularity with visitors. In contemporary writing about the Lakes, this discovery brings about first a change of tone, tempering enthusiasm with anxiety and guilt, and then a change of role, turning advocates and publicists into conservationists.

No writer illustrates the complexities of this darkening mood better than Wordsworth. I have already quoted him a good deal because his intimate knowledge of the Lake District during the critical decades when tourism was transforming it gave him special authority as its historian. Yet, of course, he was far more than that. Of all the people whom this chapter mentions, Wordsworth has most influenced our own attitude to nature, transforming the cults of the Sublime and the Picturesque, which now look like period pieces, into that complex of responses we call Romanticism, which is still part of the intellectual climate we live in. From the Picturesque he took a visual delight in the irregular, the humble and the fleeting, while liberating it from the detachment of genteel appraisal and the preoccupation with principles of taste. A moving passage towards the end of *The Prelude* rejects the 'strong infection of the age' which had encouraged his own youthful presumption in

> disliking here, and there,
> Liking, by rules of mimic art transferr'd
> To things above all art.

From the Sublime he took the central emotions of awe and reverence, while abandoning its love of violent sensation and melodramatic machinery. 'Tintern Abbey', in this respect almost a companion piece to the passage I have just quoted from *The Prelude*, looks without regret on the loss of his youthful ability to feel 'aching joys' and 'dizzying raptures' in the presence of nature, and celebrates instead his growing awareness of

> A presence that disturbs me with the joy
> Of elevated thoughts; a sense sublime
> Of something far more deeply interfused,
> Whose dwelling is the light of setting suns,
> And the round ocean and the living air,
> And the blue sky, and in the mind of man:
> A motion and a spirit, that impels,
> All thinking things, all objects of all thought,
> And rolls through all things.

No longer merely a stimulus to be exploited or a spectacle to be judged, nature has become for Wordsworth 'something far more deeply interfused': a living force embracing the individual soul and communicating with it, to console, uplift and ennoble.

Anything but local in its implications, this achievement had for contemporaries its intensely local aspect. They knew Wordsworth, with Coleridge and Southey, as a 'Lake Poet' – a misleading but persistent label which his long residence among the Lakes and the local setting of so many of his poems enforced. Wordsworth's growing fame and the growing popularity of the Lakes were, willy-nilly, yoked together. He cemented the connection in the public mind by his *Guide*, a work which makes most of the other travel books I have quoted seem two-dimensional by its larger, more rounded approach to its subject, treating landscape not as a special effect to be sought out and appreciated in isolation but connecting it to the region's geology, history and human culture. So it was inevitable that travel literature after Wordsworth's poetry and Wordsworth's *Guide* should reflect the changes he had introduced. Guidebooks no longer abbreviated the region to a series of selected views; they grew more substantial and more informative. Above all, they radiated the new seriousness of purpose appropriate to a culture which sought nature out, not as a source for cultivated amusement, but as an educational and, indeed, a religious experience.

In practice, tourism usually cannot sustain this sort of high-mindedness for very long, and when we penetrate beyond the pious and instructive generalities which make the common stock of the nineteenth-century guidebook, as the talk of taste and terror had been of their eighteenth-century predecessors, we make an abrupt descent into the trivial. Wordsworth and the other Lake Poets had become celebrities in a region otherwise lacking celebrities: they had made themselves into tourist attractions. As early as 1802 Richard Warner noted Coleridge's residence in Keswick as giving 'additional charm and interest to its impressive scenery' – a phrase whose blandness set the tone for later travel writers developing this new interest in the poets' local connections. Coleridge's stay in Keswick proved too short to satisfy the appetite but Southey filled the gap by his long, industrious years at Greta Hall. He too was 'one of the chief *lions* of the Lakes', as Edward Baines called him while exulting over a glimpse of the poet in church. Ruskin's *Iteriad*, the youthful poem he wrote after touring the Lakes with his parents in 1830, also records the spectacle of Southey at his devotions as a highlight of the visit – an ironically prophetic touch since in old age Ruskin himself would inherit the mantle of the Lake Poets as an attraction for tourists.

Wordsworth himself accepted his role as the chief lion among the Lake Poets with a certain complaisance, suffering 'the perpetual incursions of flatterers of the coarsest order' during his later years at Rydal Mount. This hostile phrase comes from Harriet Martineau, who came to live at Ambleside in the mid 1840s and observed her famous neighbour's usual way of receiving strangers in malicious detail. He took them 'the round of his garden and terraces, relating to persons whose very names he had not attended to, particulars about his writing and other affairs, which each stranger flattered himself was a confidential communication to himself' and concluded the interview by wishing them 'improved health and much enjoyment of the lake scenery'. The visitors' book at Rydal Mount contains 2,500 names for the years 1830–7, though it is by no means a complete record; there is no reason to doubt Harriet Martineau's suggestion that by the 1840s Wordsworth was receiving about five hundred people a year in the fashion she described.

Such lionisation suited the temper of an age when the Romantic cult of personality was growing into the Victorian cult of hero-worship. We have already seen how this formidable combination of forces exalted Shakespeare's reputation and Stratford's popularity to new heights in the course of the nineteenth century, so it was only natural that contemporaries should extend their practice of creating literary shrines to include living writers as well. And after Wordsworth's death he could be memorialised in the best Stratford manner. The monuments survive today as permanent items on the tourist map of the Lake District. No less than three of his houses are open to the public: his birthplace at Cockermouth; Dove Cottage in Grasmere, almost as lovingly embalmed as Shakespeare's Birthplace itself; and Rydal Mount, where the living writer first smiled on the inception of the whole cult. The churches at Grasmere, where Wordsworth and several members of his family are buried, and at Crosthwaite, where Southey rests under an epitaph by Wordsworth, make ancillary shrines. Their number was later swelled by the addition of Ruskin's home at Brantwood and his grave in the near-by village of Coniston, and of Beatrix Potter's house at Near Sawrey.

Yet this list does not even come close to exhausting the literary or even Wordsworthian associations that have nourished Lake District tourism, since it names only shrines of the sort I described in my first chapter: buildings or monuments strictly connected with the facts of a writer's birth, life and death. And, of course, by far the most significant aspect of Wordsworth's influence on tourism was the way it broadened

Rydal Water and Grasmere from Rydal Park, engraved from a drawing by
George Pickering for Thomas Rose's *Westmorland, Cumberland, Durham and
Northumberland, Illustrated* (1832).

the definition to encompass the places he mentions or describes in his
work. The literary shrine is joined, and soon overshadowed, by the
newer and more potent concept of the literary landscape. Seeing the
landscape – we might now say almost literally 'reading' the landscape –
in terms of the poems describing it became the nineteenth-century
equivalent of the earlier systems that the cults of the Sublime and the
Picturesque had established for teaching visitors what to look at, what
to see and what to feel. The cultivated tourist convinced himself that he
had experienced the distinctive atmosphere of the places he visited, or
even come to know their essential character, by opening his volume of
Wordsworth.

   At least some of his poems give the cue to this practice, not just by
locating themselves quite exactly on the map but by describing the
locations in language addressed to the visitor from elsewhere. As John
Barrell has pointed out in his study of the changing attitudes to
landscape in English poetry, Wordsworth presents the setting for his
poems not from the inside but from the outside. The result is that the

opening lines of a poem like 'Michael' speak quite openly in the tones of the guidebook directing the tourist to an interesting out-of-the-way corner which he might otherwise miss:

> If from the public way you turn your steps
> Up the tumultuous brook of Green-head Ghyll,
> You will suppose that with an upright path
> Your feet must struggle; in such bold ascent
> The pastoral mountains front you, face to face,
> But, courage! for around that boisterous brook
> The mountains have all opened out themselves
> And made a hidden valley of their own.

A similar effect is created in 'The Brothers', which begins with the vicar of Ennerdale remarking that his churchyard contains nothing to attract the tourist but immediately goes on, through his conversation with a returning native, to reveal just the sort of story about the place that would interest the tourist. Both poems are proffered as the metaphorical equivalent of those paths which Arthur Young thought needed cutting into the undiscovered corners of the landscape and which guides like Peter Crosthwaite were busy supplying.

The idea that the poem could provide a text for interpreting such places once the tourist had been led to them gets formal encouragement, indeed a sort of theoretical support, from Wordsworth's own guidebook to the Lakes. I noted earlier that this did not break entirely with West's *Guide* but used some of West's stations and even, on occasion, his language. These vestiges of the Picturesque make Wordsworth's near-silence on the subject of painters all the more striking. Claude and Poussin are mentioned only once (and then just to remark their indifference to the scenery of the Alps), Salvator not at all. The only reference to an English landscape painter comes when Turner's drawing of Hardrow Force is briefly commended during the description of the approach to the Lake District through Yorkshire. To say that Wordsworth is indifferent to landscape art only points the question of how he could manage to be, in a tradition of writing which had hitherto relied so heavily on viewing landscape in artistic terms. Here, for example, is West describing the approach to the Lake District he most admired, from the south over Lancaster Sands:

For such company as come to LANCASTER, it will be more convenient to begin the visit with CONISTON lake. By this course the lakes lie in an order more pleasing to the eye, and grateful to the imagination. The change of scenes is from what is pleasing, to what is surprising, from the delicate and elegant touches of CLAUDE, to the noble scenes of POUSSIN, and, from these, to the stupendous, romantic ideas of SALVATOR ROSA.

And here is Wordsworth, endorsing West's preference for the same route but describing it in his own terms:

The Stranger, from the moment he sets foot upon those Sands, seems to leave the turmoil and traffic of the world behind; and, crossing the majestic plain whence the sea has retired, he beholds, rising apparently from its base, the cluster of mountains among which he is going to wander, and towards whose recesses, by the Vale of Coniston, he is gradually and peacefully led.

The point is not just that Wordsworth is a better writer than West. It is that he trusts his words more. He believes that his experience of landscape can be made at home in language, and West clearly does not.

Indeed, the Picturesque movement had been very specific about the limitations of language and its inferiority to the picture. Gilpin, for example, thought words good for giving 'the great outlines of a scene' but not much more:

They can measure the dimensions of a lake. They can hang it's sides with wood. They can rear a castle on some projecting rock: or place an island near this, or the other shore. But their range extends no farther. They cannot mark the characteristic diminutions of each scene – the touches of nature – her living tints – her endless varieties, both in form and colour. – In a word, all her elegant peculiarities are beyond their reach.

The artist's pencil, on the other hand, 'offers a more perfect mode of description': 'It speaks a language more intelligible; and describes the scene in stronger, and more varied terms. The shapes and hues of objects it delineates, and marks with more exactness'. This is why William Mason welcomed Gilpin's combination of descriptive writing and aquatints as a supplement to Gray's letters about the Lakes. For all Gray's skill with language – and Mason thought that he had 'pushed its powers' – language alone remained 'defective'; the artist's pencil 'ought to be in the very hand of the writer, ready to supply with outlines every thing that his pen cannot express'.

It is in answer to such views that Wordsworth, by the time he wrote his *Guide*, had already added the footnote to his *Descriptive Sketches* of the Alps explaining that he rejected the idea of calling the poems *Picturesque Sketches* because it would have insulted the Alps. 'The cold rules of painting' could not convey the emotions stirred up by his subject: to do that he had to trust to 'nature and my feelings', and poetry. His *Guide* does the same thing for the Cumbrian mountains. Where a writer of the Picturesque school would have said that a scene was worthy of the brush of Claude or Poussin or Salvator Rosa, Wordsworth quotes a poem instead. Even when he wants to suggest how a new villa could be built in keeping with the wooded and mountainous scenery of the Lake District he ignores the visual arts with almost studied insolence, and proffers Spenser's description of Belphoebe's palace from *The Faerie Queene*. Elsewhere, when he summons 'the aid of verse' to evoke a local scene it is usually his own verse: lines from *The Excursion* about Blea Tarn, lines from *The Prelude* (then otherwise unpublished) about the calm and steady atmosphere of inland lakes, and lines originally intended for *The Recluse* about migratory birds. Two of his poems appear in their entirety, an ode to Helvellyn and, as conclusion to the *Guide*, 'The Pass of Kirkstone'.

Charles Mackay's *The Scenery and Poetry of the English Lakes*, published in 1846, is just one of the first of many books to follow Wordsworth's lead in using literature rather than painting as a guide for directing the tourist where to go and what to admire. Mackay, in fact, is early enough to be able to make Rydal Mount and Wordsworth the starting-point of his tour; thereafter he quotes *The Excursion* at Blea Tarn, 'The Somnambulist' at Aira Force, the *River Duddon* sonnets in the Duddon valley and 'Fidelity' (as well as Sir Walter Scott's poem) at Helvellyn. Where Wordsworth has left a gap in the scenery, another poet can usually be found to fill it: hence the continuing, otherwise inexplicable popularity of Southey's verses about Lodore Falls and of Sir Walter Scott's *The Bridal of Triermain*, which fixed the resemblance between Castle Rock in St John's Vale and a Gothic ruin more or less permanently in the popular imagination. Indeed, Mackay refuses to admit defeat in his search for the appropriate literary allusion, even using Shelley's brief stay in the Lakes as an excuse to quote the description of the waterfall from 'Alastor' at the otherwise uncommemorated Stockghyll Force. The tone in which he approaches these places and offers these quotations shows how happily the new religious spirit of reverence for nature combines with the familiar hero-worshipping language of the literary pilgrim. 'Lovely is the vale of Grasmere', he exclaims: 'worthy is it of all renown – and holy will it ever be in the lays of the bards who have delighted to sing of it, and in the recollections of those who love the bards.'

Mackay presented his 'summer ramble' merely as a supplement to 'the more precise and methodical information of the guide-books', yet

Aira Force, engraved by Thomas Gilks from a drawing by D. H. M'Kewan for
Charles Mackay's *The Scenery and Poetry of the English Lakes* (1846).

the guidebooks found no difficulty in assimilating his approach, telling
the visitor to Aira Force that he 'ought to know of the mournful legend
which belongs to this place, and which Wordsworth has preserved' and
nudging him with the reminder that Loughrigg Tarn is 'well known to
all readers of Wordsworth'. These particular phrases come from
Harriet Martineau's brisk, railway-age guide published in 1855, and it
says much for the popularity of the literary landscape that it should
have left its mark on a writer otherwise so sceptical of Wordsworth
and, in fact, so out of sympathy with the assumptions underlying
Wordsworthian Romanticism. Yet they could have come from any one
of the nineteenth-century guidebooks about the Lakes, so hackneyed
and formulaic has the language of the new sensibility become.

   That danger, of course, was present from the start. Indeed, it is

Lodore Falls, from John Robinson's *A Guide to the Lakes in Cumberland, Westmorland and Lancashire* (1819).

inherent in the list of poems that writers from Mackay onwards take from Wordsworth as their texts for reading the landscape. None of them is among his best work, to put it mildly, and none embodies that cleansing view of nature I began my discussion of Wordsworth by describing. Though deeply and precisely rooted in place, his poetry achieves its characteristic greatness by a process that has little, if anything, to do with topographical description. It works, as 'Tintern Abbey' does, not by literal attention to the scene at hand but by the interplay between the spirit of the place, the personal experience that the poet brings to it and the larger truths this combination helps him to glimpse. There is a sense – an important one, I believe – in which Wordsworth can help us to the Wye valley and the Wye valley can help us to Wordsworth, but that subtle process has little to do with the pious generalities or the poems which pilgrims like Mackay delight in. These poems, like the dull later sonnets plotting the course of Wordsworth's tours through other parts of England and Scotland, are more literary calling cards than anything else. They pay tribute to a particular spot by embellishing a local tale, legend or fragment of history: the death of Charles Gough on Helvellyn in 'Fidelity', the medieval lovers at Aira Force in 'The Somnambulist' or the shepherd who fell from the Pillar Rock in 'The Brothers', a poem which I have already suggested begins with an implicit invitation to the tourist.

Yet what makes these poems slight is also precisely what makes them so handy. They mark an attractive spot with the authority of the writer's name, painlessly convey a fragment of history or folklore which has its own mild interest, and briefly rouse the emotions – melodramatic, sentimental or pathetic – connected with the tale. That, presumably, is why the literary landscape spread so widely in the nineteenth century, making it by far the easiest way for tourists to convince themselves that they were feeling appropriate or edifying emotions in the presence of a particular scene without necessarily spending much time actually looking at it. Just as Wordsworth's narrative rather than his lyric or meditative poems best served the literary landscape of the Lakes, so Victorian tourists elsewhere tread in the footsteps of narrative poets or, better still, novelists: Sir Walter Scott in Scotland, R. D. Blackmore on Exmoor, Charles Kingsley in Devon and, above all, Hardy in Dorset. I say Victorian tourists but, of course, the practice continues today and has shown how easily it can accommodate itself to new media, seeking out the locations where favourite films or television series have been made.

IX

In terms of tourism, the creation of the literary landscape may well be the most widely dispersed and stubbornly enduring result of the new attitude to nature which the Romantic poets introduced. Yet it is worth returning to Wordsworth and the Lakes, if only to take a final look at him struggling with the local consequences of his own achievement. The problem is suggested by a passage in his *Guide* where he contrasts Gray's description of Grasmere, that 'unsuspected paradise' of the 1760s, with the rash of glaring white villas that were already beginning to disfigure it by the early nineteenth century:

The literary landscape on the titlepage of Mackay's book. The palette in the foreground is no longer part of the landscape painter's equipment, but is used for painting the portraits of the writers – Wordsworth, Coleridge and Southey – to whom the scenery now belongs.

It was well for the undisturbed pleasure of the Poet that he had not forebodings of the change which was soon to take place; and it might have been hoped that these words ... would of themselves have preserved the ancient franchises of this and other kindred mountain retirements from trespass; or (shall I dare say?) would have secured scenes so consecrated from profanation.

I said only that this suggests the problem, because it certainly does not face it. To us, I think, it is obvious that a poet's praise can bear unwelcome fruit and is in fact more likely to endanger its subject than to consecrate it. Wordsworth finds this truth too hard to swallow: he is left, disturbed and full of foreboding in a way that Gray was not, contemplating the disappointment of hopes that sound to us merely unrealistic. For him, the contradiction between the publicist and the man who quite naturally wished 'to preserve the native beauty' of his region remained a dilemma barely glimpsed and never resolved, though it impaled him far more sharply than it ever did James Plumptre with his fears of what his recommendation might do to Ennerdale or Captain Budworth with his regret for what his panegyrics had done to Mary Robinson. That may be an important criticism of Wordsworth, but it is not one we can make in any spirit of complacency. As tourists we follow patterns he helped to establish and as conservationists we talk a language he helped to teach us without being any closer to reconciling the roles.

We remember him as conservationist in two contexts: his remarks on threats to the Lake District in his *Guide* and his far more urgent response to the dangers in his two public letters (and the famous accompanying sonnet) opposing the Kendal and Windermere Railway in 1844. I have already quoted these sources in this chapter, but it is time now to look at each of them in its own right and distinguish between the different types, or stages, of concern they express. The first is best summed up by the memorable words which end the chapter of the *Guide* devoted to 'Changes, and Rules of Taste for Preventing their Bad Effects', arguing for the need to preserve the region from the activities of new settlers like English and Pocklington:

In this wish the author will be joined by persons of pure taste throughout the whole island, who, by their visits (often repeated) to the Lakes in the North of England, testify that they deem the district a sort of national property, in which every man has a right and interest who has an eye to perceive and a heart to enjoy.

That phrase, 'a sort of national property', has been made familiar to people who have not read Wordsworth's *Guide* by bodies like the

National Trust and the National Parks Commission, who quote it in tracing their descent from him. They have answered his call by protecting places of natural beauty against private interests on behalf of us all.

Despite being the most memorable, Wordsworth's was not the only or even the earliest voice raised in this cause. In my previous chapter we have already heard Gilpin prompted by William Aislabie's idiocies at Fountains Abbey to appeal to a 'court of taste': 'The refined code of this court does not consider an elegant ruin as a man's *property*, on which he may exercise at will the irregular sallies of a wanton imagination: but as a deposit, of which he is only the guardian, for the amusement and admiration of posterity.' And in 1802, several years before Wordsworth first attacked it in print, Pocklington's Island had already provoked Richard Warner to a similar point:

Far be it from me to wish a restraint upon the expenditure of an honest citizen's money in any way he may think proper ... but when he uses it to destroy the effect of those scenes of Nature (the common property of the public) which the general voice have pronounced to be beautiful, and thus diminishes the stock of public pleasure, and cuts off one fruitful spring of intellectual enjoyment from a whole people, I cannot but think the legislature should consider it as a sort of popular trespass, deserving prohibition if not punishment; or at least should make the promoters of false taste, in such cases as these, the objects of severe taxation.

These passages are worth setting beside Wordsworth's to show the rather different terms in which the idea of conservation could be advanced. All three writers champion the rights of visitors and the interest, in both senses of the term, they have in a scene endangered by private property owners, yet the visitors do not sound like the same group in all three accounts. Gilpin speaks the language of the Picturesque with which we are by now thoroughly familiar. His visitors take amusement from or feel admiration for an elegant sight; together, they constitute a court of taste, an élite applying a refined code of appraisal and judgement. Warner's visitors admire beauty and take pleasure, but they also embody the earnestness which I have noted as entering tourism with Romanticism and the nineteenth century, for their enjoyment stems from a fruitful spring and is intellectual. And there are obviously more of them than Gilpin's court of taste has room for, since Warner defines them in deliberately broad and democratic terms as the general voice of a whole people. The appropriate vehicle for their censure, significantly, is not a rap over the knuckles in a volume of picturesque observations but the penalties of the law.

And what about the visitors Wordsworth allies himself with? In fact, they are a curiously ill-defined and elusive group, sharing the characteristics of both Gilpin's and Warner's visitors. They begin as persons of pure taste coming, apparently, on more than one visit to the Lakes, which contrives to make them sound like the sort of visitor who came with a copy of Gilpin in their hands. Yet by the end of the passage, after rephrasing Warner's 'common property of the public' as 'national property', Wordsworth makes his appeal on behalf of 'every man' who 'has an eye to perceive and a heart to enjoy'. The words have the finely democratic ring we might expect from a Romantic poet, or at least they do until we pause to reflect that they might well fall considerably short of meaning 'every man', or, indeed, every person.

It would be unfair, as well as unprofitable, to dwell on the apparent uncertainties in this passage if they did not become crucial to Wordsworth's public letters about the Kendal and Windermere Railway. These, of course, were written in response to a very different sort of threat, for by 1844 the steam age was beginning to make possible the mass tourism whose problems we are still living with today. If not exactly invaded by the railway, the Lake District was already encircled with lines projected, approved or under construction. A system of connecting railways managed by different companies reached up the west coast, with a branch line extending from Cockermouth to Workington and Keswick. The course of the Lancaster to Carlisle line, up Shap Fell and through Penrith, marked its eastern border. The original plan for this line to pass through Kendal was modified so that it ran via Oxenholme a few miles to the east. The proposed Kendal and Windermere line would link Oxenholme with Kendal and continue to the lake shore just above the town of Bowness. It was, in other words, a branch line for the new class of tourists: weekend excursionists from the manufacturing towns of Lancashire and Yorkshire. There was even talk of making their penetration into the heartland of the Lakes more effective by an extension continuing from Windermere to Keswick via Ambleside, Rydal and Grasmere — of all local scenes, those most intimately connected with Wordsworth.

In fact, the phrases I have quoted from Wordsworth's *Guide* are directly echoed in his two public letters, though the effect is no clearer. He begins the first by defining the matter as one that concerns 'all persons of taste', and he ends the second by claiming to speak on behalf of 'every one, however humble his condition, who coming hither shall bring with him an eye to perceive, and a heart to feel and worthily enjoy'. But the issue has changed, partly because the character of the tourist Wordsworth now has immediately in his eye has changed. Whereas the *Guide* argued that the Lake District needed protecting for visitors, however vaguely they were defined or conceived, he now argues that it needs to be protected against visitors. Wordsworth's tone has changed correspondingly. The Kendal and Windermere letters throb with a horrified vision of 'cheap trains pouring out their hundreds at a time along the margin of Windermere', of the industrial towns of Lancashire and Yorkshire being able to send as many weekend excursionists to the Lake District as they did to Scarborough, of 'wrestling matches, horses and boat races without number', and of pothouses and beershops run by 'the lower class of innkeepers' keeping pace with these 'excitements and recreations'.

It is not hard to see why, when we remember Wordsworth's stand against the railway, we should prefer to take refuge in the easy, flowing rhetoric of his famous sonnet ('Is then no nook of English ground secure / From rash assault?'), rather than listen to him sounding far more snobbish and much less appeasable than the Duke of Rutland did in the face of Cook's excursionists at Belvoir. Yet such language, and all it implies, is far from unique in a nineteenth-century debate that often fed on connected fears of the steam engine, the new urban working class and the tripper. Writing thirty years after Wordsworth had lost his battle and the Kendal and Windermere Railway had been built, Ruskin deliberately echoed his words when the possibility of an extension to the line was raised again. He deplored the way the Lake District had been turned into a 'steam merry-go-round' with 'stupid herds of modern tourists' being dumped at Keswick and the shores of Windermere 'like coals from a sack', and remembered Wordsworth's lower class of innkeeper in summing up his hostility to the new breed of tourists: 'I don't want to let them see Helvellyn while they are drunk.'

Yet such disgust was not universal, and the violence of Wordsworth's tone is often the defensiveness of a man who knows he is swimming against the tide. A correspondent who replied to Wordsworth with a sonnet in the local *Whitehaven Herald* offered a very different picture of the new tourists which, incidentally, scored a neat point about Wordsworth's own role in making them want to come to the Lakes in the first place: they were 'sons of care and doubt' who found relief in getting away from the crowded streets of the manufacturing cities 'To read these scenes by light of thine own lays'. Harriet

Martineau's *Guide*, conspicuously friendly to the new tourists, was at pains to stress that 'the order of workpeople brought by the railways is of a desirable kind'. And in approving the proposed railway line, the Board of Trade report glanced obliquely at Wordsworth when it rejected arguments which would 'deprive the artisan of the offered means of occasionally changing his narrow abode, his crowded streets, his wearisome task and unwholesome toil, for the fresh air, and the healthful holiday which sends him back to his work refreshed and invigorated'.

It is disconcerting to hear the Board of Trade sounding so much closer to the central principles of Romanticism than Wordsworth does. Yet the Board states precisely the legacy which we have taken from Wordsworth, or think we have taken from Wordsworth, in seeking to explain our own need of nature and in making it the impetus for mass tourism. By contrast, the elderly poet himself cannot completely free his arguments from the taint of not-in-my-backyard selfishness or convince readers that he is more than just the spokesman for Lord Lonsdale's Tory interest and the more refined professionals among the new weekend cottagers. For much of the time his railway letters sound as if they were written by Wordsworth the Distributor of Stamps rather than Wordsworth the author of *The Prelude*.

But not all the time. Despite their manifest weaknesses, the letters still manage to raise uncomfortable points that we cannot gainsay or reconcile with the continuing demand for mass tourism any better than he could. Amidst all the confusions I have suggested about who can be trusted to preserve nature and who it needs to be preserved from, he does at least ask a related question: who can benefit from nature, and how? If surprising, his answer is depressingly honest: 'a vivid perception of romantic scenery is neither inherent in mankind, nor a necessary consequence of even a comprehensive education'. It comes after he has again glanced at the history of Pocklington's errors, and it highlights a suggestion that lurked in his much longer account of those errors in his earlier *Guide*. Pocklington's brand of 'bad taste in rural imagery' stemmed not just from the rich man's desire to make a show but from 'the common feelings of human nature'. We may all (the argument of his railway letters continues) have the inherent ability to appreciate 'ordinary varieties of rural nature', the modest effects of fields, streams and woods that more or less any English county can show, but the wild, untouched nature which attracts us to the Lakes demands a different eye. Historically speaking, our culture has only begun to acquire it in the last two hundred years or so, when we stopped feeling threatened, frightened or repelled by the mountain, the lake and the cave. Individually speaking, we cannot acquire it except by 'the habit of observing and studying the peculiar character of such scenes, and how they differ from one another'. Brief excursions do not help any more than a mastery of the genteel rules of taste, only 'a slow and gradual process of culture'. In other words, we have to live there.

I called this a depressing point. It also seems to me a formidable rebuke, coming identifiably from the author of *The Prelude* rather than the other less impressive Wordsworths who make their various contributions to the railway letters. It bespeaks the man who did not possess the simple unselfconscious rootedness of the native (which by his own argument would not have helped him much) but who became, in adult life, a returned native, rejecting city life and making a deliberate commitment to nature; its fruits were the result of a lifetime's hard work. That, presumably, is why in his poems and his *Guide* he could attempt to educate the visitor in this discipline; or, rather, why he could offer to do so before the dawn of mass tourism and the near-despair that underlies his railway letters.

Mass tourism, which is the only way most of us now experience the sort of wild nature Wordsworth was writing about, may briefly invigorate us as the Board of Trade believed it would, but otherwise it merely emphasises the gap between our fleeting interest and his impassioned service. And, as Wordsworth himself saw very clearly at the outset of the railway age, the sheer numbers in which we now indulge our fleeting interest pose their own special threats: to the modest pleasures of the tourists themselves, to the fragile communities their presence endangers, and above all to the wilderness itself. 'Done because we are too menny' – the suicide note left in an overcrowded lodging house by the itinerant, bored Father Time in Hardy's *Jude the Obscure* – is sooner or later going to be the epitaph of all tourism.

Notes

The four discussions of tourism I mention in my text are: 'Le Guide Bleu' in Roland Barthes, *Mythologies* (Paris: Editions du Seuil, 1957); chapter 3 in Daniel J. Boorstin, *The Image: A Guide to Pseudo-Events in America* (New York: Atheneum, 1973); Paul Fussell, *Abroad: British Literary Traveling Between the Wars* (Oxford: Oxford University Press, 1982); Dean MacCannell, *The Tourist: A New Theory of the Leisure Class* (London: Macmillan, 1976). Not just in my introduction but in the book as a whole I am also indebted to Esther Moir's *The Discovery of Britain: The English Tourists 1540 to 1840* (London: Routledge and Kegan Paul, 1964) and to John Barrell's comments about the viewpoint of the tourist in *The Idea of Landscape and the Sense of Place 1730–1840: An Approach to the Poetry of John Clare* (Cambridge: Cambridge University Press, 1972). Specialist works on which I have gratefully drawn in my introduction include: D. J. Hall, *English Mediaeval Pilgrimage* (London: Routledge and Kegan Paul, 1965 [1966]); Thomas M. Curley, *Samuel Johnson and the Age of Travel* (Athens, Georgia: University of Georgia Press, 1976); H. L. Beales, 'Travel and Communications' in volume 1 of *Johnson's England: An Account of the Life and Manners of His Age*, edited by A. S. Turberville, 2 volumes (Oxford: Clarendon Press, 1933); John Copeland, *Roads and Their Traffic 1750–1850* (Newton Abbot: David and Charles, 1968); John Vaughan, *The English Guide Book c.1780–1870: An Illustrated History* (Newton Abbot: David and Charles, 1974).

page
2 **roar of bombs:** George Orwell, *Homage to Catalonia* (London: Secker and Warburg, 1938), 314.
2 **acute sense of place:** Fussell, *Abroad*, 226.
5 **modern-man-in-general:** MacCannell, *The Tourist*, 1.
6 **avoiding such behaviour:** compare my argument with MacCannell's

challenge to Boorstin, in *The Tourist*, 102–7, which sensibly rejects Boorstin's attempt to posit 'an absolute separation of touristic and intellectual attitudes' as 'a part of the problem of mass tourism, not an analytical reflection on it'. Fussell, *Abroad*, 47–8, provides a witty description of what he calls 'anti-tourist behaviour' in demonstrating that 'it is hard to be a snob and a tourist at the same time'.

6 **pure cliché:** Fussell, *Abroad*, 39.

6 **bourgeois age ... proletarian movement:** Fussell, *Abroad*, 38.

8 **Magna Tabula:** see Hall, *Pilgrimage*, 63–4. The Magna Tabula is now in the possession of the Bodleian Library.

8 **thirteenth century:** see Hall, *Pilgrimage*, 70.

9 **it aspires:** Richard Twiss, *Travels through Portugal and Spain* (1775), quoted by Curley, *Johnson*, 47.

9 **as they are:** Samuel Johnson, *The Letters of Samuel Johnson*, edited by R. W. Chapman, 3 volumes (Oxford: Clarendon Press, 1952), 1, Letter No. 326, quoted by Curley, *Johnson*, 49.

9 *moving Academy*: James Howell, *Instructions for Foreine Travell* (1642), quoted by Curley, *Johnson*, 70.

10 **our own Country:** Thomas Hurtley, *A Concise Account of Some Natural Curiosities in the Environs of Malham in Craven, Yorkshire* (London, 1786), 23.

10 **journey times:** see Copeland, *Roads*, 86 and 100–1.

11 **every direction:** Arthur Young, *A General View of the Agriculture of the County of Oxford* (1809), quoted by Barrell, *Idea of Landscape*, 86, with a commentary I am indebted to.

12 **recollect exactly:** *The Torrington Diaries: Containing the Tours through England and Wales of the Hon. John Byng (Later Fifth Viscount Torrington) between the Years 1781 and 1794*, edited by C. Bruyn Andrews, 4 volumes (London: Eyre and Spottiswoode, 1934–8), 2, 102.

12 **rage of the times:** *Torrington Diaries*, 1, 69.

12 **stranger's notice:** Robert Southey, *Letters from England: By Don Manuel Alvarez Espriella. Translated from the Spanish*, second edition, 3 volumes (London, 1808), 2, 125.

12 **conventions in mapping:** see also Barrell, *Idea of Landscape*, 87.

18 **reach'd the summit:** *Torrington Diaries*, 2, 321.

18 **notion of a railway:** *Kendal and Windermere Railway. Two Letters Re-Printed from the Morning Post*, in *The Prose Works of William Wordsworth*, edited by W. J. B. Owen and Jane Worthington Smyser, 3 volumes (Oxford: Clarendon Press, 1974), 3, 341.

18 **solitary, traveller:** *Torrington Diaries*, 2, 358.

18 **counties, are tourists:** *Torrington Diaries*, 2, 171. For other uses of 'tourist', see 1, 249; 1, 350; and 2, 51.

18 **agricultural tourist:** Sydney Smith (1803), cited by OED, s.v. 'tourist'.

19 **passed over:** William Marshall, *A Review of the Reports to the Board of*

Agriculture from the Northern Department of England: Comprizing Northumberland, Durham, Cumberland, Westmoreland, Lancashire, Yorkshire; and the Mountainous Parts of Derbyshire, &c. (York, 1808), xl, quoted by Barrell, *Idea of Landscape*, 86, with a commentary I am indebted to.

19 **peaceful inhabitants:** Adam Walker, *A Tour from London to the Lakes: Containing Natural, Oeconomical, and Literary Observations, Made in the Summer of 1791. By a Gentleman* (London, 1792), 83.

19 **not be removed:** *Torrington Diaries*, 2, 321.

20 **of happiness:** William Cobbett, *Rural Rides in the Counties of Surrey, Kent, Sussex, Hampshire, Wiltshire, Gloucestershire, Herefordshire, Worcestershire, Somersetshire, Oxfordshire, Berkshire, Essex, Suffolk, Norfolk, and Hertfordshire: with Economical and Political Observations Relative to Matters Applicable to, and Illustrated by, the State of those Counties Respectively* (London, 1830), 345–6.

1 LITERARY SHRINES AND LITERARY PILGRIMS

A House of Kings: The History of Westminster Abbey, edited by Edward Carpenter (London: John Baker, 1966) makes a good introduction to its subject. Among the numerous studies of Shakespeare and Stratford, I have found the following particularly useful. For local history and buildings: Levi Fox, *The Borough Town of Stratford-upon-Avon* (Stratford-upon-Avon: Corporation of Stratford-upon-Avon, 1953) and, by the same author, 'The Heritage of Shakespeare's Birthplace', *Shakespeare Survey*, 1 (1948), 79–88. For the facts of the poet's life: Samuel S. Schoenbaum, *William Shakespeare: A Documentary Life* (Oxford: Clarendon Press, and London: Scolar Press, 1975). For the myths and their local uses: Ivor Brown and George Fearon, *Amazing Monument: A Short History of the Shakespeare Industry* (London: Heinemann, 1939) and F. E. Halliday, *The Cult of Shakespeare* (London: Duckworth, 1957). For the Jubilee: Christian Deelman, *The Great Shakespeare Jubilee* (London: Michael Joseph, 1964) and Johanne M. Stochholm, *Garrick's Folly: The Shakespeare Jubilee of 1769 at Stratford and Drury Lane* (London: Methuen, 1964).

22 **two million visits a year:** this very rough estimate is taken from statistics kindly provided by the British Tourist Authority.

23 **his Tombe:** William Camden, *The Historie of the Most Renowned and Victorious Princesse Elizabeth, Late Queene of England* (London, 1630), 135.

25 **fowerfold Tombe:** *The Works of Ben Jonson*, edited by C. H. Herford, E. M. Simpson and Percy Simpson, 11 volumes (Oxford: Clarendon Press, 1925–52), 11, 145.

25 **praise to giue:** *Works of Jonson*, 8, 391.

25 **Mansion keep:** *The Poetical Works of Sir John Denham*, edited by Theodore Howard Banks, Jr (New Haven: Yale University Press, 1928), 150.

25 **no Poets:** *Spectator* essay No. 26 in *The Spectator*, edited by Donald F. Bond, 5 volumes (Oxford: Clarendon Press, 1965), 1, 110.

25 **not disagreeable:** *Spectator*, 1, 108–9.

26 **Appearance together:** *Spectator*, 1, 111.

26 **unbounded Sway:** John Dart, *Westmonasterium: or The History and Antiquities of the Abbey Church of St Peter's Westminster*, 2 volumes (London, [1742]), 1, xi.

26 ***Augustus* lies:** Dart, *Westmonasterium*, 1, xl.

27 **nameless stone:** *The Poems of Alexander Pope*, general editor John Butt, Twickenham Edition, 11 volumes (London: Methuen, and New Haven: Yale University Press, 1961–9), 6, 208.

27 **set off none:** Dart, *Westmonasterium*, 1, 90.

27 **have with Shakespeare:** *Horace Walpole's Correspondence*, edited W. S. Lewis, Yale Edition, 48 volumes (London: Oxford University Press, and New Haven: Yale University Press, 1937–83), 35, 151.

27 **natural, free, and easy:** quoted by *Poems of Pope*, 6, 395n.

27 **Benson's name:** *Poems of Pope*, 6, 395.

28 **Westminster Abbey:** *Poems of Pope*, 6, 376.

28 **admission charges:** see Carpenter, *House of Kings*, 251–2.

28 **from the mob:** *Walpole's Correspondence*, 38, 111.

28 **merit inspire:** *The Collected Works of Oliver Goldsmith*, edited by Arthur Friedman, 5 volumes (Oxford: Clarendon Press, 1966), 2, 57.

29 **all must live:** *Works of Goldsmith*, 2, 60–1.

29 **ecclesiastical beggars:** *Works of Goldsmith*, 2, 62.

29 **very decay:** 'Westminster Abbey', *The Sketch Book of Geoffrey Crayon, Gent.*, edited by Haskell Springer, in *The Complete Works of Washington Irving*, general editors Henry A. Pochmann, Herbert Kleinfield and Richard Dilworth Rust, 29 volumes (Madison, Wisconsin: University of Wisconsin Press; and Boston: Twayne Publishers, 1969–81), 8, 134.

29 **an inscription:** 'Westminster Abbey', *Works of Irving*, 8, 135.

29 **the sculptor:** 'Westminster Abbey', *Works of Irving*, 8, 136.

29 **longest about them:** 'Westminster Abbey', *Works of Irving*, 8, 136.

29 **author and reader:** 'Westminster Abbey', *Works of Irving*, 8, 136.

29 **crowd too great:** quoted by Leslie Marchand, *Byron: A Biography*, 3 volumes (London: John Murray, 1957), 3, 1254.

31 **English-speaking people:** from a letter by Dean Herbert Kyle to *The Times* of 19 July 1924, quoted by J. O. Bailey, *The Poetry of Thomas Hardy: A Handbook and Commentary* (Chapel Hill: University of North Carolina Press, 1972), 557.

31 **ensconce Swinburne:** No. 778 in *The Complete Poems of Thomas Hardy*, edited by James Gibson, New Wessex Edition (London: Macmillan, 1976).

31 **strong representations:** quoted by Gordon S. Haight, *George Eliot: A Biography* (Oxford: Clarendon Press, 1968), 548.

31 **literary excellence:** *The Daily Telegraph* of 5 October 1889, quoted by Kenneth Robinson, *Wilkie Collins: A Biography* (London: Davis-Poynter, 1974), 548.

31 **heathen annexe:** quoted by Jack Lindsay, *George Meredith: His Life and Work* (London: The Bodley Head, 1956), 332.

33 **sole mausoleum:** 'Stratford-on-Avon', *Sketch Book* in *Works of Irving*, 8, 223–4.

33 **among your own:** John R. Wise, *Shakspere: His Birthplace and Its Neighbourhood* (London, 1861), 22.

33 **little mercate town:** William Camden, *Britain, Or A Choro-Graphicall Description of the Most Flourishing Kingdomes, England, Scotland, and Ireland, the Ilands Adioyning, out of the Depth of Antiquitie*, translated by Philemon Holland (London, 1610), 565.

33 **Hall 6/-:** quoted by Deelman, *Shakespeare Jubilee*, 34.

36 **in yᵗ matter:** quoted by Fox, *Stratford*, 142.

36 **more vermilion:** *Walpole's Correspondence*, 9, 120.

36 **James Ist's reign:** *The Journal of Sir Walter Scott*, edited by W.E.K. Anderson (Oxford: Clarendon Press, 1972), 454.

37 **very curious indeed:** *Nicholas Nickleby*, 354, in *The Nonesuch Dickens*, edited by Arthur Waugh, Hugh Walpole, Walter Dexter and Thomas Hatton, 25 volumes (London: Nonesuch Press, 1937–8).

37 **of this figure:** Samuel Ireland, *Picturesque Views on the Upper, or Warwickshire Avon* (London, 1795), 211.

37 **upon a scroll:** Robert Bell Wheler, *History and Antiquities of Stratford-upon-Avon* (Stratford, 1806), 71.

37 **no stranger to:** Wheler, *History*, 72.

39 **totally useless:** Wheler, *Collectanea de Stratford*, quoted by Schoenbaum, *Shakespeare*, 78.

41 **its inhabitants:** Wheler, *History*, 138.

42 **for Mulberry-wood:** quoted by Wheler, *History*, 137n–138n.

43 **ever divine:** quoted by Wheler, *History*, 199, in the appendix reprinting *Shakespeare's Garland*, a collection of Jubilee songs.

44 **in all Britain:** quoted by Deelman, *Shakespeare Jubilee*, 289.

44 **aeconomy and abstinence:** *The Torrington Diaries: Containing the Tours through England and Wales of the Hon. John Byng (Later Fifth Viscount Torrington) between the Years 1781 and 1794*, edited by C. Bruyn Andrews, 4 volumes (London: Eyre and Spottiswoode, 1934–8), 1, 226.

44 **every spectator:** *Torrington Diaries*, 1, 225.

44 **poor and numerous:** Ireland, *Warwickshire Avon*, 206.

44 **courting chair:** Ireland, *Warwickshire Avon*, 207.

44 **to our Shakspeare:** Ireland, *Warwickshire Avon*, 208.

45 **had purchased:** Ireland, *Warwickshire Avon*, 209.

46 **growing light:** quoted by Deelman, *Shakespeare Jubilee*, 203.

47 **cheerless appearance:** Robert Bell Wheler, *An Historical Account of the Birth-Place of Shakespeare, Reprinted from the Edition of 1824, With a Few Prefatory Remarks by J. O. Halliwell, Esq. F.R.S.* (Stratford, 1863), 9.

47 **to let:** Wheler, *Birth-Place*, 16.

47 **the bed room:** *Torrington Diaries*, 1, 224.

47 **tobacco stopper:** *Torrington Diaries*, 1, 224.

48 **Lady of Loretto:** Ireland, *Warwickshire Avon*, 189.

48 **stamped paper:** Ireland, *Warwickshire Avon*, 190.

48 **at the tomb:** 'Stratford-on-Avon', *Works of Irving*, 8, 210.

48 **costs nothing:** 'Stratford-on-Avon', *Works of Irving*, 8, 210.

48 **dirty cap:** 'Stratford-on-Avon', *Works of Irving*, 8, 210.

49 **levity and folly:** Wheler, *A Guide to Stratford-upon-Avon* (Stratford, 1814), 13.

49 **Nature was born:** quoted by Fox, 'Shakespeare's Birthplace', 82.

49 **to rest upon:** *The Illustrated London News* (18 September 1847), 189–90.

51 **exceedingly clean:** Nathaniel Hawthorne, 'Recollections of a Gifted Woman', *Our Old Home: A Series of English Sketches* in *The Works of Nathaniel Hawthorne*, general editors William Charvat, Roy Harvey Pearce, Claude M. Simpson and Matthew J. Bruccoli, Centenary Edition, 14 volumes (Columbus, Ohio: Ohio State University Press, 1962–80), 5, 98.

51 **intelligence about Shakspere:** 'Recollections of a Gifted Woman', *Works of Hawthorne*, 5, 98.

51 **homes and haunts:** 'Recollections of a Gifted Woman', *Works of Hawthorne*, 5, 98–9.

51 **a word in England:** 'Recollections of a Gifted Woman', *Works of Hawthorne*, 5, 99.

51 **had been purchased:** Preface to Wheler, *Birth-Place*, 7.

52 **million visits a year:** figures for the nineteenth century are taken from the graph in Levi Fox, *In Honour of Shakespeare: The History and Collections of the Shakespeare Birthplace Trust* (Norwich: Jarrold and Sons, and the Shakespeare Birthplace Trust, 1972). Modern figures (for 1983) were kindly supplied by the British Tourist Authority.

54 **world's greatest men:** Wise, *Shakspere*, 15.

54 **called Hamnet:** quoted by Brian Masters, *Now Barabbas Was a Rotter: The Extraordinary Life of Marie Corelli* (London: Hamish Hamilton, 1978), 162.

54 **divine Shakespeare:** quoted by Masters, *Corelli*, 98.

55 **her masterpieces:** *Punch* for 6 March 1901, quoted by Masters, 167.

55 **ugly doubt:** 'Recollections of a Gifted Woman', *Works of Hawthorne*, 5, 97.

55 **common showman:** quoted by J. L. Bradley, 'Joseph Skipsey', *Notes and Queries*, 223 (August 1978), 320.

55 **grave doubt:** quoted by Bradley, 'Skipsey', 320–1.

56 **every day:** Henry James, 'The Birthplace' in *The Novels and Tales of Henry James*, New York Edition, 26 volumes (London: Macmillan, 1908–70), 17, 180.

56 **keep it up:** 'The Birthplace' in *Novels and Tales of James*, 17, 181.

56 **the imagination:** 'Recollections of a Gifted Woman', *Works of Hawthorne*, 5, 99.

57 **age of Elizabeth:** 'In Warwickshire' in *English Hours* (London: William Heinemann, 1905), 201.

2 ENVIOUS SHOW

For my purposes the most useful study of country houses is Mark Girouard's *Life in the English Country House: A Social and Architectural History* (New Haven and London: Yale University Press, 1978); readers will notice my debt to chapters 5, 6 and 7 in particular. The history of country-house visiting has been a curiously neglected subject, though I have profited from two preliminary essays: Bernard Denvir, 'Visiting Country Houses 200 Years Ago', *Country Life*, 120 (25 October 1956), 934–6, and Esther Moir, chapter 6 of *The Discovery of Britain: The English Tourists 1540 to 1840* (London: Routledge and Kegan Paul, 1964).

The phrase 'envious show' in my title for this chapter comes from the opening line of Ben Jonson's 'To Penshurst': 'Thou art not PENSHURST, built to envious show'.

58 **the sixteenth century:** Evelyn Waugh, Preface to *Brideshead Revisited: The Sacred and Profane Memories of Captain Charles Ryder*, second edition (London: Chapman and Hall, 1960), 10.

59 **the sixteenth century:** quoted by John Butler, *The Economics of Historic Country Houses*, Policy Studies Institute No. 591 (January 1981), 1–2.

59 **250 houses:** the figure comes from the book accompanying the exhibition my text goes on to mention, *The Destruction of the Country House 1875–1975*, edited by Roy Strong, Marcus Binney and John Harris (London: Thames and Hudson, 1975), 8.

59 **Lord Marchmain:** Preface to *Brideshead Revisited*, 10.

59 **16-million mark:** see Butler, *Economics*, 29.

60 **lives of the owners:** Butler, *Economics*, 30.

64 **rank or fortune:** *The Life of Richard Nash* in *The Collected Works of Oliver Goldsmith*, edited by Arthur Friedman, 5 volumes (Oxford: Clarendon Press, 1966), 3, 300. Goldsmith's phrases are also quoted by Girouard, *English Country House*, 183.

65 **water at the pump:** Tobias Smollett, *The Expedition of Humphry*

Clinker, edited by Lewis M. Knapp, Oxford English Novels (London: Oxford University Press, 1966), 49.

65 **order and urbanity:** Smollett, *Humphry Clinker*, 51.

65 **Beaumont and Disney:** *A New Tour thro' England, Perform'd in the Summers of 1765, 1766, and 1767 ... Describing Whatever is Curious, in the Several Counties, Cities, Boroughs, Market Towns, and Villages of Note in the Kingdom: Including All the Cathedral, Collegiate, and Parochial Churches; Palaces Antient and Modern; Seats of the Nobility and Gentry; Remains of British, Roman and Saxon Antiquities, Worthy the Inspection of Gentlemen or Others, Who Travel for Amusement, Instruction, or Business. With a New Map of England by Kitchen, Accurately Engraved, and Finely Coloured. With the Exact Distances by the Milestones* (London, [1768]).

65 **Paterson:** *A New and Accurate Description of all the Direct and Principal Cross Roads in Great Britain*, of which I have seen the second edition (London, 1772) and *Paterson's British Itinerary Being A New and Accurate Delineation of all the Direct and Principal Cross Roads in Great Britain*, 2 volumes (London, 1785).

65 **Mogg ... railway guides:** Mogg, who took over the format of 'Paterson's Roads' in 1822, himself adapted its principles to the railway system, beginning (apparently) with *Mogg's Pocket Itinerary; or, An Entirely New and Accurate Description of the Direct and Cross Roads of England and Wales, with Part of the Roads of Scotland, Shewing the Seats of the Nobility and Gentry ... To Which is Now First Added an Appendix of the Rail Roads* (London, 1837).

65 **without viewing it:** Arthur Young, *A Six Weeks Tour through the Southern Counties of England and Wales* (London, 1768), 2.

66 **history by 1749 ... guidebook by 1755:** see Joseph Pote, *The History and Antiquities of Windsor Castle, and the Royal College, and Chapel of St George: with the Institution, Laws, and Ceremonies of the Most Noble Order of the Garter* (Eton, 1749) and *Les Delices de Windsore; or, A Description of Windsor Castle, and the Country Adjacent* (Eton, 1755).

66 **his claptrap:** Carl Philip Moritz, *Journeys of a German in England in 1782*, translated and edited by Reginald Nettel (London: Jonathan Cape, 1965), 114.

66 **like recovery:** Louis Simond, *An American in Regency England: The Journal of a Tour in 1810–1811*, edited by Christopher Hibbert (London: Robert Maxwell, 1968), 124.

66 **by travellers:** Arthur Young, *A Six Months Tour through the North of England*, 4 volumes (London, 1770), 2, 107.

66 **yew hedge gardens:** *The Torrington Diaries: Containing the Tours through England and Wales of the Hon. John Byng (Later Fifth Viscount Torrington) between the Years 1781 and 1794*, edited by C. Bruyn Andrews, 4 volumes (London: Eyre and Spottiswoode, 1934–8), 2, 221.

67 **satisfactory manner:** William MacRitchie, *Diary of a Tour through Great Britain in 1795*, with an introduction and notes by David MacRitchie (London, 1897), 143.

67 **Arundel:** see, for example, Thomas Pennant, *A Journey from London to the Isle of Wight*, 2 volumes (London, 1801), 2, 99.

67 **Five's Court:** *Torrington Diaries*, 4, 161–2.

67 **Knight errant:** *The Diary of John Evelyn*, edited by E. S. de Beer, 6 volumes (Oxford: Clarendon Press, 1955), 3, 120.

67 **perfect order:** *Torrington Diaries*, 1, 230.

67 **Conisbrough Castle:** see *Torrington Diaries*, 3, 27.

67 **any neighbour:** *Torrington Diaries*, 1, 351.

67 **the kingdom:** *Torrington Diaries*, 2, 354.

68 **roof'd the hall:** *Torrington Diaries*, 2, 198.

68 **Castle of Belvoir:** *Torrington Diaries*, 2, 42.

68 **of the weather:** *The Works of the Late Edward Dayes Containing an Excursion through the Principal Parts of Derbyshire and Yorkshire*, edited by E. W. Brayley (London, 1805), 12.

68 **tolerable dwelling:** *Horace Walpole's Correspondence*, edited by W. S. Lewis, Yale Edition, 48 volumes (London: Oxford University Press and New Haven: Yale University Press, 1937–83), 9, 296.

68 **ever saw:** *Torrington Diaries*, 2, 33.

68 **creeping in:** *Walpole's Correspondence*, 9, 297.

68 **warm it well:** *Torrington Diaries*, 2, 35.

69 **generous Temper:** Daniel Defoe, *A Tour thro' the Whole Island of Great Britain*, with an introduction by G. D. H. Cole, 2 volumes (London: Frank Cass, 1968), 2, 427.

69 **infamous:** Young, *North of England*, 4, 575.

69 **houling Wilderness:** Defoe, *Tour*, 2, 567.

70 **Genius for Building:** Defoe, *Tour*, 2, 513.

72 **foolish glare:** *Torrington Diaries*, 2, 37.

72 **King of Poland:** *Walpole's Correspondence*, 9, 289.

72 **Pounds *Sterl*.:** Defoe, *Tour*, 2, 427.

72 **no connoisseur:** Young, *Southern Counties*, 197.

72 **size of rooms:** see Young, *Southern Counties*, 280–1, and *North of England*, 4, 594.

73 **very fine place:** *Pride and Prejudice* in *The Novels of Jane Austen*, edited by R. W. Chapman, third edition, 5 volumes (London: Oxford University Press, 1933), 2, 241.

73 **admiration of his taste:** *Pride and Prejudice* in *Novels of Austen*, 2, 246.

74 **marbles it contains:** Young, *North of England*, 2, 41.

74 **lately from *Italy*:** Young, *North of England*, 2, 76.

74 **into the river:** *Walpole's Correspondence*, 35, 296.

74 **subject's in Europe:** Richard Joseph Sulivan, *Tour through Different Parts of England, Scotland, and Wales* (1778), as paraphrased in

William Mavor, *The British Tourists; or Traveller's Pocket Companion, through England, Wales, Scotland, and Ireland. Comprehending the Most Celebrated Tours in the British Islands*, 6 volumes (London, 1798–1800), 3, 40.

75 **Worksop Manor:** see Young, *North of England*, 1, 366.

75 **Raby Castle:** see *Torrington Diaries*, 3, 74.

76 **sight of the place:** *Torrington Diaries*, 1, 231.

76 **16 miles:** *Torrington Diaries*, 1, 237.

76 **civil deportment:** *Torrington Diaries*, 2, 204.

76 **beauty of the place:** William Bray, *Tour through Some of the Midland Counties, into Derbyshire and Yorkshire by William Bray, F.A.S. Performed in 1777* (1783), as paraphrased in Mavor, *The British Tourists*, 2, 344.

76 **her apartment:** Young, *North of England*, 1, 148.

76 **Clumber Park:** see *Torrington Diaries*, 2, 9–11.

76 **green paper:** Young, *Southern Counties*, 31.

76 **most sumptuous:** *Walpole's Correspondence*, 10, 91.

77 **easy entrance:** *Passages from the Diaries of Mrs Philip Lybbe Powys of Hardwick House, Oxon. A.D. 1756 to 1808*, edited by Emily J. Climenson (London, 1899), 15.

77 **genteelest taste:** *Diaries of Mrs Powys*, 11.

77 **come again:** *Torrington Diaries*, 4, 127.

77 **in dudgeon:** *Torrington Diaries*, 1, 364.

77 **advancing Possessors:** *The Journals and Letters of Fanny Burney (Madame D'Arblay)*, edited by Joyce Hemlow and others, 12 volumes (Oxford: Clarendon Press, 1972–84), 1, 22. The editors mark 'doings' and 'thirty' in this passage as doubtful readings.

78 **distinct articulator:** Boswell, *Life of Samuel Johnson*, edited by George Birkbeck Hill and revised by L. F. Powell, 6 volumes (Oxford: Clarendon Press, 1934–50), 3, 161.

78 **superannuated housekeeper:** *Torrington Diaries*, 1, 230.

78 **Temple Newsam:** see Young, *North of England*, 1, 390.

78 **the Murderer:** *Torrington Diaries*, 4, 134.

78 **fees were taken:** Young, *North of England*, 3, 102.

78 **half a crown:** *Walpole's Correspondence*, 19, 443.

79 **cloud their houses:** Young, *North of England*, 1, 148.

79 **castellated style:** see Girouard, *English Country House*, 242.

79 **showing the castle:** *The Annual Register*, 76 (1834), 233. Mrs Home's fortune is also mentioned in *The Destruction of the Country House*, 163.

79 **Wilton:** see *Diaries of Mrs Powys*, 165.

79 **Woburn:** see *Torrington Diaries*, 2, 127.

79 **days in a week:** 'Horace Walpole's Journals of Visits to Country Seats, &c.', edited by Paget Toynbee, *The Walpole Society*, 16 (1927–8), 29.

79 **Blenheim:** see William Mavor, *A Description of Blenheim, The Seat of His Grace, The Duke of Marlborough: Containing a Full and Accurate Account of the Paintings, Tapestry, and Furniture; A Picturesque Tour of the Gardens and Park; A General Delineation of the China Gallery, Private Gardens, &c.; To Which Are Also Added, An Itinerary; An Account of the Roman Villa, Near Northleigh, &c. &c.: with a Preliminary Essay on Landscape Gardening*, twelfth edition (Oxford, not dated).

79 **Chiswick House:** see Young, *North of England*, 1, 148, and *Walpole's Correspondence*, 2, 274.

80 *sit down:* Simond, *Regency England*, 63.

80 **guidance and direction:** 'Advertisement' in Joseph Pote, *Les Delices de Windsore*.

80 **half-crown catalogue:** Young, *Southern Counties*, 159–60. The catalogue is *A New Description of the Pictures, Statues, Bustos, Basso Relievos, and Other Curiosities, in the Earl of Pembroke's House, at Wilton*, of which I have seen the ninth edition (Salisbury, 1779).

80 **Chatsworth servants:** see *Torrington Diaries*, 2, 37.

80 **its favour:** William Bray, *Tour*, in Mavor, *British Tourists*, 2, 334.

81 **insolent gardener:** Mavor, *British Tourists*, 2, 334n.

81 **servants' wages:** Hon. Mrs Murray [Sarah Aust], *A Companion and Useful Guide to the Beauties of Scotland, to the Lakes of Westmorland, Cumberland, and Lancashire; and to the Curiosities in the District of Craven in the West Riding of Yorkshire. To Which is Added, a More Particular Description of Scotland, Especially That Part of It, Called the Highlands* (London, 1799), 7.

81 **rich travellers:** *Torrington Diaries*, 1, 53.

81 **ravenous:** *Walpole's Correspondence*, 10, 309.

81 **well deserves:** Young, *Southern Counties*, 96–7.

81 **through the house:** Simond, *Regency England*, 122–3.

82 **be overdressed:** *Walpole's Correspondence*, 9, 348.

82 **sit upon it:** *Walpole's Correspondence*, 2, 275.

82 **customers:** see, for example, *Walpole's Correspondence*, 11, 25.

83 **plenty as flounders:** *Walpole's Correspondence*, 37, 269.

84 **ever saw:** *Walpole's Correspondence*, 37, 269.

85 **my housekeeper:** *Walpole's Correspondence*, 1, 166.

85 **many rudenesses:** *Walpole's Correspondence*, 2, 275.

85 **longer a paragraph:** *Walpole's Correspondence*, 25, 423.

85 **Mr Walpole shoot:** *Walpole's Correspondence*, 11, 25.

86 **pocketed the piece:** *Walpole's Correspondence*, 11, 293.

86 **my rules:** *Walpole's Correspondence*, 33, 435.

86 **particular indulgence:** *Walpole's Correspondence*, 12, 222.

86 **appointment book:** printed in *Walpole's Correspondence*, 12, 219–52.

87 **Victorian idealist:** the point is made by Edmund Swinglehurst, *Cook's Tours: The Story of Popular Travel* (Poole, Dorset: Blandford Press, 1982), 12.

89 **wise is enough:** Thomas Cook, *Hand-Book of Belvoir Castle: Designed as a Guide to an Excursion Party from Leicester to Belvoir, Aug. 29, 1848; with a Description of the Route from Leicester, and Places of Interest in the Locality of the Castle* (Leicester, 1848), 22.

89 **of any article:** quoted by *Cook's Excursionist and Cheap Trip Advertiser* (3 June 1858), 2.

89 **visitors behave:** *Cook's Excursionist* (3 June 1858), 1.

90 **universal humanity:** *Cook's Exhibition Herald and Excursion Advertiser*, 1 (31 May 1851), 9.

90 **legitimate claim:** Cook, *Hand-Book of Belvoir*, 3–4.

91 **permission of entrance:** *Torrington Diaries*, 3, 74.

3 A PROPER STATE OF DECAY

Rose Macaulay's *Pleasure of Ruins* (London: Thames and Hudson, 1953) is the fullest survey of its subject, taking in a far wider historical and geographical range than I attempt in this chapter. Other works I have found helpful are: Carl Paul Barbier's *William Gilpin: His Drawings, Teaching, and Theory of the Picturesque* (Oxford: Clarendon Press, 1963); Martin S. Briggs' *Goths and Vandals: A Study of the Destruction, Neglect and Preservation of Historical Buildings in England* (London: Constable, 1952); Kenneth Clark's *The Gothic Revival: An Essay in the History of Taste*, third edition (London: John Murray, 1962); Paul Frankl's *The Gothic: Literary Sources and Interpretations through Eight Centuries* (Princeton, New Jersey: Princeton University Press, 1960); Christopher Hussey's *The Picturesque: Studies in a Point of View* (1927, reprinted London: Frank Cass, 1967); 'The First Gothic Revival and the Return to Nature' in Arthur O. Lovejoy's *Essays in the History of Ideas* (Baltimore: The Johns Hopkins Press, 1948); Stuart Piggott's *Ruins in a Landscape: Essays in Antiquarianism* (Edinburgh: Edinburgh University Press, 1976), particularly the title essay and the one on 'The Origins of the English County Archaeological Societies'; and Kenneth Woodbridge's *Landscape and Antiquity: Aspects of English Culture at Stourhead 1718 to 1838* (Oxford: Clarendon Press, 1970). Unfortunately Malcolm Andrews' *The Search for the Picturesque: Landscape, Aesthetics and Tourism in Britain, 1760–1800* (Aldershot: Scolar Press, 1989) appeared too late to help me in my work, though I am glad of the opportunity to recommend it.

Of the many works about Stonehenge, I am particularly indebted to Christopher Chippindale's witty and erudite *Stonehenge Complete* (London: Thames and Hudson, 1983), to Louis Hawes' *Constable's Stonehenge* (London: Her Majesty's Stationery Office, 1975) and to the relevant sections

of Stuart Piggott's *William Stukeley: An Eighteenth-Century Antiquary*
(Oxford: Clarendon Press, 1950).

92 **powers erected:** William Gilpin, *Observations on the Western Parts of
England, Relative Chiefly to Picturesque Beauty, To Which Are Added,
a Few Remarks on the Picturesque Beauties of the Isle of Wight* (London,
1798), 77.

93 **devil is it:** Canto 11, stanza 25 of *Don Juan*, edited by Truman Guy
Steffan and Willis W. Pratt, second edition, 4 volumes (Austin: University of Texas Press, 1971), 3, 280.

94 **one of the uprights:** see William Smith, *The Particular Description of
England. 1588. With Views of Some of the Chief Towns and Armorial
Bearings of Nobles and Bishops*, edited by Henry B. Wheatley and
Edmund W. Ashbee (London: privately issued, 1879), plate 22; also
reproduced as colour plate 1 in Chippindale, *Stonehenge*.

95 **pleasingly awful:** *Passages from the Diaries of Mrs Philip Lybbe Powys
of Hardwick House, Oxon. AD 1756 to 1808*, edited by Emily J.
Climenson (London, 1899), 53.

95 **them polished:** *Diaries of Mrs Powys*, 52.

96 **our laughing:** *Diaries of Mrs Powys*, 173–4.

96 **the hut:** John Smith, *Choir Gaur; The Grand Orrery of the Ancient
Druids, Commonly Called Stonehenge, on Salisbury Plain, Astronomically Explained, and Mathematically Proved to be a Temple Erected in
the Earliest Ages, for Observing the Motions of the Heavenly Bodies*
(Salisbury, 1771), 58.

98 **some 20,000:** for these figures see Chippindale, *Stonehenge*, 164 and
253.

99 **live again:** see Piggott, *Stukeley*, 15.

99 ***The Prelude:*** see A.L. Owen, *The Famous Druids: A Survey of Three
Centuries of English Literature on the Druids* (Oxford: Clarendon Press,
1962).

101 **Danish invasions:** see Clark, *Gothic Revival*, 236.

101 **Destroyers than Builders:** quoted by Briggs, *Goths and Vandals*,
107.

103 **sultry climate:** quoted by Clark, *Gothic Revival*, 36–7.

103 **Arts nor Learning:** quoted by Briggs, *Goths and Vandals*, 107.

104 **fantastical and licentious:** John Evelyn, *Account of Architects and
Architecture* (1697), quoted by Lovejoy, *Essays*, 138.

104 ***Cut-Work* and *Crinkle-Crankle*:** quoted by Lovejoy, *Essays*, 138.

104 **Proportion, Use or Beauty:** quoted by Lovejoy, *Essays*, 138.

105 **impervious to the sunbeams:** Tobias Smollett, *The Expedition of
Humphry Clinker*, edited by Lewis M. Knapp, Oxford English Novels
(London: Oxford University Press, 1966), 180.

105 **through his shoulder:** Smollett, *Humphry Clinker*, 181.

106 **vile and barbarous:** Arthur Young, *A Six Weeks Tour through the Southern Counties of England and Wales* (London, 1768), 92.

106 **great or pleasing:** Arthur Young, *A Six Months Tour through the North of England*, 4 volumes (London, 1770), 1, 200.

107 **unletter'd vulgar:** William Mason, *The English Garden: A Poem in Four Books* (York, 1783), Book 1, lines 355–71.

107 **superstition are in ruin:** Sir Uvedale Price, *An Essay on the Picturesque*, quoted by Piggott, *Ruins in a Landscape*, 120.

107 **Oliver Cromwell:** *The Torrington Diaries: Containing the Tours through England and Wales of the Hon. John Byng (Later Fifth Viscount Torrington) between the Years 1781 and 1794*, edited by C. Bruyn Andrews, 4 volumes (London: Eyre and Spottiswoode, 1934–8), 1, 6.

107 **really committed:** *Torrington Diaries*, 1, 6.

108 **priory stood:** *Torrington Diaries*, 2, 359–60.

108 **and brambles:** *Torrington Diaries*, 3, 56.

109 **pull'd down:** *Torrington Diaries*, 1, 297n.

109 **industrial degradation:** see *Wild Wales*, in *The Works of George Borrow*, edited by Clement Shorter, Norwich Edition, 16 volumes (London: Constable, 1923–4), 13, 397–400.

109 **family seat:** *Torrington Diaries*, 1, 294.

109 **oiled paper:** E. D. Clarke, *A Tour through the South of England, Wales, and Part of Ireland, Made in 1791* (London, 1793), 191.

109 **impended over it:** *The Journeys of Sir Richard Colt Hoare through England and Wales 1793–1810*, edited by M. W. Thompson (Gloucester: Alan Sutton, 1983), 211. Hoare's comments about Margam are also quoted by Woodbridge, *Landscape and Antiquity*, 170.

109 **sad relics:** *Journeys of Hoare*, 211.

110 **for repairs:** *Torrington Diaries*, 2, 158.

110 **dwelt therein:** *Torrington Diaries*, 2, 163.

110 **abbey wall:** contemporary account quoted by *Memorials of the Abbey of St Mary of Fountains*, edited by John Richard Walbram, Volume 2, Part 1, published as Volume 67 of *The Publications of the Surtees Society* (Durham, London and Edinburgh, 1878), 120.

111 **body of it:** quoted by *Memorials of Fountains*, 108.

112 **style of improvement:** Thomas Pennant, *A Tour from Alston-Moor to Harrowgate, and Brimham Crags* (London, 1804), 74.

113 **ceaselessly regretted:** *Memorials of Fountains*, 121.

113 **noble ruin:** Young, *North of England*, 2, 322–3.

113 **it's execution:** William Gilpin, *Observations, Relative Chiefly to Picturesque Beauty, Made in the Year 1772, on Several Parts of England: Particularly the Mountains, and Lakes of Cumberland, and Westmoreland*, 2 volumes (London, 1786), 2, 181.

113 **trim polish:** Gilpin, *Mountains and Lakes*, 2, 184.

114 **formal framework:** see Christopher Hussey, *English Gardens and Land-scapes 1700–1750* (London: Country Life, 1967), 138.

114 **flowering shrubs:** Gilpin, *Mountains and Lakes*, 2, 187.

114 **human industry:** Gilpin, *Mountains and Lakes*, 2, 187.

114 **awkward patchwork:** Gilpin, *Mountains and Lakes*, 2, 186.

114 **be obtained:** Gilpin, *Mountains and Lakes*, 2, 186.

114 **heathen statue:** Gilpin, *Mountains and Lakes*, 2, 188.

114 **in the valley:** Gilpin, *Mountains and Lakes*, 2, 187.

114 **about eighteen inches:** see *Memorials of Fountains*, 110.

114 **chief extravagancies:** *Memorials of Fountains*, 112.

115 **too spruce:** *Torrington Diaries*, 3, 47.

115 **melancholy reflexion:** *Torrington Diaries*, 3, 48.

115 **wonderfully done:** *Torrington Diaries*, 3, 47.

116 **than of art:** Gilpin, *Mountains and Lakes*, 2, 188.

116 **architectural evidence:** see M. W. Thompson, *Ruins: Their Preservation and Display* (London: British Museum Publications, 1981), 20–1.

117 **defaced and ruined:** quoted by Harold Brakspear and Morton Evans, *Tintern Abbey, Monmouthshire* (London: His Majesty's Stationery Office, 1908), 51.

117 **fury and indecency:** Charles Heath, *Historical and Descriptive Accounts of the Ancient and Present State of Tintern Abbey* (Monmouth, not dated), not paginated. The preface is dated 1801.

117 **considerable height:** Heath, *Tintern Abbey*, not paginated.

117 **survived at all:** see the description of Tintern in Francis Grose, *The Antiquities of England*, 4 volumes (London, 1773–6), 4, not paginated.

118 **of the natives:** Rev. Stebbing Shaw, *A Tour to the West of England, in 1788* (London, 1789), 204.

118 **bring with them:** Heath, *Tintern Abbey*, not paginated.

118 **chearful solitude:** Gilpin, *Mountains and Lakes*, 2, 180.

118 **piece of scenery:** William Gilpin, *Observations on the River Wye, and Several Parts of South Wales &c. Relative Chiefly to Picturesque Beauty; Made in the Summer of the Year 1770* (London, 1782), 32.

118 **shabby houses:** Gilpin, *River Wye*, 33.

119 **readers complained ... idealised aquatints:** see Barbier, *Gilpin*, 71.

121 **wretchedness within:** Gilpin, *River Wye*, 36.

121 **many cripples:** *Torrington Diaries*, 1, 271.

121 ***temporary inhabitants*:** Heath, *Tintern Abbey*, not paginated.

122 **confound the perspective:** Gilpin, *River Wye*, 32–3.

122 **King's College Chapel:** *The Seven Lamps of Architecture*, in *The Works of John Ruskin*, edited by E. T. Cook and Alexander Wedderburn, Library Edition, 39 volumes (London: George Allen, 1903–12), 8, 164.

122 **formal appearance:** William Coxe, *An Historical Tour in Monmouth-shire; Illustrated with Views by Sir R. C. Hoare, Bart.*, 2 volumes (London, 1801), 2, 352.

124 **undoubtedly *does*:** Gilpin, *River Wye*, 35.

124 **details of the carvings:** see Henry Penruddocke Wyndham, *A Gentleman's Tour through Monmouthshire and Wales in the Months of June and July 1774* (London, 1775), 4–5.

124 **brokenness and irregularity:** Samuel Ireland, *Picturesque Views on the River Wye, from Its Source at Plinlimmon Hill to Its Junction with the Severn below Chepstow: with Observations on the Public Buildings, and Other Works of Art, in Its Vicinity* (London, 1797), 137.

124 **do there:** *Torrington Diaries*, 1, 24.

124 **decayed Abbey:** Grose, *Antiquities*, 2, not paginated.

124 **guess or explore:** Grose: *Antiquities*, 2, not paginated.

124 **tales of the nursery:** Grose, *Antiquities*, 2, not paginated.

124 **ruin to appear in:** Young, *North of England*, 2, 323.

125 **limits of reality:** Young, *North of England*, 2, 324.

125 **thrown it into:** Young, *North of England*, 2, 325.

125 **torch below:** Joseph Cottle, *Reminiscences of Samuel Taylor Coleridge and Robert Southey* (London, 1847), 34.

125 **minor key:** Preface to the second edition of *The Seven Lamps*, in *Works of Ruskin*, 8, 8.

129 **finishing to a ruin:** Gilpin, *River Wye*, 33–4.

4 RASH ASSAULT

Three studies of attitudes to nature and landscape have been particularly useful to me: Keith Thomas, *Man and the Natural World: Changing Attitudes in England 1500–1800* (London: Allen Lane, 1983), notably chapter 7; Marjorie Hope Nicolson, *Mountain Gloom and Mountain Glory: The Development of the Aesthetics of the Infinite* (Ithaca, New York: Cornell University Press, 1959); and John Barrell, *The Idea of Landscape and the Sense of Place 1730–1840: An Approach to the Poetry of John Clare* (Cambridge: Cambridge University Press, 1972), whose comments about the viewpoint of the tourist influences my discussion here as well as in my introduction. My account of the Picturesque movement continues the debt to Christopher Hussey's *The Picturesque* and Carl Paul Barbier's *William Gilpin* noted in my previous chapter.

The best general history of the Lake District I have found is the volume by Roy Millward and Adrian Robinson in the Regions of Britain series (London: Eyre and Spottiswoode, 1970). Norman Nicholson's *The Lakers: The Adventures of the First Tourists* (London: Robert Hale, 1955) is lively and thoughtful but often wayward in its handling of detail. Reliable detail about Pocklington's Island, Belle Isle and other episodes in the history of the Lakes is best found in W. J. B. Owen and Jane Worthington Smyser's annotation to their complete edition of Wordsworth's prose works and in the various items by Peter Bicknell, all cited more fully in my notes below. Peter Bicknell's edition, *The Illustrated Wordsworth's Guide to the Lakes* (Exeter: Webb and Bower, 1984), which reprints the Kendal and Windermere Railway letters as an appendix, is a rich mine of information about the Lake District in the visual arts.

The phrase 'rash assault' in my chapter title comes, of course, from Wordsworth's sonnet opposing the Kendal and Windermere railway line.

130 **another world:** *A Relation of a Short Survey of 26 Counties Observed in a Seven Weeks Journey Begun on August 11, 1634 by a Captain, a Lieutenant, and an Ancient All Three of the Military Company in Norwich*, edited by L. G. Wickham Legg (London: F. E. Robinson, 1904), 41.

132 **Mount, and Pit:** Thomas Hobbes, *De Mirabilibus Pecci: Being the Wonders of the Peak in Darby-shire, Commonly Called The Devil's Arse of Peak. In English and Latine. The Latine Written by Thomas Hobbes of Malmsbury. The English by a Person of Quality* (London, 1678), 14; quoted by Nicolson, *Mountain Gloom*, 63.

132 **shames and Ills:** Charles Cotton, *The Wonders of the Peake* (London, 1681), 76; quoted by Nicolson, *Mountain Gloom*, 67.

132 *Warts ... Wens ...* **imposthumated boyles:** Cotton, *Wonders*, 1 and 2; quoted by Nicolson, *Mountain Gloom*, 66.

132 **houling Wilderness:** Daniel Defoe, *A Tour thro' the Whole Island of Great Britain*, with an introduction by G. D. H. Cole, 2 volumes (London: Frank Cass, 1968), 2, 567.

133 *Wonderless* **Wonders of the Peak:** Defoe, *Tour*, 2, 576.

133 **varieties of furniture:** *Journal of a Three Weeks Tour in 1797 through Derbyshire to the Lakes by a Gentleman of the University of Oxford*, as paraphrased in William Mavor, *The British Tourists; or Traveller's Pocket Companion, through England, Wales, Scotland, and Ireland. Comprehending the Most Celebrated Tours in the British Islands*, 6 volumes (London, 1798–1800), 5, 221. Moir in *The Discovery of Britain* and Nicholson in *The Lakers* follow the British Library catalogue in identifying the anonymous author as J. Grant, otherwise unknown.

133 **pedantic puppy:** *The Torrington Diaries: Containing the Tours through England and Wales of the Hon. John Byng (Later Fifth Viscount Torrington) between the Years 1781 and 1794*, edited by C. Bruyn Andrews, 4 volumes (London: Eyre and Spottiswoode, 1934–8), 2, 62.

133 **petrified spars:** *Pride and Prejudice*, in *The Novels of Jane Austen*, edited by R. W. Chapman, third edition, 5 volumes (London: Oxford University Press, 1933), 2, 239.

133 **colour of Blue John:** Richard Warner, *A Tour through the Northern Counties of England, and the Borders of Scotland*, 2 volumes (Bath, 1802), 1, 176.

133 **keep her:** Cotton, *Wonders*, 6.

133 **Strangers the Place:** *Four Topographical Letters, Written in July 1755, upon a Journey through Bedfordshire, Northamptonshire, Leicestershire, Nottinghamshire, Derbyshire, Warwickshire, &c. from a Gentleman of London, to His Brother and Sister in Town: Giving a Description of the Country thro' Which He Pass'd; with Observations on Every Thing That Occurred to Him, Either Curious or Remarkable* (Newcastle upon Tyne, 1757), 38.

133 **comes to visit:** *Four Topographical Letters*, 25–6.

133 **little Town:** Defoe, *Tour*, 2, 579.

133 **wretched Countenances:** *Four Topographical Letters*, 27.

134 **among the whole:** *Three Weeks Tour* in Mavor, *British Tourists*, 5, 233.

136 **the Chancel:** William Bray, *Tour through Some of the Midland Counties, into Derbyshire and Yorkshire by William Bray, F.A.S. Performed in 1777* (1783), as paraphrased in Mavor, *British Tourists*, 2, 338–9.

136 **mouth of the cave:** Hon. Mrs Murray [Sarah Aust], *A Companion and Useful Guide to the Beauties of Scotland, to the Lakes of Westmorland, Cumberland, and Lancashire; and to the Curiosities in the District of Craven in the West Riding of Yorkshire. To Which Is Added, a More Particular Description of Scotland, Especially That Part of It, Called the Highlands* (London, 1799), 8.

136 **confederate furies:** *Three Weeks Tour* in Mavor, *British Tourists*, 5, 232–3.

136 **rock asunder:** *Three Weeks Tour* in Mavor, *British Tourists*, 5, 232.

137 **Imps of Darkness:** *Four Topographical Letters*, 27.

137 **witches in *Macbeth*:** see, for example, William MacRitchie, *Diary of a Tour through Great Britain in 1795*, with an introduction and notes by David MacRitchie (London, 1897), 55.

137 **crossing the Styx:** *Three Weeks Tour* in Mavor, *British Tourists*, 5, 232.

137 **begun to inspire:** Carl Philip Moritz, *Journeys of a German in England in 1782*, translated and edited by Reginald Nettel (London: Jonathan Cape, 1965), 161.

137 **avengers of murder:** *Three Weeks Tour* in Mavor, *British Tourists*, 5, 222.

137 **to our eyes:** *Three Weeks Tour* in Mavor, *British Tourists*, 5, 231.

138 **mind together:** Thomas West, *A Tour to the Caves, in the Environs of Ingleborough and Settle, in the West-Riding of Yorkshire. With Some Philosophical Conjectures on the Deluge and the Alterations on the Surface and Interior Parts of the Earth Occasioned by This Great Revolution of Nature* (London, 1780), 11.

139 **before us:** John Housman, *A Descriptive Tour, and Guide to the Lakes, Caves, Mountains, and Other Natural Curiosities in Cumberland, Westmoreland, Lancashire, and a Part of the West Riding of Yorkshire* (Carlisle, 1800), 36.

139 **not without shuddering:** *The Works of Thomas Gray; Containing His*

Poems, and Correspondence with Several Eminent Literary Characters. To Which Are Added, Memoirs of His Life and Writings, by W. Mason, M.A., third edition, 2 volumes (London, 1807), 2, 287.

139 **awful, great, and grand:** West, *Caves*, 33.

140 **falling water:** Murray, *Companion*, 30.

140 **Sublime on canvas:** see Edward J. Nygren's study, *James Ward's Gordale Scar: An Essay in the Sublime* (London: Tate Gallery, 1982).

141 **trembling visitant:** Housman, *Descriptive Tour*, 23–4.

142 **broken world:** Thomas Burnet, sixth edition (1726) of *The Sacred Theory of the Earth*, quoted by Nicolson, *Mountain Gloom*, 200. Burnet first published his work in Latin as *Telluris Theoria Sacra* in 1681 and issued his first English version in 1684. I am indebted to Nicolson's discussion of Burnet in chapter 5 of *Mountain Gloom*. Wordsworth and Coleridge were among later writers who kept the memory of Burnet's work alive, taking particular interest in his untranslated Latin chapter 'De Montibus'.

142 **Rocks, and Cliffs:** Burnet, quoted by Nicolson, *Mountain Gloom*, 206.

142 **Gothic taste:** *Four Topographical Letters*, 28.

142 **ruined castle:** *Three Weeks Tour* in Mavor, *British Tourists*, 5, 213.

142 **Castle Rock:** for a striking example of a description of Castle Rock as a Gothic ruin, see William Hutchinson, *An Excursion to the Lakes, in Westmoreland and Cumberland, August 1773* (London, 1774), 104–5.

143 **Preserver of the Universe:** Thomas Hurtley, *A Concise Account of Some Natural Curiosities in the Environs of Malham in Craven, Yorkshire* (London, 1786), 59.

143 **desultory Tourist:** Hurtley, *Craven*, 28.

143 *Immensity* **united:** Hurtley, *Craven*, 63.

143 **immensity united:** John Brown, *Description of the Lake and Vale of Keswick*, reprinted in and here quoted from Hutchinson, *Excursion*, 110n. Apparently first published at Newcastle in 1767, the letter became famous by being reprinted in other sources, including West's *Guide* as well as Hutchinson; see Barbier, *Gilpin*, 40, n2, for an interesting note on Brown and his connection with Gilpin.

143 **poor miniatures:** Brown, in Hutchinson, *Excursion*, 108n.

143 **excessively disappointed:** *Pride and Prejudice*, in *Novels of Austen*, 2, 239.

146 **sequestered spots:** *A Guide through the District of the Lakes*, in *The Prose Works of William Wordsworth*, edited by W. J. B. Owen and Jane Worthington Smyser, 3 volumes (Oxford: Clarendon Press, 1974), 2, 207. The text used here, and cited throughout this chapter, is that of the fifth edition (1835).

146 **thing neamed:** *Kendal and Windermere Railway. Two Letters Re-Printed from the Morning Post,* in *Prose Works of Wordsworth*, 3, 342. The letters appeared in the newspaper in 1844 and as a pamphlet twice

issued in 1845. The text used here, and cited throughout this chapter, is that of the second pamphlet issue.

146 **lap of Horrour**: William Gilpin, *Observations, Relative Chiefly to Picturesque Beauty, Made in the Year 1772, on Several Parts of England; Particularly the Mountains, and Lakes of Cumberland, and Westmoreland*, 2 volumes (London, 1786), 1, 183.

146 **primeval horror**: *Three Weeks Tour* in Mavor, *British Tourists*, 5, 271.

147 **overwhelm a caravan**: *Works of Gray*, 2, 263.

147 **every summer's day**: Robert Southey, *Letters from England: By Don Manuel Alvarez Espriella. Translated from the Spanish*, second edition, 3 volumes (London, 1808), 2, 162.

147 **terrify below**: Gilpin, *Mountains and Lakes*, 1, 187.

147 **heard of**: Gilpin, *Mountains and Lakes*, 1, 188.

148 **above the water**: Gilpin, *Mountains and Lakes*, 1, 188.

148 **high-colouring**: the term is used by Gilpin in an interesting discussion of the degree of exaggeration proper to picturesque observation, in *Mountains and Lakes*, 1, xix.

148 **horrid uproar**: Hutchinson, *Excursion*, 160.

149 **presumption and impiety**: Hutchinson, *Excursion*, 160.

150 **awful scene**: Hutchinson, *Excursion*, as paraphrased in Mavor, *British Tourists*, 2, 276.

150 **crush of worlds**: *Three Weeks Tour* in Mavor, *British Tourists*, 5, 268.

150 **discharge of the guns**: Hutchinson, *Excursion*, 70.

150 **into the Lake**: Hutchinson, *Excursion*, 70–1.

150 **general ruin**: Gilpin, *Mountains and Lakes*, 2, 61.

150 **agitation of a storm**: Gilpin, *Mountains and Lakes*, 2, 61.

150 **thousand symphonies**: Gilpin, *Mountains and Lakes*, 2, 62.

151 **desires it**: James Clarke, *A Survey of the Lakes of Cumberland, Westmorland and Lancashire: Together with an Account, Historical, Topographical, and Descriptive, of the Adjacent Country. To Which Is Added, a Sketch of the Border Laws and Customs* (London, 1787), 25.

151 **varied tones**: Clarke, *Survey*, 26.

151 **reach of art**: Clarke, *Survey*, 26.

151 **for the purpose**: West, *Caves*, 14.

151 **tumble into ruins**: Warner, *Northern Counties*, 1, 170.

152 **soldier's daughter**: Edward Baines, *A Companion to the Lakes of Cumberland, Westmoreland and Lancashire; in a Descriptive Account of a Family Tour, and Excursions on Horseback and on Foot. With a New, Copious, and Correct Itinerary*, third edition (London, 1834), 134–5.

152 **shilling and sixpence**: see James Plumptre, 'A Narrative of a Pedestrian Journey through Some Parts of Yorkshire, Durham and Northumberland to the Highlands of Scotland and Home by the Lakes and Some Parts of Wales in the Summer of the Year 1799', 3 volumes (unpublished manuscript, Cambridge University Library Add. 5814–16), 3, 21.

152 **traveller can indulge:** Southey, *Letters from England*, 2, 153.

152 **will be lost:** John Robinson, *A Guide to the Lakes in Cumberland, Westmorland and Lancashire, Illustrated with Twenty Views of Local Scenery, and a Travelling Map of the Adjacent Country* (London, 1819), 134.

152 **super-extra-double-superfine:** Southey, *Letters from England*, 2, 153.

152 **consistent whole:** *Guide*, in *Prose Works of Wordsworth*, 2, 181.

153 **Richard Payne Knight:** Hussey, *The Picturesque*, especially chapter 3, has a useful account of Burke's *Philosophical Enquiry into the Origin of Our Ideas of the Sublime and Beautiful* and the exchanges between Price and Knight.

153 **pleases the eye:** quoted by Barbier, *Gilpin*, 98.

154 *in a picture*: William Gilpin, *Observations on the Western Parts of England, Relative Chiefly to Picturesque Beauty. To Which Are Added, a Few Remarks on the Picturesque Beauties of the Isle of Wight* (London, 1798), 328.

154 **impending mountains:** Brown, in Hutchinson, *Excursion*, 110–11n.

154 **landscape:** see OED, s.v. 'landscape', and the discussion of the word's meanings in Barrell, *Idea of Landscape*, 1–3.

155 **thousand pounds:** *Works of Gray*, 2, 267–8.

155 **among the mountains:** Thomas West, *A Guide to the Lakes: Dedicated to the Lovers of Landscape Studies, and to All Who Have Visited, or Intend to Visit the Lakes in Cumberland, Westmorland, and Lancashire* (London, 1778), 15.

155 **recommended by guidebooks:** see, for example, Joseph Mawman, *An Excursion to the Highlands of Scotland, and the English Lakes, with Recollections, Descriptions, and References to Historical Fact* (London, 1805), 235.

155 **science demonstrate:** West, *Lakes*, 15.

155 *correctly picturesque*: Gilpin, *Mountains and Lakes*, 1, 119.

156 **unequal in composition:** William Gilpin, *Observations on the River Wye, and Several Parts of South Wales &c. Relative Chiefly to Picturesque Beauty; Made in the Summer of the Year 1770* (London, 1782), 18.

156 **within its scope:** Gilpin, *River Wye*, 18.

156 *The Seasons*: the hilltop view is discussed in Barrell, *Idea of Landscape*, particularly 21–7.

156 **poor and diminutive:** *Works of Gray*, 2, 267.

156 **all prospects:** William Mason, in *Works of Gray*, 2, 267n.

156 **levelled ... elevated:** Gilpin, *Mountains and Lakes*, 1, 96.

157 *vallies*: Gilpin, *Mountains and Lakes*, 1, 103.

157 **water boundary:** Gilpin, *Mountains and Lakes*, 1, 95–6.

157 **islands:** see Gilpin, *Mountains and Lakes*, 1, 97.

157 **shining round them:** West, *Lakes*, 89–90.

157 **to the left:** West, *Lakes*, 7.

158 **magnificent lake:** West, *Lakes*, 59–60.

158 **at your feet:** West, *Lakes*, 50–1.

158 **West's guide:** Plumptre, 'Pedestrian Journey 1799', 2, 288.

158 **his friends:** Jonathan Otley, *A Concise Description of the English Lakes* (Keswick, 1823), 16.

159 **most becoming attire:** *Works of Gray*, 2, 273.

160 **on this head:** Plumptre, 'Pedestrian Journey 1799', 2, 252.

160 **king's dominions:** Arthur Young, *A Six Months Tour through the North of England*, 4 volumes (London, 1770), 3, 176.

160 **be conceived:** Gilpin, *Mountains and Lakes*, 1, 135.

161 **shewing too much:** Gilpin, *Mountains and Lakes*, 1, 137.

161 **middle of the island:** Gilpin, *Mountains and Lakes*, 1, 138.

161 **sycamore grove:** West, *Lakes*, 63.

161 **apparently in 1773:** most scholarly sources give 1774 as the date when English began operations, apparently on the assumption that Hutchinson, whom I quote below, saw the work in progress that year; in fact, he came in August 1773.

162 **beauty of the country:** *Kendal and Windermere Railway*, in *Prose Works of Wordsworth*, 3, 342.

162 **left undone:** Gilpin, *Mountains and Lakes*, 1, 139n.

162 **Dutch Burgomaster's palace:** Hutchinson, *Excursion*, 178.

163 **high wind:** Clarke, *Survey*, 139.

163 **Isabella Curwen:** see Humphrey Ward and W. Roberts, *Romney: A Biographical and Critical Essay with a Catalogue Raisonné of His Works*, 2 volumes (London: Thomas Agnew and Sons, 1904), 2, 29.

163 **towards its beauties:** Housman, *Descriptive Tour*, 168.

163 **Nottinghamshire:** *Kendal and Windermere Railway*, in *Prose Works of Wordsworth*, 3, 342. In fact, Pocklington came from a banking family in the Newark area.

163 ***tea-garden taste*:** Plumptre, 'Pedestrian Journey 1799', 3, 7.

164 **grievous eye-sore:** William Green, *The Tourist's New Guide, Containing a Description of the Lakes, Mountains, and Scenery, in Cumberland, Westmorland, and Lancashire, with Some Account of Their Bordering Towns and Villages. Being the Result of Observations Made during a Residence of Eighteen Years in Ambleside and Keswick*, 2 volumes (Kendal, 1819), 2, 64.

164 **had been, and was:** *Guide*, in *Prose Works of Wordsworth*, 2, 209.

165 **1796:** most modern sources are reluctant to offer an exact date for Pocklington's sale of his island to Peachy. I take 1796 from Bicknell's edition of Wordsworth's *Guide*, 54.

165 **puerilities:** *Guide*, in *Prose Works of Wordsworth*, 2, 209.

165 **pleasure-grounds:** Baines, *Companion to Lakes*, 127.

165 **upon his island:** Green, *Tourist's New Guide*, 2, 64.

165 **King Pocky:** *The Notebooks of Samuel Taylor Coleridge*, edited by

Kathleen Coburn, 3 volumes (London: Routledge and Kegan Paul, 1957–73), 1, part 1, 542.

165 **white-washed house:** *Three Weeks Tour* in Mavor, *British Tourists*, 5, 271.

165 **each gate:** Plumptre, 'Pedestrian Journey 1799', 2, 305.

165 **white and scarlet:** Plumptre, 'Pedestrian Journey 1799', 2, 309.

167 **old woman:** Southey, *Letters from England*, 2, 164–5.

167 **profitable trade:** Green, *Tourist's New Guide*, 2, 133–4.

167 **nature's images:** Green, *Tourist's New Guide*, 2, 134.

167 **which he belongs:** Green, *Tourist's New Guide*, 2, 134.

168 **acquainted with society:** West, *Lakes*, 103.

168 **some halfpence:** Ann Radcliffe, *A Journey Made in the Summer of 1794, through Holland and the Western Frontier of Germany, with a Return down the Rhine: To Which Are Added Observations during a Tour to the Lakes of Lancashire, Westmoreland, and Cumberland* (London, 1795), 397.

168 **account of illness:** *Three Weeks Tour* in Mavor, *British Tourists*, 5, 263.

168 **officiate as guide:** Joseph Budworth, *A Fortnight's Ramble to the Lakes in Westmoreland, Lancashire, and Cumberland. By a Rambler*, first edition (London, 1792), 111. Budworth changed his name in 1811, and so is sometimes remembered as Joseph Palmer.

168 **great people:** Budworth, *Fortnight's Ramble*, first edition, 117–18.

169 **aged parent:** Radcliffe, *Journey*, 461.

169 **well informed:** James Denholm, *A Tour to the Principal Scotch and English Lakes* (Glasgow, 1804), 282.

169 **bitter enemies:** Plumptre, 'Pedestrian Journey 1799', 2, 303.

169 **criticised Pocklington's Island:** see Plumptre, 'Pedestrian Journey 1799', 2, 304.

169 **rank and fashion:** quoted by Nicholson, *Lakers*, 107.

172 **use in Cumberland:** Plumptre, 'Pedestrian Journey 1799', 2, 303.

172 **Guides of the Lakes:** Plumptre, 'Pedestrian Journey 1799', 3, 25.

172 **accurate information:** *Guide*, in *Prose Works of Wordsworth*, 2, 158n.

172 **representations of his country:** quoted in the useful short catalogue note on Green in Peter Bicknell and Robert Woof, *The Lake District Discovered 1810–1850: The Artists, The Tourists and Wordsworth* (Grasmere: Trustees of Dove Cottage, 1983), 36.

172 **pleasurable enjoyment:** Gilpin, *Mountains and Lakes*, 2, 68.

173 **row on:** Budworth, *Fortnight's Ramble*, first edition, xii.

173 **dishonest means:** Gilpin, *Mountains and Lakes*, 2, 67.

173 **pastoral simplicity:** Plumptre, 'Pedestrian Journey 1799', 2, 267.

174 **Maid of Buttermere:** Wordsworth, Book 7, line 321 of the 1805–6 text of *The Prelude*, edited by Ernest de Selincourt, second edition, revised by Helen Darbishire (Oxford: Clarendon Press, 1959), 236. In my account I am indebted to chapter 6 of Nicholson, *Lakers*, which points out that

contemporaries viewed Mary Robinson's fate as 'a kind of allegory' (75) of the destruction of the old society by the new, and to Donald H. Reiman, 'The Beauty of Buttermere as Fact and Romantic Symbol', *Criticism*, 26 (Spring 1984), 139–70.

174 **as a phenomenon:** Budworth, *Fortnight's Ramble*, first edition, 202.

174 **very comfortably:** Murray, *Companion*, 19.

175 **of the valley:** Budworth, *Fortnight's Ramble*, first edition, 203.

175 **against his return:** see *Three Weeks Tour*, in Mavor, *British Tourists*, 5, 275–6.

175 **upon your guard:** Joseph Budworth, *A Fortnight's Ramble to the Lakes in Westmoreland, Lancashire, and Cumberland*, third edition (London, 1810), 407. Budworth's description of his second visit to Buttermere, originally published in *The Gentleman's Magazine* for January 1800, is reprinted as an appendix to this edition. His final thoughts on Mary's fate, written after her betrayal by Hatfield, are also added as a note to the text.

176 **sad fate:** Denholm, *Scotch and English Lakes*, 298.

176 **public notice:** Book 7, lines 337–9 of the 1805–6 text of *The Prelude*, 238.

176 **ready utterance:** Green, *Tourist's New Guide*, 2, 185.

176 **bold bad Man:** Wordsworth drew the phrase from Spenser's *The Faerie Queene* and used it of Hatfield in Book 7, line 322 of the 1805–6 text of *The Prelude*, 238.

177 **blush unseen:** Budworth, *Fortnight's Ramble*, third edition, 254n.

177 **would astonish:** Young, *North of England*, 3, 155–6.

178 **infection of the age:** Book 11, line 156 of the 1805–6 text of *The Prelude*, 438.

178 **above all art:** Book 11, lines 153–5 of the 1805–6 text of *The Prelude*, 438.

178 **acting joys ... dizzying raptures:** 'Lines Composed a Few Miles above Tintern Abbey', lines 84 and 85, in *The Poetical Works of William Wordsworth*, edited by Ernest de Selincourt and Helen Darbishire, 5 volumes (Oxford: Clarendon Press, 1940–9), 2, 261.

178 **through all things:** 'Tintern Abbey', lines 94–102, in *Poetical Works of Wordsworth*, 2, 261–2.

179 **impressive scenery:** Warner, *Northern Counties*, 2, 100–1.

179 *lions* **of the lakes:** Baines, *Companion*, 185.

179 *Iteriad:* see *The Works of John Ruskin*, edited by E. T. Cook and Alexander Wedderburn, Library Edition, 39 volumes (London: George Allen, 1903–12), 2, 297. A later passage in the *Iteriad* (not printed in full by Cook and Wedderburn but quoted at 2, 315, n2) describes a rather less impressive glimpse of Wordsworth in Rydal chapel.

180 **coarsest order:** *Harriet Martineau's Autobiography*, third edition, 3 volumes (London, 1877), 2, 240.

180 **lake scenery:** *Martineau's Autobiography*, 2, 241–2.

180 **2,500 names:** see Bicknell and Woof, *Lake District Discovered*, 82.

180 **five hundred people a year:** *Martineau's Autobiography*, 2, 241.

181 **Barrell:** *Idea of Landscape*, 183, which quotes the passage from 'Michael' I go on to discuss.

182 **of their own:** 'Michael', lines 1–8, in *Poetical Works of Wordsworth*, 2, 80–1.

182 **Claude and Poussin:** *Guide*, in *Prose Works of Wordsworth*, 2, 234.

182 **Turner:** *Guide*, in *Prose Works of Wordsworth*, 2, 156.

183 SALVATOR ROSA: **West,** *Lakes*, 14–15.

183 **peacefully led:** Guide, in *Prose Works of Wordsworth*, 2, 160.

183 **with more exactness:** Gilpin, *Mountains and Lakes*, 2, 10.

183 **cannot express:** *Works of Gray*, 2, 288n.

183 **my feelings:** *Descriptive Sketches*, in *Poetical Works of Wordsworth*, 1, 62.

184 *The Faerie Queene*: *Guide*, in *Prose Works of Wordsworth*, 2, 213.

184 **aid of verse:** *Guide*, in *Prose Works of Wordsworth*, 2, 183.

184 **Blea Tarn:** *Guide*, in *Prose Works of Wordsworth*, 2, 159–60.

184 **inland lakes:** *Guide*, in *Prose Works of Wordsworth*, 2, 179.

184 **migratory birds:** *Guide*, in *Prose Works of Wordsworth*, 2, 183.

184 **ode to Helvellyn:** *Guide*, in *Prose Works of Wordsworth*, 2, 234–44.

184 **Pass of Kirkstone:** *Guide*, in *Prose Works of Wordsworth*, 2, 251–3.

184 **love the bards:** Charles Mackay, *The Scenery and Poetry of the English Lakes. A Summer Ramble* (London, 1846), 25.

184 **the guide-books:** Mackay, *Scenery and Poetry*, 2.

185 **Wordsworth has preserved:** Harriet Martineau, *A Complete Guide to the English Lakes* (Windermere, 1855), 39.

185 **readers of Wordsworth:** Martineau, *Complete Guide*, 47.

189 **from profanation:** *Guide*, in *Prose Works of Wordsworth*, 2, 208.

189 **native beauty:** *Guide*, in *Prose Works of Wordsworth*, 2, 223.

189 **heart to enjoy:** *Guide*, in *Prose Works of Wordsworth*, 2, 225.

190 **admiration of posterity:** Gilpin, *Mountains and Lakes*, 2, 188.

190 **severe taxation:** Warner, *Northern Counties*, 2, 99.

191 **all persons of taste:** *Kendal and Windermere Railway*, in *Prose Works of Wordsworth*, 3, 340.

192 **worthily enjoy:** *Kendal and Windermere Railway*, in *Prose Works of Wordsworth*, 3, 355.

192 **margin of Windermere:** *Kendal and Windermere Railway*, in *Prose Works of Wordsworth*, 3, 345–6.

192 **races without number:** *Kendal and Windermere Railway*, in *Prose Works of Wordsworth*, 3, 346.

192 **class of innkeepers:** *Kendal and Windermere Railway*, in *Prose Works of Wordsworth*, 3, 346.

192 **excitements and recreations:** *Kendal and Windermere Railway*, in *Prose Works of Wordsworth*, 3, 346.

192 **steam merry-go-round:** 'The Extension of Railways in the Lake District:

A Protest', in *Works of Ruskin*, 34, 141. The essay originally appeared as the preface, dated 1876, to a miscellaneous collection of pamphlets by Robert Somervell, *A Protest against the Extension of Railways in the Lake District* (Windermere, 1877).

192 **modern tourists:** 'Extension of Railways', in *Works of Ruskin*, 34, 140.

192 **from a sack:** 'Extension of Railways', in *Works of Ruskin*, 34, 140.

192 **they are drunk:** 'Extension of Railways', in *Works of Ruskin*, 34, 142.

192 **thine own lays:** quoted by the editors of *Prose Works of Wordsworth*, 3, 332.

193 **desirable kind:** Martineau, *Complete Guide*, 141.

193 **refreshed and invigorated:** *Reports of the Railway Department of the Board of Trade on Schemes for Extending Railway Communications, and on Amalgamation of Railways* (London, 1845), quoted by the editors of *Prose Works of Wordsworth*, 3, 334.

193 **comprehensive education:** *Kendal and Windermere Railway*, in *Prose Works of Wordsworth*, 3, 342–3.

193 **rural imagery:** *Guide*, in *Prose Works of Wordsworth*, 2, 211.

193 **human nature:** *Guide*, in *Prose Works of Wordsworth*, 2, 211.

193 **varieties of rural nature:** *Kendal and Windermere Railway*, in *Prose Works of Wordsworth*, 3, 343.

194 **from one another:** *Kendal and Windermere Railway*, in *Prose Works of Wordsworth*, 3, 344.

194 **process of culture:** *Kendal and Windermere Railway*, in *Prose Works of Wordsworth*, 3, 349.

Works consulted

PRIMARY: TRAVEL BOOKS, GUIDE BOOKS, WORKS OF
LITERATURE, ETC. MAINLY WRITTEN BEFORE 1900

Addison, Joseph and others. *The Spectator.* Edited by Donald F. Bond. 5 volumes. Oxford: Clarendon Press, 1965.

Aikin, John. *England Delineated; or, A Geographical Description of Every County in England and Wales: with a Concise Account of Its Most Important Products, Natural and Artificial. For the Use of Young Persons.* Second edition. London, 1790.

Anon. *Black's Picturesque Tourist and Road-Book of England and Wales. With a General Travelling Map; Charts of Roads, Railroads, and Interesting Localities; and Engraved Views of the Scenery.* Edinburgh, 1843.

Anon. *History and Description of Woburn and Its Abbey.* London, 1890.

Anon. *Four Topographical Letters, Written in July 1755, upon a Journey through Bedfordshire, Northamptonshire, Leicestershire, Nottinghamshire, Derbyshire, Warwickshire, &c. from a Gentleman of London, to His Brother and Sister in Town: Giving a Description of the Country thro' Which He Pass'd; with Observations on Every Thing That Occurred to Him, Either Curious or Remarkable.* Newcastle upon Tyne, 1757.

Anon. *Journal of a Three Weeks Tour in 1797 through Derbyshire to the Lakes by a Gentleman of the University of Oxford*, paraphrased in Volume 5 of William Mavor, *The British Tourists; or Traveller's Pocket Companion, through England, Wales, Scotland, and Ireland. Comprehending the Most Celebrated Tours in the British Islands.* 6 volumes. London, 1798–1800.

Anon. *A New Description of the Pictures, Statues, Bustos, Basso Relievos, and Other Curiosities, in the Earl of Pembroke's House, at Wilton.* Ninth edition. Salisbury, 1779.

Anon. *A Relation of a Short Survey of 26 Counties Observed in a Seven Weeks*

Journey Begun on August 11, 1634 by a Captain, a Lieutenant and an Ancient All Three of the Military Company in Norwich. Edited by L. G. Wickham Legg. London: F. E. Robinson, 1904.

Anon. *Sylvan's Pictorial Handbook to the English Lakes*. London, 1847.

Austen, Jane. *The Novels of Jane Austen*. Edited by R. W. Chapman. Third edition. 5 volumes. London: Oxford University Press, 1933.

Bacon, Delia. *The Philosophy of the Plays of Shakespere Unfolded*. London, 1857.

Baedeker, Karl. *Great Britain: England, Wales, and Scotland as Far as Loch Maree and the Cromarty Firth. Handbook for Travellers*. First edition. Leipzig and London, 1887.

Great Britain: Handbook for Travellers. Third edition. Leipzig and London, 1894.

London and Its Environs, Including Excursions to Brighton, the Isle of Wight, etc.: Handbook for Travellers. First edition. Leipzig and London, 1878.

Baines, Edward. *A Companion to the Lakes of Cumberland, Westmoreland and Lancashire; in a Descriptive Account of a Family Tour, and Excursions on Horseback and on Foot. With a New, Copious, and Correct Itinerary*. Third edition. London, 1834.

Beaumont, George and Disney, Captain Henry. *A New Tour thro' England, Perform'd in the Summers of 1765, 1766, and 1767 ... Describing Whatever is Curious, in the Several Counties, Cities, Boroughs, Markets Towns, and Villages of Note in the Kingdom: Including All the Cathedral, Collegiate, and Parochial Churches; Palaces Antient and Modern; Seats of the Nobility and Gentry; Remains of British, Roman and Saxon Antiquities, Worthy the Inspection of Gentlemen or Others, Who Travel for Amusement, Instruction, or Business. With a New Map of England by Kitchen, Accurately Engraved, and Finely Coloured. With the Exact Distances by the Milstones*. London, [1768].

[Black, Adam and Charles]. *Black's Picturesque Tourist and Road-Book of England and Wales*. First edition. Edinburgh, 1843.

Black's Picturesque Tourist and Road and Railway Guide Book through England and Wales. Third edition. Edinburgh, 1853.

Black's Picturesque Tourist and Road and Railway Guide Book through England and Wales. Fourth edition. Edinburgh, 1862.

London and Its Environs: A Practical Guide to the Metropolis and Its Vicinity. First edition. Edinburgh, 1862.

Borrow, George. *The Works of George Borrow*. Edited by Clement Shorter. Norwich Edition. 16 volumes. London: Constable, 1923–4.

Boswell, James. *Life of Samuel Johnson*. Edited by George Birkbeck Hill and revised by L. F. Powell. 6 volumes. Oxford: Clarendon Press, 1934–50.

Bray, William. *Tour through Some of the Midland Counties, into Derbyshire and Yorkshire by William Bray, F.A.S. Performed in 1777* (1783), paraphrased in Volume 2 of William Mavor, *The British Tourists; or Traveller's Pocket Companion, through England, Wales, Scotland, and Ireland. Comprehending the Most Celebrated Tours in the British Islands.* 6 volumes. London, 1798–1800.

Brayley, Edward Wedlake. *The History and Antiquities of the Abbey Church of St Peter, Westminster.* Illustrated by John Preston Neale. 2 volumes. London, 1818–23.

Britton, John. *The Beauties of Wiltshire, Displayed in Statistical, Historical and Descriptive Sketches Illustrated by Views of Principal Seats &c., with Anecdotes of the Arts.* 3 volumes. London, 1801–25.

Picturesque Antiquities of the English Cities. London, 1830.

Browne, H. *An Illustration of Stonehenge and Abury, in the County of Wilts, Pointing out Their Origin and Character, through Considerations Hitherto Unnoticed.* Salisbury, 1823.

Buck, Samuel and Nathaniel. *Buck's Antiquities; or Venerable Remains of Above Four Hundred Castles, Monasteries, Palaces, &c., &c. in England and Wales.* 3 volumes. London, 1774.

Buckler, J. and Buckler, J. C. *Views of Eaton Hall in Cheshire, the Seat of the Right Honourable Earl of Grosvenor.* London, 1826.

Budworth, Joseph [Joseph Palmer]. *A Fortnight's Ramble to the Lakes in Westmoreland, Lancashire, and Cumberland. By a Rambler.* First edition. London, 1792.

A Fortnight's Ramble to the Lakes in Westmoreland, Lancashire, and Cumberland. Second edition. London, 1795.

A Fortnight's Ramble to the Lakes in Westmoreland, Lancashire, and Cumberland. Third edition. London, 1810.

Burney, Fanny. *The Journals and Letters of Fanny Burney (Madame D'Arblay).* Edited by Joyce Hemlow and others. 12 volumes. Oxford: Clarendon Press, 1972–84.

Byng, Hon. John. *The Torrington Diaries: Containing the Tours through England and Wales of the Hon. John Byng (Later Fifth Viscount Torrington) between the Years 1781 and 1794.* Edited by C. Bruyn Andrews. 4 volumes. London: Eyre and Spottiswoode, 1934–8.

Byron, George Gordon, Lord. *Don Juan.* Edited by Truman Guy Steffan and Willis W. Pratt. Second edition. 4 volumes. Austin: University of Texas Press, 1971.

Camden, William. *Britain, Or A Choro-Graphicall Description of the Most Flourishing Kingdomes, England, Scotland, and Ireland, and the Ilands Adioyning, out of the Depth of Antiquitie.* Translated by Philemon Holland. London, 1610.

The Historie of the Most Renowned and Victorious Princesse Elizabeth, Late Queene of England. London, 1630.

Campbell, Colen. *Vitruvius Britannicus or the British Architect, Containing the Plans, Elevations, and Sections of the Regular Buildings, both Publick and Private, in Great Britain.* 3 volumes. London, 1715–25.

Campbell, Colen and others. *Vitruvius Britannicus or the British Architect and The New Vitruvius Britannicus.* Edited by Paul Breman and Denise Addis. 4 volumes. New York: Benjamin Blom, 1967–72.

Cary, John. *Cary's Traveller's Companion, or a Delineation of the Turnpike Roads of England and Wales; Shewing the Immediate Rout to Every Market and Borough Town throughout the Kingdon. Laid Down from the Best Authorities, on a New Set of County Maps. To Which is Added an Alphabetical List of all the Market Towns, with the Days on Which They Are Held.* London, 1791.

Clarke, E.D. *A Tour through the South of England, Wales, and Part of Ireland, Made in 1791.* London, 1793.

Clarke, James. *A Survey of the Lakes of Cumberland, Westmorland and Lancashire: Together with an Account, Historical, Topographical, and Descriptive, of the Adjacent Country. To Which Is Added, a Sketch of the Border Laws and Customs.* London, 1787.

Cobbett, William. *Rural Rides in the Counties of Surrey, Kent, Sussex, Hampshire, Wiltshire, Gloucestershire, Herefordshire, Worcestershire, Somersetshire, Oxfordshire, Berkshire, Essex, Suffolk, Norfolk, and Hertfordshire: with Economical and Political Observations Relative to Matters Applicable to, and Illustrated by, the State of those Counties Respectively.* London, 1830.

Coleridge, Samuel Taylor. *The Notebooks of Samuel Taylor Coleridge.* Edited by Kathleen Coburn. 3 volumes. London: Routledge and Kegan Paul, 1957–73.

Combe, William. *The History of the Abbey Church of St Peter's Westminster, Its Antiquities and Monuments.* 2 volumes. London, 1812.

    The Second Tour of Doctor Syntax, in Search of Consolation. London, 1820.

    The Third Tour of Doctor Syntax, in Search of a Wife. A Poem. London, 1821.

    The Tour of Doctor Syntax in Search of the Picturesque. A Poem. Fifth edition. London, 1820.

Cook, Thomas. *Hand-Book of Belvoir Castle: Designed as a Guide to an Excursion Party from Leicester to Belvoir, Aug. 29, 1848; with a Description of the Route from Leicester, and Places of Interest in the Locality of the Castle.* Leicester, 1848.

Cotman, John Sell. *Specimens of Architectural Remains, in Various Counties in England, But Principally in Norfolk.* With notes by Dawson Turner and Thomas Rickman. 2 volumes. London, 1838.

Cottle, Joseph. *Reminiscences of Samuel Taylor Coleridge and Robert Southey.* London, 1847.

Cotton, Charles. *The Genuine Works of Charles Cotton, Esq.; Containing I. Scarronnides, or Virgil Travestie. II. Lucian Burlesqued, or the Scoffer Scoft. III. The Wonders of the Peake. IV. The Planters Manual.* London, 1715.

   The Wonders of the Peake. London, 1681.

Coxe, William. *An Historical Tour in Monmouthshire; Illustrated with Views by Sir R. C. Hoare, Bart.* 2 volumes. London, 1801.

Crull, J. *The Antiquities of St Peters, or the Abbey Church of Westminster.* London, 1711.

Dalton, John. *A Descriptive Poem Addressed to Two Ladies at their Return from Viewing the Mines near Whitehaven.* London, 1755.

Dart, John. *Westmonasterium: or The History and Antiquities of the Abbey Church of St Peter's Westminster.* 2 volumes. London, [1742].

Dayes, Edward. *The Works of the Late Edward Dayes Containing an Excursion through the Principal Parts of Derbyshire and Yorkshire.* Edited by E. W. Brayley. London, 1805.

Defoe, Daniel. *A Tour thro' the Whole Island of Great Britain.* With an introduction by G. D. H. Cole. 2 volumes. London: Frank Cass, 1968.

Denham, Sir John. *The Poetical Works of Sir John Denham.* Edited by Theodore Howard Banks, Jr. New Haven: Yale University Press, 1928.

Denholm, James. *A Tour to the Principal Scotch and English Lakes.* Glasgow, 1804.

Dibdin, Charles. *Observations on a Tour through Almost the Whole of England, and a Considerable Part of Scotland.* 2 volumes. London, not dated but in fact 1801.

Dickens, Charles. *The Nonesuch Dickens.* Edited by Arthur Waugh, Hugh Walpole, Walter Dexter and Thomas Hatton. 25 volumes. London: Nonesuch Press, 1937–8.

Dodd, S. *An Historical and Topographical Account of the Town of Woburn, Its Abbey, and Vicinity, Containing Also a Concise Genealogy of the House of Russell, and Memoirs of the Late Francis Duke of Bedford.* Woburn, 1818.

Dugdale, Sir William. *The Antiquities of Warwickshire, Illustrated. From Records, Leiger-Books, Manuscripts, Charters, Evidences, Tombes and Armes.* Coventry, 1765.

   Monasticon Anglicanum, or, The History of the Ancient Abbies, and Other Monasteries, Hospitals, Cathedral and Collegiate Churches in England and Wales ... Collected, and Published in Latin by Sir William Dugdale, Knt. late Garter King of Arms ... And Now Epitomized in English, Page by Page. London, 1693.

Elmes, James. *London and Its Environs in the Nineteenth Century.* Illustrated by Thomas Shepherd. London, 1829.

Evelyn, John. *The Diary of John Evelyn.* Edited by E. S. de Beer. 6 volumes. Oxford: Clarendon Press, 1955.

Fiennes, Celia. *The Journeys of Celia Fiennes*. Edited by Christopher Morris. Second edition. London: Cresset Press, 1949.

Freeling, Arthur. *The London and Birmingham Railway Companion*. London, not dated.

Freeling, Arthur (editor). *Picturesque Excursions; Containing Upwards of Four Hundred Views at and near Places of Popular Resort; with Descriptions of Each Locality*. London, not dated.

Gent, Thomas. *The Antient and Modern History of the Loyal Town of Rippon: Introduc'd by a Poem on the Surprizing Beauties of Studley-Park, with a Description of the Venerable Ruins of Fountains-Abbey*. York, 1733.

Gilpin, William. *Observations on the River Wye, and Several Parts of South Wales &c. Relative Chiefly to Picturesque Beauty; Made in the Summer of the Year 1770*. London, 1782.

Observations on the Western Parts of England, Relative Chiefly to Picturesque Beauty, To Which Are Added, a Few Remarks on the Picturesque Beauties of the Isle of Wight. London, 1798.

Observations, Relative Chiefly to Picturesque Beauty, Made in the Year 1772, on Several Parts of England; Particularly the Mountains, and Lakes of Cumberland, and Westmoreland. 2 volumes. London, 1786.

Goldsmith, Oliver. *The Collected Works of Oliver Goldsmith*. Edited by Arthur Friedman. 5 volumes. Oxford: Clarendon Press, 1966.

Gray, Thomas. *The Works of Thomas Gray; Containing His Poems, and Correspondence with Several Eminent Literary Characters. To Which Are Added, Memoirs of His Life and Writings, by W. Mason, M.A.* Third edition. 2 volumes. London, 1807.

Green, William. *Seventy Eight Studies from Nature. Engraved by William Green, from Drawings Made by Himself*. London, 1809.

The Tourist's New Guide, Containing a Description of the Lakes, Mountains, and Scenery, in Cumberland, Westmorland, and Lancashire, with Some Account of Their Bordering Towns and Villages. Being the Result of Observations Made during a Residence of Eighteen Years in Ambleside and Keswick. 2 volumes. Kendal, 1819.

Grose, Francis. *The Antiquities of England*. 4 volumes. London, 1773–6.

Hardy, Thomas. *The Complete Poems of Thomas Hardy*. Edited by James Gibson. New Wessex Edition. London: Macmillan, 1976.

Hassell, John. *Tour of the Isle of Wight*. 2 volumes. London, 1790.

Hawthorne, Nathaniel. *The Works of Nathaniel Hawthorne*. General editors William Charvat, Roy Harvey Pearce, Claude M. Simpson and Matthew J. Bruccoli. Centenary Edition. 14 volumes. Columbus, Ohio: Ohio State University Press, 1962–80.

Heath, Charles. *Historical and Descriptive Accounts of the Ancient and Present State of Tintern Abbey*. Monmouth, not dated.

Hoare, Sir Richard Colt. *The Journeys of Sir Richard Colt Hoare through*

England and Wales 1793–1810. Edited by M. W. Thompson. Gloucester: Alan Sutton, 1983.

Hobbes, Thomas. *De Mirabilibus Pecci: Being the Wonders of the Peak in
Darby-shire, Commonly Called The Devil's Arse of Peak. In English and
Latine. The Latine Written by Thomas Hobbes of Malmsbury. The
English by a Person of Quality.* London, 1678.

Horne, T. H. *The Lakes of Lancashire, Westmorland, and Cumberland;
Delineated in Forty-Three Engravings. From Drawings by Joseph Farington, R.A.* London, 1816.

Housman, John. *A Descriptive Tour, and Guide to the Lakes, Caves,
Mountains, and Other Natural Curiosities in Cumberland, Westmoreland, Lancashire, and a Part of the West Riding of Yorkshire.* Carlisle,
1800.

Hurtley, Thomas. *A Concise Account of Some Natural Curiosities in the
Environs of Malham in Craven, Yorkshire.* London, 1786.

Hutchinson, William. *An Excursion to the Lakes, in Westmoreland and
Cumberland, August 1773.* London, 1774.

*Excursion to the Lakes, with a Tour through Part of the North of England,
in 1773 and 1774,* paraphrased in Volume 2 of William Mavor, *The
British Tourists; or Traveller's Pocket Companion, through England,
Wales, Scotland, and Ireland. Comprehending the Most Celebrated
Tours in the British Islands.* 6 volumes. London, 1798–1800.

*The History of the Country of Cumberland, and Some Places Adjacent,
from the Earliest Accounts to the Present Time.* 2 volumes. Carlisle,
1794.

Ireland, Samuel. *Picturesque Views on the River Wye, from its Source at
Plinlimmon Hill to Its Junction with the Severn below Chepstow: with
Observations on the Public Buildings, and Other Works of Art, in Its
Vicinity.* London, 1797.

Picturesque Views on the Upper, or Warwickshire Avon. London, 1795.

Irving, Washington. *The Complete Works of Washington Irving.* General
editors Henry A. Pochmann, Herbert Kleinfield and Richard Dilworth
Rust. 29 volumes. Madison, Wisconsin: University of Wisconsin Press,
and Boston: Twayne Publishers, 1969–81.

James, Henry. *English Hours.* London: William Heinemann, 1905.

The Novels and Tales of Henry James. New York Edition. 26 volumes.
London: Macmillan, 1908–70.

Jewitt, Llewellynn and Hall, S. C. *The Stately Homes of England.* London,
1874.

Johnson, Samuel. *The Letters of Samuel Johnson.* Edited by R. W. Chapman.
3 volumes. Oxford: Clarendon Press, 1952.

Jonson, Ben. *The Works of Ben Jonson.* Edited by C. H. Herford, E. M.
Simpson and Percy Simpson. 11 volumes. Oxford: Clarendon Press,
1925–52.

Kennedy, J. *A Description of the Antiquities and Curiosities in Wilton-House*, Salisbury, 1786.

Kip, Johannes and Knyff, Leonard. *Britannia Illustrata or Views of Several of the Queens Palaces as Also of the Principal Seats of the Nobility and Gentry of Great Britain Curiously Engraven on 80 Copper Plates.* London, 1707.

Kitchiner, William. *The Traveller's Oracle; or, Maxims for Locomotion: Containing Precepts for Promoting the Pleasures and Hints for Preserving the Health of Travellers.* Third edition. London, 1828.

Leigh, Charles. *The Natural History of Lancashire, Cheshire, and the Peak in Derbyshire.* Oxford, 1700.

Loveday, John. *Diary of a Tour in 1732 through Parts of England, Wales, Ireland and Scotland Made by John Loveday of Caversham. Now for the First Time Printed from a Manuscript in the Possession of his Great-Grandson John Edward Taylor Loveday.* Edinburgh, 1890.

Mackay, Charles. *The Scenery and Poetry of the English Lakes. A Summer Ramble.* London, 1846.

MacRitchie, William. *Diary of a Tour through Great Britain in 1795.* With an introduction and notes by David MacRitchie. London, 1897.

Marshall, William. *A Review of the Reports to the Board of Agriculture from the Northern Department of England: Comprizing Northumberland, Durham, Cumberland, Westmoreland, Lancashire, Yorkshire; and the Mountainous Parts of Derbyshire, &c.* York, 1808.

Martineau, Harriet. *A Complete Guide to the English Lakes.* Windermere, 1855.

Harriet Martineau's Autobiography. Third edition. 3 volumes. London, 1877.

Mason, William. *The English Garden: A Poem in Four Books.* York, 1783.

Mavor, William. *Blenheim, A Poem. To Which is Added, A Blenheim Guide. Inscribed to Their Graces, the Duke and Duchess of Marlborough.* London, 1787.

The British Tourists; or Traveller's Pocket Companion, through England, Wales, Scotland, and Ireland. Comprehending the Most Celebrated Tours in the British Islands. 6 volumes. London, 1798–1800.

A Description of Blenheim, the Seat of His Grace, the Duke of Marlborough: Containing a Full and Accurate Account of the Paintings, Tapestry, and Furniture; A Picturesque Tour of the Gardens and Park; A General Delineation of the China Gallery, Private Gardens, &c.; To Which Are Also Added, An Itinerary; An Account of the Roman Villa, Near Northleigh, &c. &c.: with a Preliminary Essay on Landscape Gardening. Twelfth edition. Oxford, not dated.

Mawman, Joseph. *An Excursion to the Highlands of Scotland, and the English Lakes, with Recollections, Descriptions, and References to Historical Fact.* London, 1805.

Mogg, Edward. *Mogg's Pocket Itinerary; or, An Entirely New and Accurate Description of the Direct and Cross Roads of England and Wales, with Part of the Roads of Scotland, Shewing the Seats of the Nobility and Gentry . . . To Which is Now First Added an Appendix of the Rail Roads.* London, 1837.

Moore, Thomas. *The Fudges in England; Being a Sequel to the 'Fudge Family in Paris'. By Thomas Brown the Younger.* Second edition. London, 1835.

Moritz, Carl Philip. *Journeys of a German in England in 1782.* Translated and edited by Reginald Nettel. London: Jonathan Cape, 1965.

[Murray, John]. *Handbook for England and Wales; Alphabetically Arranged for the Use of Travellers.* First edition. London, 1878.

Handbook for England and Wales; Alphabetically Arranged for the Use of Travellers. Second edition. London, 1890.

Murray's Handbook for Modern London. First edition. London, 1851.

Murray, Hon. Mrs [Sarah Aust]. *A Companion and Useful Guide to the Beauties of Scotland, to the Lakes of Westmorland, Cumberland, and Lancashire; and to the Curiosities in the District of Craven in the West Riding of Yorkshire. To Which Is Added, a More Particular Description of Scotland, Especially That Part of It, Called the Highlands.* London, 1799.

Neale, John Preston. *Views of the Seats of Noblemen and Gentlemen, in England, Wales, Scotland, and Ireland.* 6 volumes. London, 1822–3.

Norden, John. *England, An Intended Guide for English Travellers.* London, 1625.

Ogilby, John. *Britannia, Volume the First: or An Illustration of the Kingdom of England and the Dominion of Wales: by a Geographical and Historical Description of the Principal Roads thereof. Actually Admeasured and Delineated in a Century of Whole-Sheet Copper-Sculps. Accomodated with the Ichnography of the Several Cities and Capital Towns; and Compleated by an Accurate Account of the More Remarkable Passages of Antiquity, Together with a Novel Discourse of the Present State.* London, 1675.

The Traveller's Pocket-Book; or Ogilby and Morgan's Book of the Roads Improved and Amended, in a Method Never Before Attempted. Fourth edition. London, 1752.

The Traveller's Pocket-Book; or Ogilby and Morgan's Book of the Roads Improved and Amended, in a Method Never Before Attempted. Twenty-second edition. London, 1785.

Orwell, George. *Homage to Catalonia.* London: Secker and Warburg, 1938.

Otley, Jonathan. *A Concise Description of the English Lakes, the Mountains in Their Vicinity, and the Roads by Which They May Be Visited; with Remarks on the Mineralogy and Geology of the District.* Keswick, 1823.

Parry, J. D. *Guide to Woburn Abbey.* Woburn, 1831.

Paterson, Daniel. *A New and Accurate Description of all the Direct and*

Principal Cross Roads in Great Britain. Second edition. London, 1772.

Paterson's British Itinerary Being A New and Accurate Delineation of all the Direct and Principal Cross Roads in Great Britain. 2 volumes. London, 1785.

Pennant, Thomas. *The Journey from Chester to London.* London, 1782.

A Journey from London to the Isle of Wight. 2 volumes. London, 1801.

A Tour from Alston-Moor to Harrowgate, and Brimham Crags. London, 1804.

A Tour in Scotland, and Voyage to the Hebrides; 1772. 2 volumes. Chester, 1774.

Pepys, Samuel. *The Diary of Samuel Pepys.* Edited by Robert Latham and William Matthews. 11 volumes. London: Bell and Hyman, 1970–83.

Plumptre, James. 'A Journal of a Pedestrian Tour by the Caves in the West Riding of Yorkshire to the Lakes and Home thro Parts of North Wales in the Year 1797'. Unpublished manuscript. Cambridge University Library.

The Lakers: A Comic Opera in Three Acts. London, 1798.

'A Narrative of a Pedestrian Journey through Some Parts of Yorkshire, Durham and Northumberland to the Highlands of Scotland and Home by the Lakes and Some Parts of Wales in the Summer of the Year 1799'. Unpublished manuscript, Cambridge University Library.

Pococke, Richard. *The Travels through England of Dr Richard Pococke.* Edited by James Joel Cartwright. 2 volumes. London, 1888–9.

Pope, Alexander. *The Poems of Alexander Pope.* General editor John Butt. Twickenham Edition. 11 volumes. London: Methuen, and New Haven: Yale University Press, 1961–9.

Pote, Joseph. *The History and Antiquities of Windsor Castle, and the Royal College, and Chapel of St George: with the Institution, Laws, and Ceremonies of the Most Noble Order of the Garter.* Eton, 1749.

Les Delices de Windsore; or, A Description of Windsor Castle, and the Country Adjacent. Eton, 1755.

Les Delices de Windsor; or, A Pocket Companion to Windsor Castle; and the Country Adjacent ... The Third Edition, with the Necessary Alterations to the Present Time. Eton, 1771.

Powys, Mrs Philip Lybbe. *Passages from the Diaries of Mrs Philip Lybbe Powys of Hardwick House, Oxon. A.D. 1756 to 1808.* Edited by Emily J. Climenson. London, 1899.

Prothero, R. E. *The Life and Correspondence of Arthur Penrhyn Stanley.* 2 volumes. London, 1893.

Radcliffe, Ann. *A Journey Made in the Summer of 1794, through Holland and the Western Frontier of Germany, with a Return down the Rhine: To Which Are Added Observations during a Tour to the Lakes of Lancashire, Westmoreland, and Cumberland.* London, 1795.

Reed, Edwin. *The Truth Concerning Stratford-upon-Avon, and Shakspere, with Other Essays.* Boston: Coburn Publishing Co., 1907.

Robinson, John. *A Guide to the Lakes in Cumberland, Westmorland and Lancashire, Illustrated with Twenty Views of Local Scenery, and a Travelling Map of the Adjacent Country*. London, 1819.

Robinson, Peter Frederick. *Vitruvius Britannicus. History of Woburn Abbey: Illustrated by Plans, Elevations, and Internal Views of the Apartments, from Actual Measurement*. London, 1827.

Rose, Thomas. *Picturesque Rambles in Westmorland, Cumberland, Durham and Northumberland*. London, 1847.

Westmorland, Cumberland, Durham and Northumberland, Illustrated. London, 1832.

Rowlandson, Thomas. *Rowlandson's Drawings for a Tour in a Post Chaise*. Edited by Robert R. Wark. San Marino, California: Huntington Library Publications, 1964.

Ruskin, John. *The Works of John Ruskin*. Edited by E. T. Cook and Alexander Wedderburn. Library Edition. 39 volumes. London: George Allen, 1903–12.

Scott, Sir Walter. *The Journal of Sir Walter Scott*. Edited by W. E. K. Anderson. Oxford: Clarendon Press, 1972.

Shaw, Rev. Stebbing. *A Tour to the West of England, in 1788*. London, 1789.

Shelley, Henry C. *Shakespeare and Stratford*. London: Simpkin, Marshall, Hamilton, Kent, 1913.

Simond, Louis. *An American in Regency England: The Journal of a Tour in 1810–1811*. Edited by Christopher Hibbert. London: Robert Maxwell, 1968.

Smith, John. *Choir Gaur; The Grand Orrery of the Ancient Druids, Commonly Called Stonehenge, on Salisbury Plain, Astronomically Explained, and Mathematically Proved to be a Temple Erected in the Earliest Ages, for Observing the Motions of the Heavenly Bodies*. Salisbury, 1771.

Smith, William. *The Particular Description of England, 1588. With Views of Some of the Chief Towns and Armorial Bearings of Nobles and Bishops*. Edited by Henry B. Wheatley and Edmund W. Ashbee. London: privately issued, 1879.

Smollett, Tobias. *The Expedition of Humphry Clinker*. Edited by Lewis M. Knapp. Oxford English Novels. London: Oxford University Press, 1966.

Somervell, Robert. *A Protest against the Extension of Railways in the Lake District*. With a Preface by John Ruskin. Windermere, 1877.

Southey, Robert. *Letters from England: By Don Manuel Alvarez Espriella. Translated from the Spanish*. Second edition. 3 volumes. London, 1808.

Speed, John. *England Wales Scotland and Ireland Described and Abridged . . . from a Farr Larger Voulume*. London, 1627.

Theatrum Imperii Magnae Britanniae. London, 1616.

Spelman, Sir Henry. *The History and Fate of Sacrilege, Discover'd by Examples of Scripture, of Heathens, and of Christians; From the Beginning of the World, Continually to this Day*. London, 1698.

Stanley, Arthur Penrhyn. *Historical Memorials of Westminster Abbey.* London, 1882.

Sulivan, Richard Joseph. *Tour through Different Parts of England, Scotland, and Wales* (1778), paraphrased in Volume 3 of William Mavor, *The British Tourists; or Traveller's Pocket Companion, through England, Wales, Scotland, and Ireland. Comprehending the Most Celebrated Tours in the British Islands.* 6 volumes. London 1798–1800.

Torrington, Viscount. See Byng, Hon. John.

Tuvar, Lorenzo [Wilson Armistead]. *Tales and Legends of the English Lakes and Mountains Collected from the Best and Most Authentic Sources.* London, 1851.

Walbram, John Richard (editor). *Memorials of the Abbey of St Mary of Fountains.* Volume 67 of *The Publications of the Surtees Society.* Durham, London and Edinburgh, 1878.

Walker, Adam. *A Tour from London to the Lakes: Containing Natural, Oeconomical, and Literary Observations, Made in the Summer of 1791. By a Gentleman.* London, 1792.

Walpole, Horace. *A Description of the Villa of Mr Horace Walpole, Youngest Son of Sir Robert Walpole, Earl of Orford, at Strawberry-Hill near Twickenham, Middlesex. With an Inventory of the Furniture, Pictures, Curiosities, &c.* Strawberry Hill, 1784.

Horace Walpole's Correspondence. Edited by W. S. Lewis. Yale Edition. 48 volumes. London: Oxford University Press, and New Haven: Yale University Press, 1937–83.

'Horace Walpole's Journals of Visits to Country Seats, &c.', edited by Paget Toynbee, *The Walpole Society*, 16 (1927–8), 9–80.

Warner, Richard. *A Tour through the Northern Counties of England, and the Borders of Scotland.* 2 volumes. Bath, 1802.

Waugh, Edwin. *Rambles in the Lake Country and its Borders.* London, 1861.

Waugh, Evelyn. *Brideshead Revisited: The Sacred and Profane Memories of Captain Charles Ryder.* Second edition. London: Chapman and Hall, 1960.

Weever, John. *Ancient Funerall Monuments within the United Monarchie of Great Britaine, Ireland, and the Islands Adiacent, with the Dissolued Monasteries therein Contained: Their Founders, and What Eminent Persons Haue Beene in the Same Interred.* London, 1631.

West, Thomas. *The Antiquities of Furness. Illustrated with Engravings. A New Edition with Additions by William Close.* Ulverston, 1805.

A Guide to the Lakes: Dedicated to the Lovers of Landscape Studies, and to All Who Have Visited, or Intend to Visit the Lakes in Cumberland, Westmorland, and Lancashire. London, 1778.

A Tour to the Caves, in the Environs of Ingleborough and Settle, in the West-Riding of Yorkshire. With Some Philosophical Conjectures on the Deluge and the Alterations on the Surface and Interior Parts of the Earth Occasioned by This Great Revolution of Nature. London, 1780.

Westall, William. *Views of the Caves near Ingleton, Gordale Scar, and Malham Cove, in Yorkshire.* London, 1818.

Wheler, Robert Bell. *A Guide to Stratford-upon-Avon.* Stratford, 1814.

An Historical Account of the Birth-Place of Shakespeare, Reprinted from the Edition of 1824, With a Few Prefatory Remarks by J. O. Halliwell, Esq., F.R.S. Stratford, 1863.

History and Antiquities of Stratford-upon-Avon. Stratford, 1806.

Whitaker, Thomas Dunham. *The History and Antiquities in the Deanery of Craven, in the County of York.* Second edition. London, 1812.

Widmore, Richard. *An History of the Church of St Peter, Westminster, Commonly Called Westminster Abbey.* London, 1751.

Wilkinson, Thomas. *Tours to the British Mountains, with the Descriptive Poems of Lowther and Emont Vale.* London, 1824.

Wise, John R. *Shakspere: His Birthplace and Its Neighbourhood.* London, 1861.

Wordsworth, William. *The Illustrated Wordsworth's Guide to the Lakes.* Edited by Peter Bicknell. Exeter: Webb and Bower, 1984.

The Poetical Works of William Wordsworth. Edited by Ernest de Selincourt and Helen Darbishire. 5 volumes. Oxford: Clarendon Press, 1940–9.

The Prelude: or The Growth of a Poet's Mind. Edited by Ernest de Selincourt. Second edition, revised by Helen Darbishire. Oxford: Clarendon Press, 1959.

The Prose Works of William Wordsworth. Edited by W. J. B. Owen and Jane Worthington Smyser. 3 volumes. Oxford: Clarendon Press, 1974.

Wyndham, Henry Penruddocke. *A Gentleman's Tour through Monmouthshire and Wales in the Months of June and July 1774.* London, 1775.

A Gentleman's Tour through Monmouthshire and Wales Made in the Months of June, and July, 1774 and in the Months of June, July, and August, 1777. Second edition. Salisbury, 1781.

Young, Arthur. *A Six Months Tour through the North of England.* 4 volumes. London, 1770.

A Six Weeks Tour through the Southern Counties of England and Wales. London, 1768.

SECONDARY: WORKS OF ART HISTORY, ARCHAEOLOGY, BIOGRAPHY, HISTORY, LITERARY CRITICISM, ETC. PUBLISHED AFTER 1900

Aston, Margaret. 'English Ruins and English History: The Dissolution and the Sense of the Past', *Journal of the Warburg and Courtauld Institutes*, 36 (1973), 231–55.

Bailey, J. O. *The Poetry of Thomas Hardy: A Handbook and Commentary.* Chapel Hill, North Carolina: University of North Carolina Press, 1972.

Barbier, Carl Paul. *William Gilpin: His Drawings, Teaching, and Theory of the Picturesque.* Oxford: Clarendon Press, 1963.

Barrell, John. *The Idea of Landscape and the Sense of Place 1730–1840: An Approach to the Poetry of John Clare*. Cambridge: Cambridge University Press, 1972.

Barthes, Roland, 'Le Guide Bleu' in *Mythologies*. Paris: Editions du Seuil, 1957.

Beales, H. L. 'Travel and Communications' in *Johnson's England: An Account of the Life and Manners of His Age*. Edited by A. S. Turberville. 2 volumes. Oxford: Clarendon Press, 1933.

Bicknell, Peter. *Beauty, Horror and Immensity: Picturesque Landscape in Britain 1750–1850*. Exhibition Catalogue. Cambridge: Cambridge University Press, 1981.

Bicknell, Peter and Woof, Robert. *The Lake District Discovered 1810–1850: The Artists, The Tourists, and Wordsworth*. Exhibition Catalogue. Grasmere: Trustees of Dove Cottage, 1983.

Boorstin, Daniel J. *The Image: A Guide to Pseudo-Events in America*. New York: Atheneum, 1973.

Bradley, J. L. 'Joseph Skipsey', *Notes and Queries*, 223 (August 1978), 320–1.

Brakspear, Harold and Evans, Morton. *Tintern Abbey, Monmouthshire*. London: His Majesty's Stationery Office, 1908.

Briggs, Martin S. *Goths and Vandals: A Study of the Destruction, Neglect and Preservation of Historical Buildings in England*. London: Constable, 1952.

Brown, Ivor and Fearon, George. *Amazing Monument: A Short History of the Shakespeare Industry*. London: Heinemann, 1939.

Burke, Thomas. *Travel in England: From Pilgrim and Pack-Horse to Car and Plane*. London: Batsford, 1942.

Burton, Anthony and Pip. *The Green Bag Travellers: Britain's First Tourists*. London: André Deutsch, 1978.

Butler, John. *The Economics of Historic Country Houses*, Policy Studies Institute No. 591 (January 1981).

Carpenter, Edward (editor). *A House of Kings: The History of Westminster Abbey*. London: John Baker, 1966.

Chippindale, Christopher. *Stonehenge Complete*. London: Thames and Hudson, 1983.

Clark, Kenneth. *The Gothic Revival: An Essay in the History of Taste*. Third edition. London: John Murray, 1962.

Copeland, John. *Roads and Their Traffic 1750–1850*. Newton Abbot: David and Charles, 1968.

Curley, Thomas M. *Samuel Johnson and the Age of Travel*. Athens, Georgia: University of Georgia Press, 1976.

Deelman, Christian. *The Great Shakespeare Jubilee*. London: Michael Joseph, 1964.

Denvir, Bernard, 'Visiting Country Houses 200 Years Ago', *Country Life*, 120 (25 October 1956), 934–6.

Edel, Leon. *Henry James: The Master, 1901–1916*. London: Rupert Hart-Davis, 1972.

Fordham, Sir Herbert George. *'Paterson's Roads': Daniel Paterson, His Maps and Itineraries, 1738–1825*. London: Oxford University Press, 1925.

Fox, Levi. *The Borough Town of Stratford-upon-Avon*. Stratford-upon-Avon: Corporation of Stratford-upon-Avon, 1953.

'The Heritage of Shakespeare's Birthplace', *Shakespeare Survey*, 1 (1948), 79–88.

In Honour of Shakespeare: The History and Collections of the Shakespeare Birthplace Trust. Norwich: Jarrold and Sons, and the Shakespeare Birthplace Trust, 1972.

Frankl, Paul. *The Gothic: Literary Sources and Interpretations through Eight Centuries*. Princeton, New Jersey: Princeton University Press, 1960.

Fussell, Paul. *Abroad: British Literary Traveling between the Wars*. Oxford: Oxford University Press, 1980.

Gibson, H. N. *The Shakespeare Claimants: A Critical Survey of the Four Principal Theories Concerning the Authorship of the Shakespearean Plays*. London: Methuen, 1962.

Girouard, Mark. *Life in the English Country House: A Social and Architectural History*. New Haven and London: Yale University Press, 1978.

Haight, Gordon S. *George Eliot: A Biography*. Oxford: Clarendon Press, 1968.

Hall, D. J. *English Mediaeval Pilgrimage*. London: Routledge and Kegan Paul, 1965 [1966].

Halliday, F. E. *The Cult of Shakespeare*. London: Duckworth, 1957.

Harris, John. *The Artist and the Country House: A History of Country House and Garden View Painting in Britain 1540–1870*. London: Sotheby Parke Bernet, 1979.

Hawes, Louis. *Constable's Stonehenge*. London: Her Majesty's Stationery Office, 1975.

Hindley, Geoffrey. *Tourists, Travellers and Pilgrims*. London: Hutchinson, 1983.

Hunter, Michael. *John Aubrey and the Realm of Learning*. London: Duckworth, 1975.

Hussey, Christopher. *English Gardens and Landscapes 1700–1750*. London: Country Life, 1967.

The Picturesque: Studies in a Point of View. 1927, reprinted London: Frank Cass, 1967.

Johnson, Edgar. *Charles Dickens: His Tragedy and Triumph*. 2 volumes. London: Victor Gollancz, 1953.

Knight, Jeremy. *Tintern and the Romantic Movement*. London: Her Majesty's Stationery Office, 1977.

Lees-Milne, James. *Earls of Creation: Five Great Patrons of Eighteenth-Century Art*. London: Hamish Hamilton, 1962.

Lennard, Reginald (editor). *Englishmen at Rest and Play: Some Phases of English Leisure, 1558–1714*. Oxford: Clarendon Press, 1931.

Lindsay, Jack. *George Meredith: His Life and Work*. London: The Bodley Head, 1956.

Lovejoy, Arthur O. *Essays in the History of Ideas*. Baltimore: The Johns Hopkins Press, 1948.

Macaulay, Rose. *Pleasure of Ruins*. London: Thames and Hudson, 1953.

MacCannell, Dean. *The Tourist: A New Theory of the Leisure Class*. London: Macmillan, 1976.

Manwaring, Elizabeth Wheeler. *Italian Landscape in Eighteenth Century England: A Study Chiefly of the Influence of Claude Lorrain and Salvator Rosa on English Taste 1700–1800*. New York: Oxford University Press, 1925.

Marchand, Leslie. *Byron: A Biography*. 3 volumes. London: John Murray, 1957.

Masters, Brian. *Now Barabbas Was a Rotter: The Extraordinary Life of Marie Corelli*. London: Hamish Hamilton, 1978.

Millward, Roy and Robinson, Adrian. *The Lake District*. The Regions of Britain. London: Eyre and Spottiswoode, 1970.

Moir, Esther. *The Discovery of Britain: The English Tourists 1540 to 1840*. London: Routledge and Kegan Paul, 1964.

'Touring Country Houses in the Eighteenth Century'. *Country Life*, 126 (22 October 1959), 586–8.

Moorman, Mary. *William Wordsworth: A Biography*. 2 volumes. Oxford: Clarendon Press, 1957–65.

Nicholson, Norman. *The Lakers: The Adventures of the First Tourists*. London: Robert Hale, 1955.

Nicolson, Marjorie Hope. *Mountain Gloom and Mountain Glory: The Development of the Aesthetics of the Infinite*. Ithaca, New York: Cornell University Press, 1959.

Nygren, Edward J. *James Ward's Gordale Scar: An Essay in the Sublime*. London: Tate Gallery, 1982.

Owen, A. L. *The Famous Druids: A Survey of Three Centuries of English Literature on the Druids*. Oxford: Clarendon Press, 1962.

Parkes, Joan. *Travel in England in the Seventeenth Century*. London: Oxford University Press, 1925.

Perkins, Jocelyn. *Westminster Abbey: The Empire's Crown*. London: Duckworth, 1937.

Piggott, Stuart. *Ruins in a Landscape: Essays in Antiquarianism*. Edinburgh: Edinburgh University Press, 1976.

William Stukeley: An Eighteenth-Century Antiquary. Oxford: Clarendon Press, 1950.

Pimlott, J. A. R. *The Englishman's Holiday: A Social History*. London: Faber and Faber, 1947.

Reiman, Donald H. 'The Beauty of Buttermere as Fact and Romantic Symbol', *Criticism*, 26 (Spring 1984), 139–170.

Robinson, Kenneth. *Wilkie Collins: A Biography*. London: Davis-Poynter, 1974.

Royal Commission on Historical Monuments (England). *An Inventory of the Historical Monuments in London*. 5 volumes. London: His Majesty's Stationery Office, 1924.

Russell, A. L. N. *Westminster Abbey: The Story of the Church and the Monastery with Some Account of the Life of the Monks, a Guide to the Buildings and Monuments and an Explanation of Their Styles*. London: Chatto and Windus, 1934.

Sadleir, Michael. *Things Past*. London: Constable, 1944.

Schoenbaum, Samuel S. *William Shakespeare: A Documentary Life*. Oxford: Clarendon Press, and London: Scolar Press, 1975.

Slack, Margaret. *Lakeland Discovered: From No Man's Land to National Park*. London: Robert Hale, 1982.

Smith, Valerie L. (editor). *Hosts and Guests: The Anthropology of Tourism*. Oxford: Basil Blackwell, 1977.

Stochholm, Johanne M. *Garrick's Folly: The Shakespeare Jubilee of 1769 at Stratford and Drury Lane*. London: Methuen, 1964.

Strong, Roy; Binney, Marcus; and Harris, John. *The Destruction of the Country House 1875–1975*. London: Thames and Hudson, 1975.

Swinglehurst, Edmund. *Cook's Tours: The Story of Popular Travel*. Poole, Dorset: Blandford Press, 1982.

  The Romantic Journey: The Story of Thomas Cook and Victorian Travel. London: Pica, 1974.

Thomas, Keith. *Man and the Natural World: Changing Attitudes in England 1500–1800*. London: Allen Lane, 1983.

Thompson, M. W. *Ruins: Their Preservation and Display*. London: British Museum Publications, 1981.

Trewin, J. C. *The Story of Stratford-upon-Avon*. London and New York: Staples Press, 1950.

Turner, Lois and Ash, John. *The Golden Hordes: International Tourism and the Pleasure Periphery*. London: Constable, 1975.

Vaughan, John. *The English Guide Book c.1780–1870: An Illustrated History*. Newton Abbot and London: David and Charles, 1974.

Ward, Humphrey and Roberts, W. *Romney: A Biographical and Critical Essay with a Catalogue Raisonné of His Works*. 2 volumes. London: Thomas Agnew and Sons, 1904.

Woodbridge, Kenneth. *Landscape and Antiquity: Aspects of English Culture at Stourhead 1718 to 1838*. Oxford: Clarendon Press, 1970.

Wyatt, John. *The Lake District National Park*. Exeter: Webb and Bower, 1987.

Index

Page numbers in italics refer to illustrations and captions rather than the main text